IMAGES
of America

SOUTHERN ARIZONA CEMETERIES

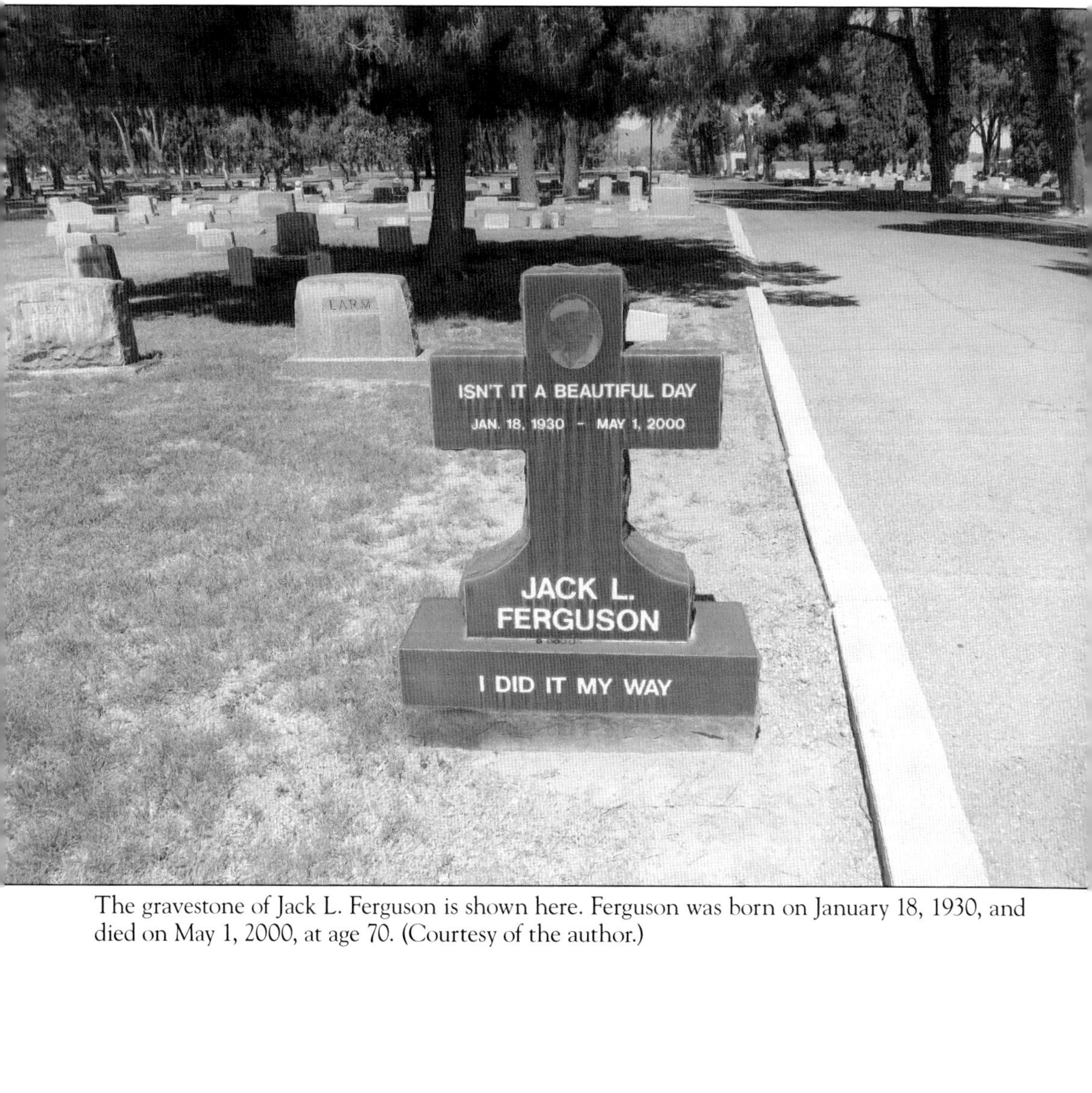

The gravestone of Jack L. Ferguson is shown here. Ferguson was born on January 18, 1930, and died on May 1, 2000, at age 70. (Courtesy of the author.)

On the Cover: A woman clasping a cross and holding a crown of thorns adorns the grave of Eloisa H. Durazo (1862–1911) in Holy Hope Cemetery in Tucson, Arizona. (Courtesy of the author.)

IMAGES
of America

SOUTHERN ARIZONA CEMETERIES

Jane Eppinga

ARCADIA
PUBLISHING

ISBN 978-1-4671-3123-0

Published by Arcadia Publishing
Charleston, South Carolina

Printed in the United States of America

Library of Congress Control Number: 2013946007

For all general information, please contact Arcadia Publishing:
Telephone 843-853-2070
Fax 843-853-0044
E-mail sales@arcadiapublishing.com
For customer service and orders:
Toll-Free 1-888-313-2665

Visit us on the Internet at www.arcadiapublishing.com

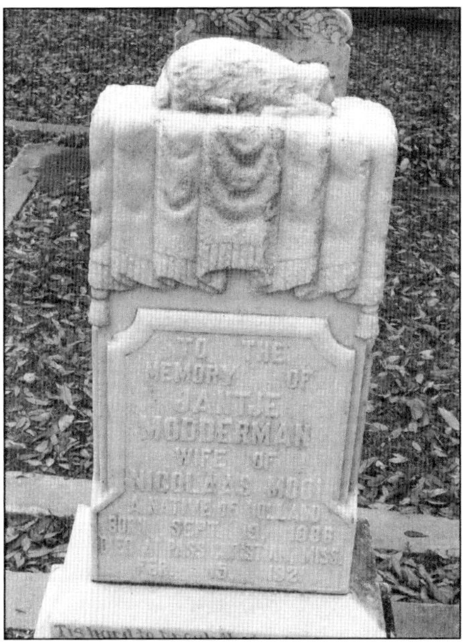

*Dedicated to my grandmother,
Jantje Modderman Mooi, who died
in 1921, at the age of 34, while
giving birth to her 14th child.*

Contents

Acknowledgments

The work of a book is never entirely the work of one person, and so it is with *Southern Arizona Cemeteries*. Now is the time to list the individuals and organizations that have generously given their assistance. The Arizona Historical Society Libraries and Archives, the Library of Congress, Stephen Gregory (Fort Huachuca Museum), Khaleel Saba and Leslie Matthaei at the Western Archeological and Conservation Center (WACC), Kristin Sanderson and Fort Bowie, Susan and Brian Ballard, John Horne from the Baseball Hall of Fame, Carolyn O'Bagy Davis, Jeanette Done, Mary Kasulaitis, Catherine Sutherland Hartline (niece of Frank O. Sutherland and great-granddaughter of William H. Sutherland), and Richard Lapidus all supplied images and information. Eileen Grade and Anne Vandenberg (with Evergreen Cemetery) and Kay Mullenax and Tammy Turner (with Holy Hope Cemetery) were especially helpful. Ilona Smerekanich and Andy Haratyk provided information on the Evergreen Cemetery in Bisbee. Lincoln Chin, from the Tucson Chinese Cultural Center, translated Chinese tombstones. My "cemeterying" friends include Alene Fletcher, Betty Barr, and Betty Leavengood. No book sees the light of day without the aid of a publisher and editor, and I am grateful to Alyssa Jones and the Arcadia Publishing staff. Finally, the biggest contributors are those pioneers who left their stones on a place called Southern Arizona.

Unless otherwise noted, all images appear courtesy of the author.

INTRODUCTION

Throughout the ages, humans have had a need to mark the time and place when and where people make the final stop on their journey from this world to the next. Sometimes the marker is a simple cross on rock-covered earth; at other times, it is an elaborate tombstone that tells something of the individual's life. Early graves were placed close together without regard to religion, fraternal association, or nationality, but as urban areas grew, people became more picky about whom they did the final big sleepover with. One commonality across these disparate groups is the observance of rituals that are supposed to ward off evil spirits and guarantee the deceased a safe journey to heaven. The tombstones might be simple wooden crosses with inscriptions or structures richly covered with symbolism. Some rituals—the firing of guns, the ringing of funeral bells, the wailing of chants—are intended to scare away other ghosts. In many cemeteries, graves are oriented so that bodies lie with their heads to the west, a practice attributed to the belief that the final summons to judgment will come from the east.

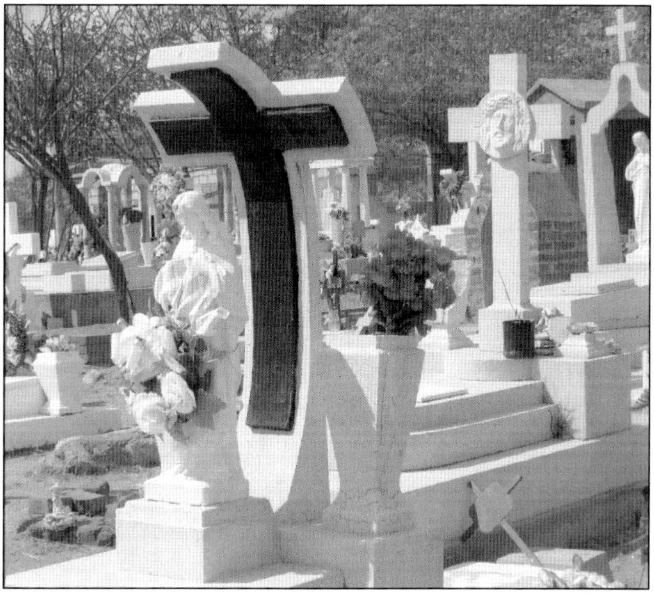

Sasabe, Arizona, and Sasabe, Sonora, Mexico, grew out of a private development by rancher Carlos Escalante. Situated on the border, a customhouse for these two towns was erected in 1935. The Sasabe cemeterio, pictured here while decorated for the Day of the Dead, reflects the influence of the culture that shaped Arizona. Día de los Muertos (Day of the Dead) is a festive occasion characterized by families visiting cemeteries, placing marigolds on headstones, making offerings to the dead, and exchanging sugar skeletons and skulls.

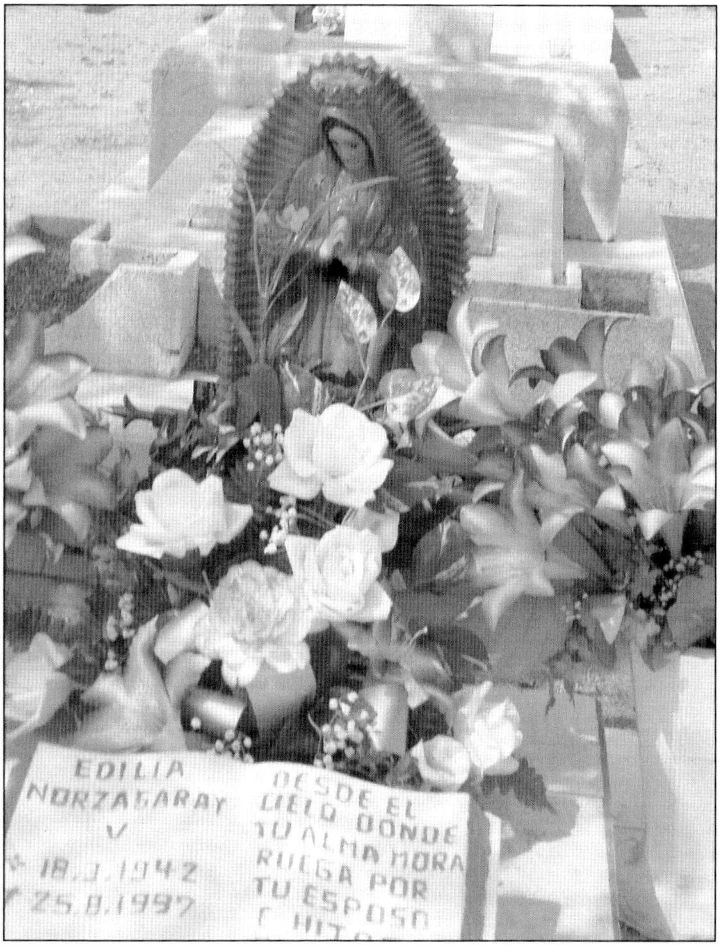

Our Lady of Guadalupe is the only saint who wears a full-body halo, or *esplendora*. While walking from his village to Mexico City on December 9, 1531, a peasant named Juan Diego saw a woman surrounded by light. He recognized the Virgin Mary and told his story to Archbishop Zumárraga, who instructed him to ask her for a miraculous sign to prove her identity. The Virgin told Juan Diego to gather flowers from the top of Tepeyac Hill even though it was December. He found roses, which he took to the archbishop. When he opened his cloak before Zumárraga, the roses fell to the floor and left the image of the Virgin of Guadalupe on the fabric.

One

Babyland

There are few things as poignant as a tiny tombstone marking the death of a child whose time on earth is measured in just a few minutes or a few years. Children's tombstones often speak of angels called to heaven. Sometimes, angels are used for comfort and to show protection. Lambs, imparting the innocence of children, are often found on graves. Family photographs may be taken with the deceased. Customs surrounding the burial of children in Southern Arizona are especially influenced by the Mexican Day of the Dead celebrations. On October 31, families welcome the souls of the deceased back to earth for one day. Their graves are decorated with flowers, fruits, and—in the case of children—toys. For three years after the death of a child, the godparents decorate arches over the graves in the belief that the soul enters eternity through arches. The church bells ring, calling children's souls and the living relatives, and incense provides an aroma to guide the returning spirits.

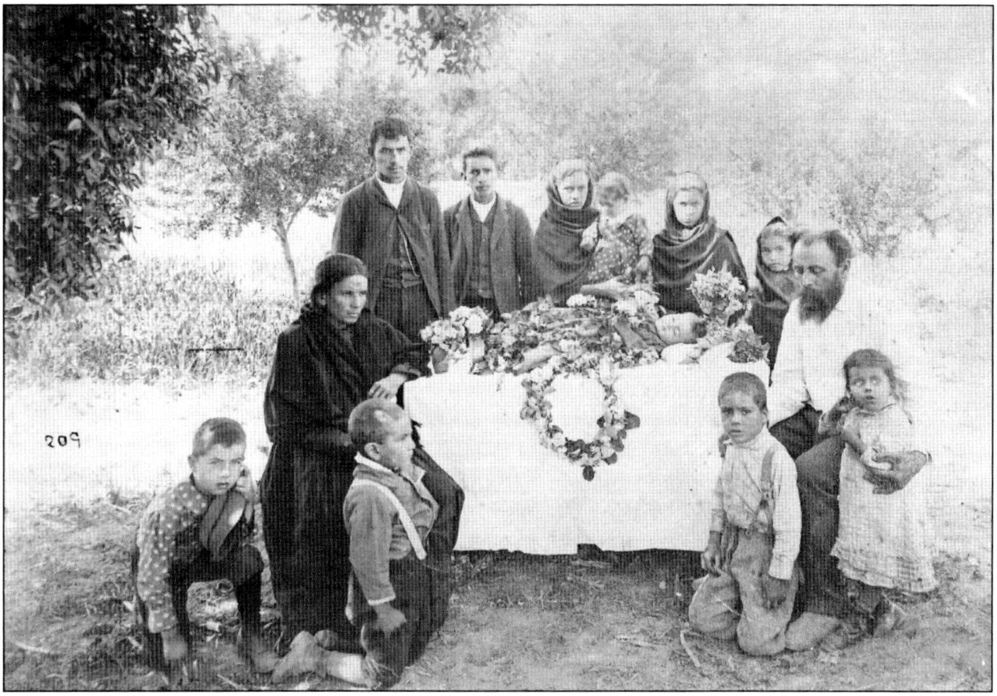

Pioneer families like Leonardo Romero's often had portraits—like this 1890 photograph—taken with a deceased person. From left to right are Feliciano, Librada, Ysidro (kneeling), Leonardo Jr., Diego, Ramona, three unidentified people, Leonardo Sr., and two unidentified children. With the advent of photography, memories could finally be made tangible. (Courtesy of the Arizona Historical Society.)

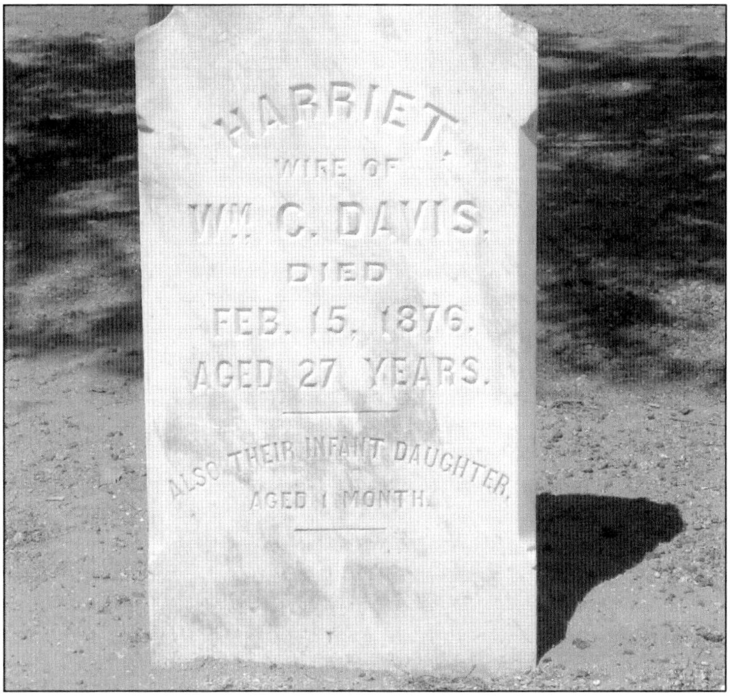

The death of a young mother and her one-month-old infant daughter is all the more heartrending when one considers that she is buried in the Pima County indigent cemetery. Harriet Davis died on February 15, 1876. She was 27 years old when she died, but her birth date is not known. She and her daughter were originally buried in Tucson's downtown cemetery.

Edith Bessy Riggs was born into a prominent southeastern Arizona ranching family, but she spent barely more than a year on this earth. The daughter of Swedish immigrants, she was born on August 2, 1884, and died on August 9, 1885. At the time, there was little in the way of medical assistance when anyone—especially a child—became sick or hurt on the frontier.

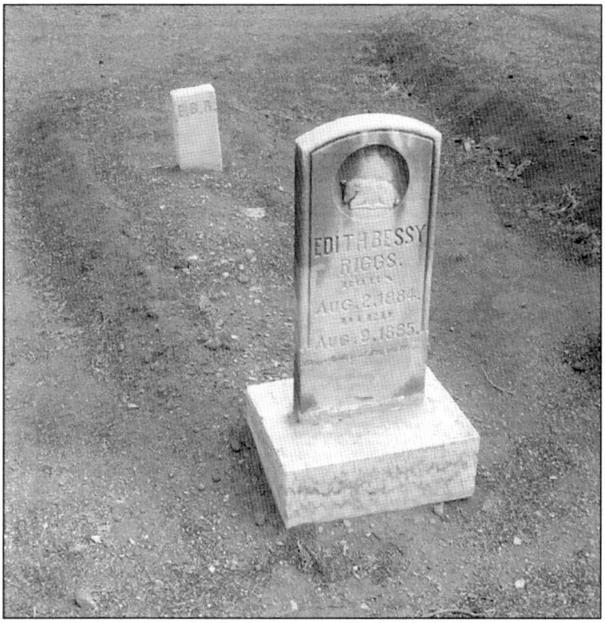

Christian Keith Ongley's grave marker says it all. Born on October 2, 1996, he died on October 4, 1996. His grave, located in Tucson's Evergreen Cemetery, is decorated with a baby picture, several toy cars, and, of course, an innocent lamb.

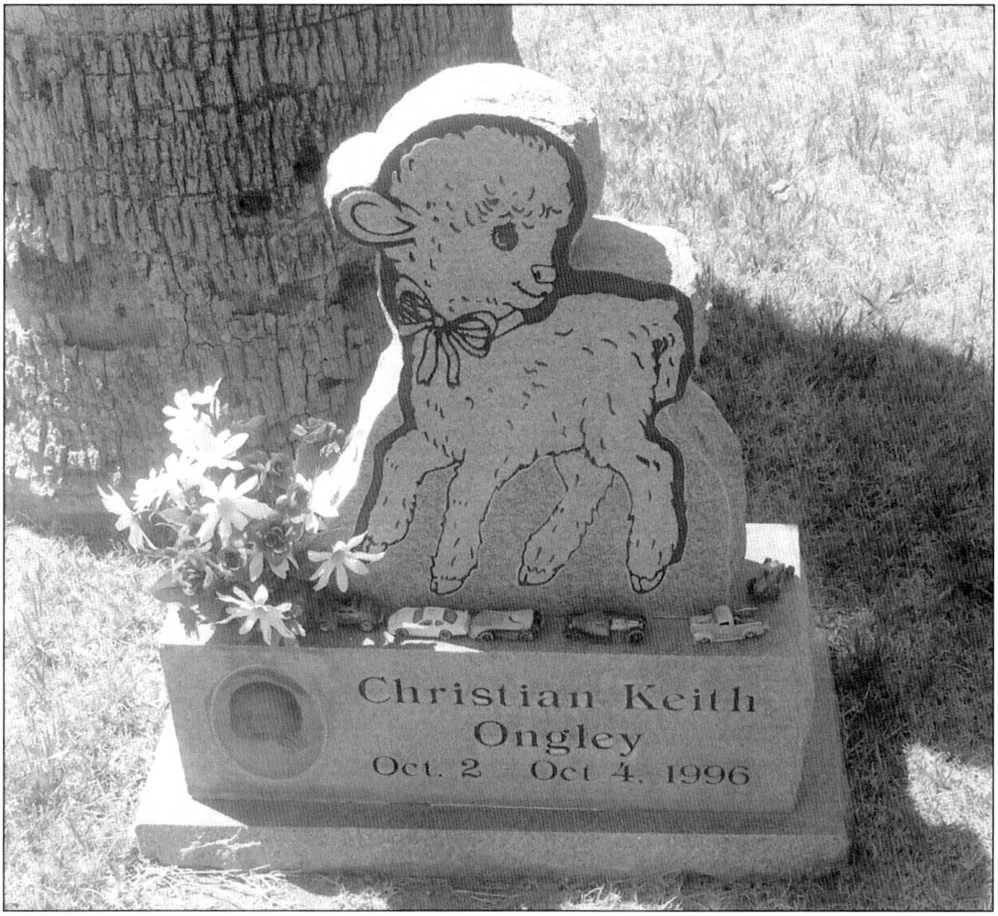

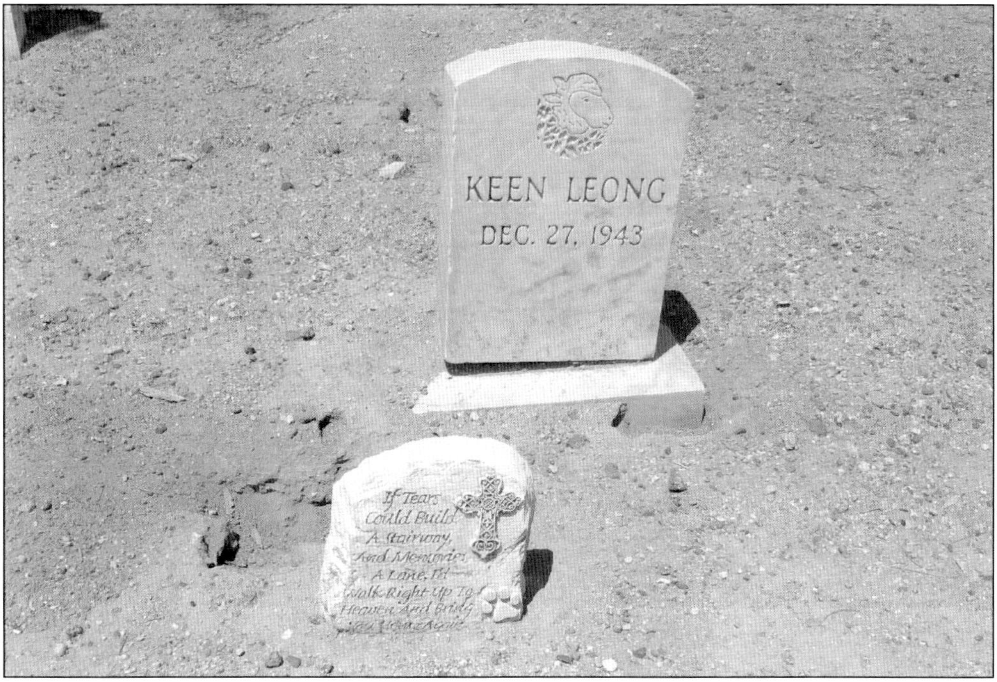

There is no name on this grave, but a wonderful verse appears on a tiny marker: "If tears could build a stairway/and thoughts a memory lane/I'd walk right up to heaven/and bring you home again."

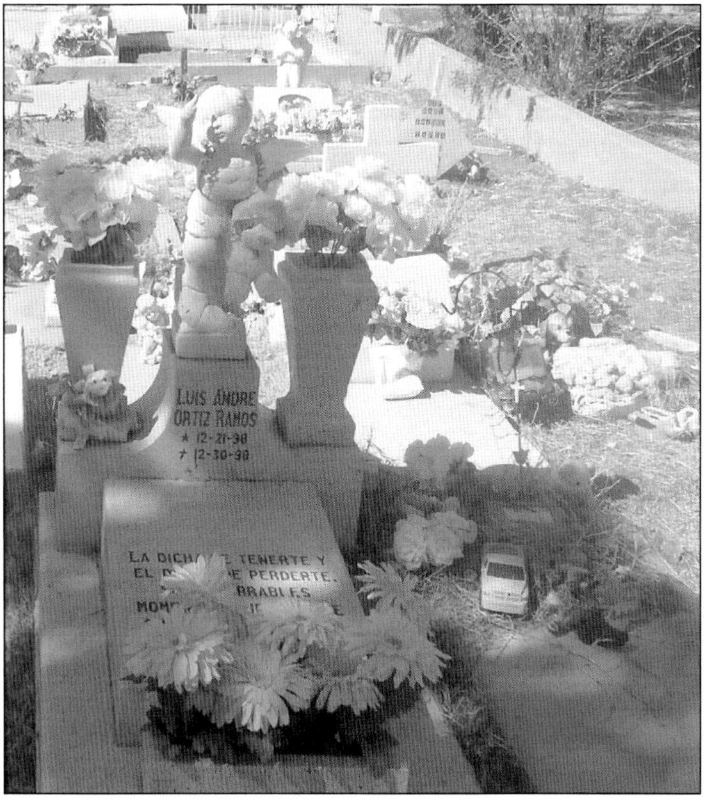

Little Luis Andre Ortiz Ramos will not lack for toys with his cars, teddy bears, and angel pointing toward heaven while clutching a stuffed dog. He was born on December 21, 1998, and died on December 30, 1998, and is buried in the Nogales cemetery.

Don Jack Han, buried in Tucson's Evergreen Cemetery, was born in Tucson on July 9, 1901, and died on March 25, 1914. His tombstone includes a number of Chinese characters.

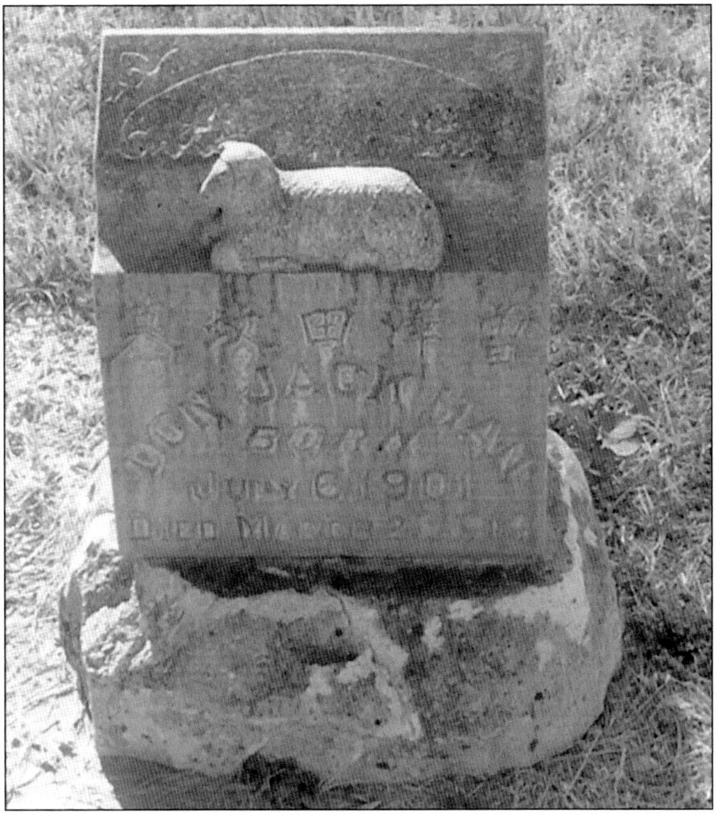

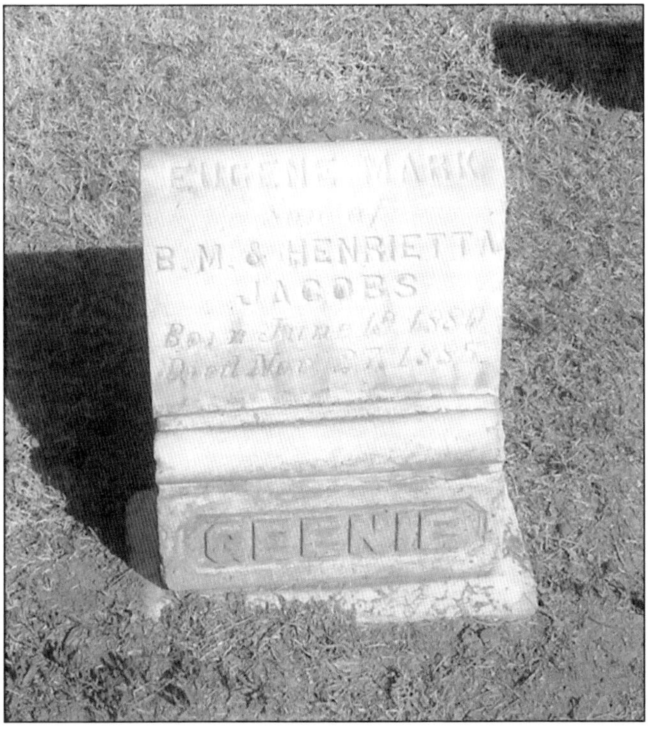

Eugene "Geenie" Mark Jacobs, the son of B.M. and Henrietta Jacobs, was born June 19, 1880, and died November 27, 1885. He is buried in Tucson's Evergreen Cemetery.

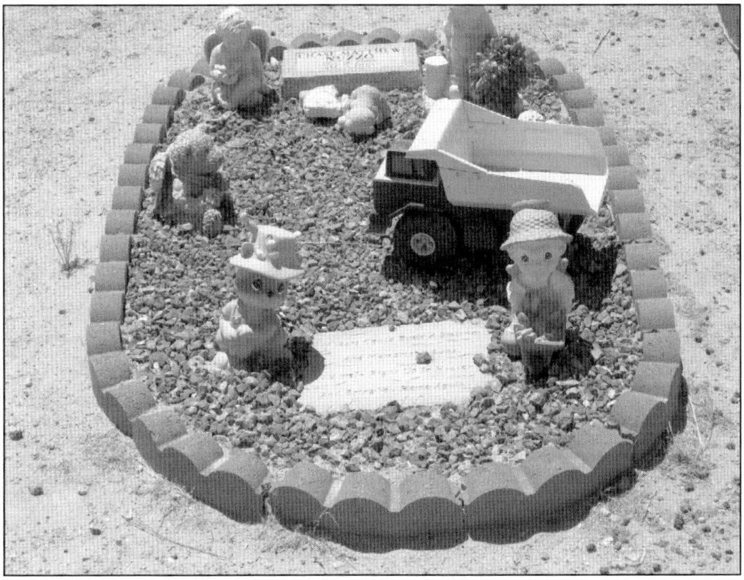

Chase Matthew Nuzzo, son of Amanda Joyce Nuzzo, died on December 3, 2003, in Tucson. Chase has a wonderful playground grave marker in Sunset Cemetery in Willcox. He was survived by his mother and a twin brother, Logan.

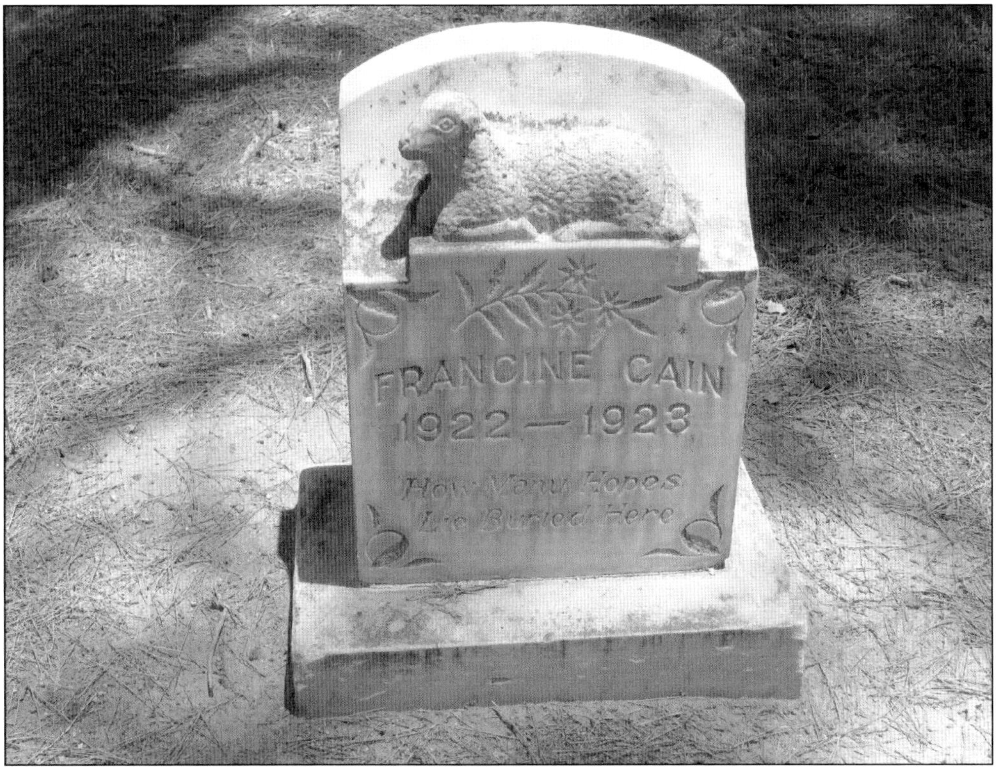

The inscription on Francine Cain's grave marker reads, "How Many Hopes Lie Buried Here," which reflected the family's deep loss. Besides the lamb of innocence, ferns adorn her tombstone. Ferns, which grow deep in the forest, are only found by those who have honestly searched.

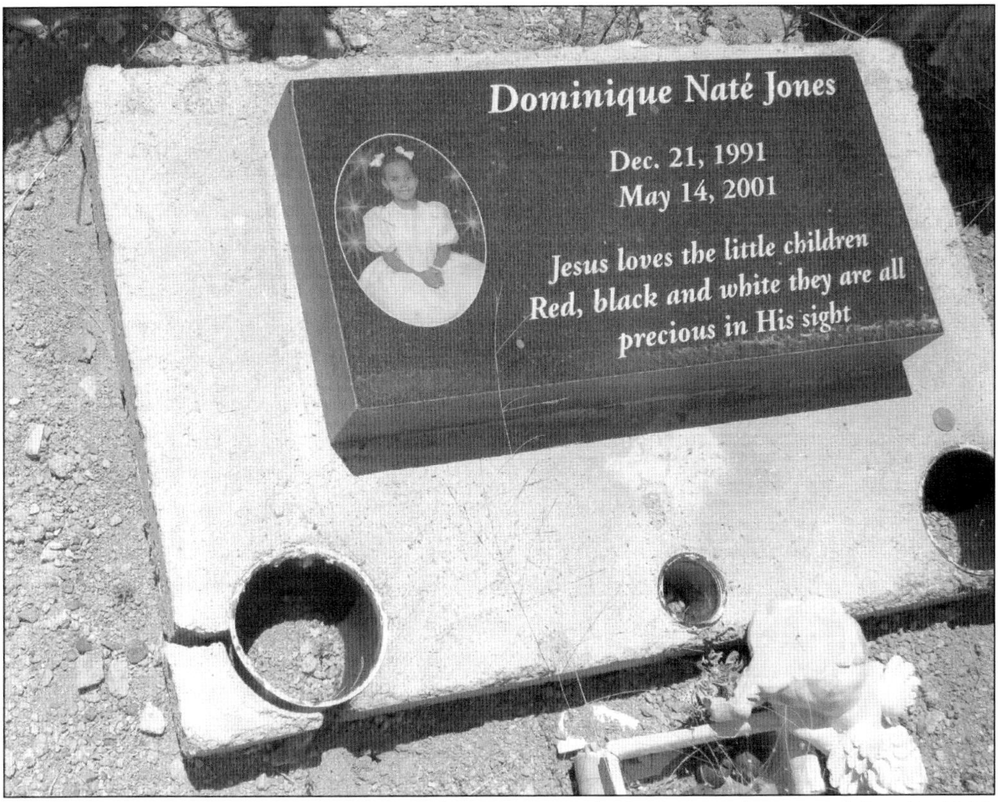

Dominique Naté Jones, born on December 21, 1991, died of appendicitis on May 14, 2001. She is buried in the Arivaca Cemetery. Her stone's inscription is a verse from "Jesus Loves the Little Children."

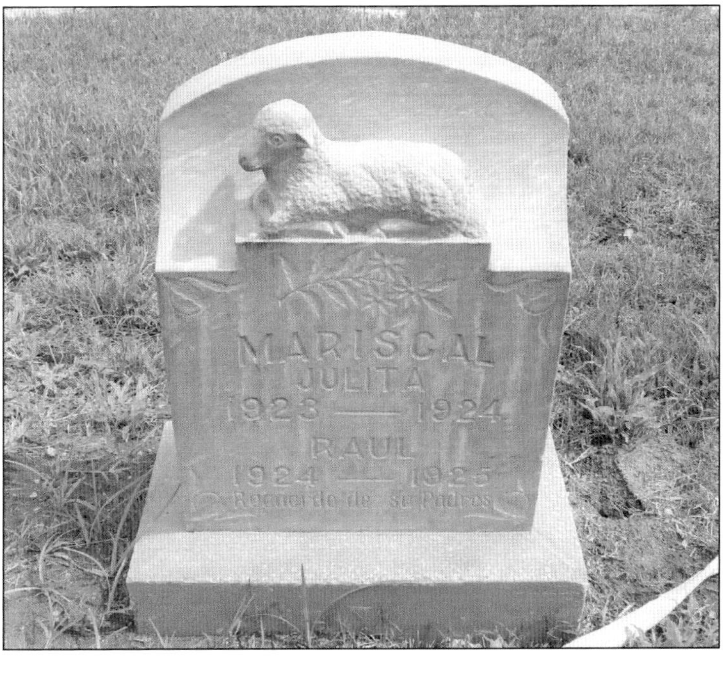

One can only imagine the grief of the Mariscal family, who lost two young children in a year. A daughter, Julita, died in 1924, and their son Raul died in 1925. The children are buried in a common grave in Tucson's Evergreen Cemetery.

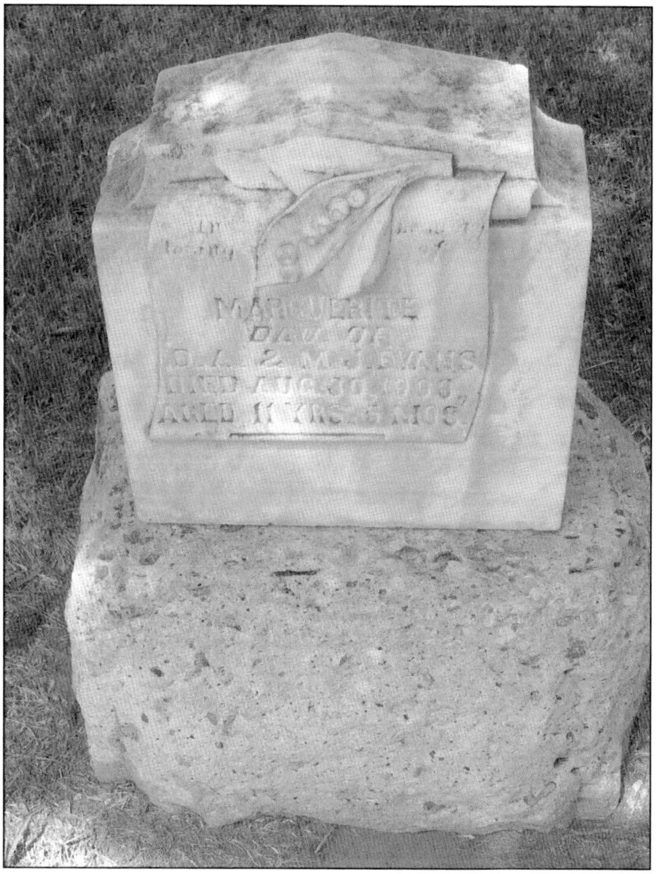

Marguerite Evans's birthday is not known, but she died in Tucson on August 30, 1900, at the age of 11 years and 5 months. Her elegant tombstone in Evergreen Cemetery has an inscribed scroll and a lily of the valley decoration. The lily of the valley, one of the first flowers to bloom in the spring, symbolizes both renewal and the resurrection of Christ.

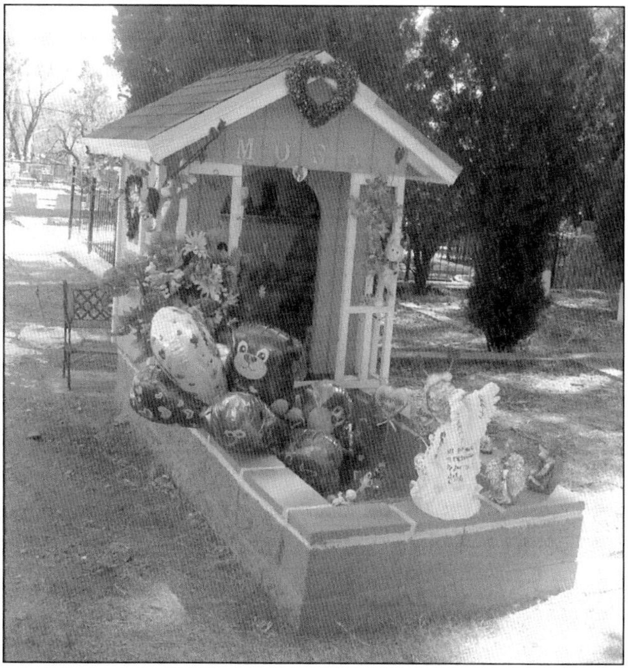

This child buried in the Nogales Cemetery has everything, including a house where he can rest and where offerings can be made. The Mexican American practice of decorating grave sites has roots in the belief that time is a never-ending cycle of life and death.

Two

Potter's Field

The term "potter's field" dates from the Biblical story of Judas Iscariot and his 30 pieces of silver, which he returned to the temple and, since it was blood money, the priests used to purchase land owned by a potter. The term was also in use in Ancient Greece; according to the book *Ceramicus Redivivus: The Early Iron Age Potters' Field in the Area of the Classical Athenian Agora*, by John K. Papadopoulos, "Although this usage ultimately derives from the passage in Matthew 27:7, which refers to the purchase of a potter's field for use as a graveyard, the association of potters' quarters and burial grounds has a much older ancestry." Every county in Arizona provides for burial of the dead who have no funds or family to pay funeral expenses. Many are simply buried in a city cemetery, but Pima County has a special cemetery for the indigent that is operated by the county's Public Fiduciary. The indigent cemetery began in 1907, the same time as Evergreen Cemetery. For many years, Evergreen took care of burying the indigent.

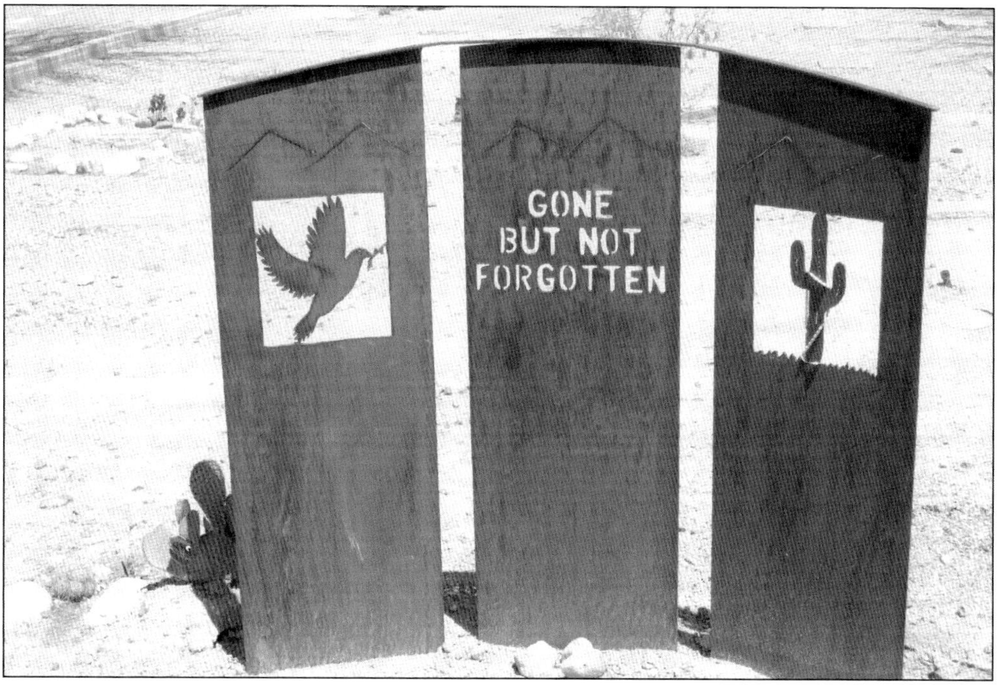

The Pima County indigent cemetery is located at the western corner of Evergreen Cemetery in Tucson. Small cacti near the graves are wrapped in black veils, as if the desert vegetation mourns the loss. This three-paneled rustic steel sculpture, created by local artist Ray Rizzo, was installed in 2013. One panel depicts a dove with an olive branch, the second reads "Gone but not forgotten," and the third has a saguaro. Many of the graves are marked "John Doe" or "Jane Doe."

John Brackett Allen was born in Maine on October 22, 1818. He died in Tucson on June 13, 1899. After his education in Boston schools, the lure of gold brought him to California, then to Arizona in 1857. One year later, he was baking and selling apple pies, an enterprise that earned him the nickname "Pie" Allen. He sold the pies to soldiers for $1, and many a soldier was known to eat the whole pie in one sitting. Following the silver strike in Tombstone, Arizona, Allen served as mayor of Tucson from 1875 to 1877, during which time he used prison inmates to implement the city's first street-sweeping program. He was elected to the Arizona legislature in 1867 and served as Arizona territorial treasurer from 1867 to 1872. He introduced the first honeybees to Arizona in 1877. Allen opened a store in the fall of 1878 at Gird's Camp on the bank of the nearby San Pedro River. He operated a mercantile business in a canvas tent at Millville and served as Millville's first and only postmaster.

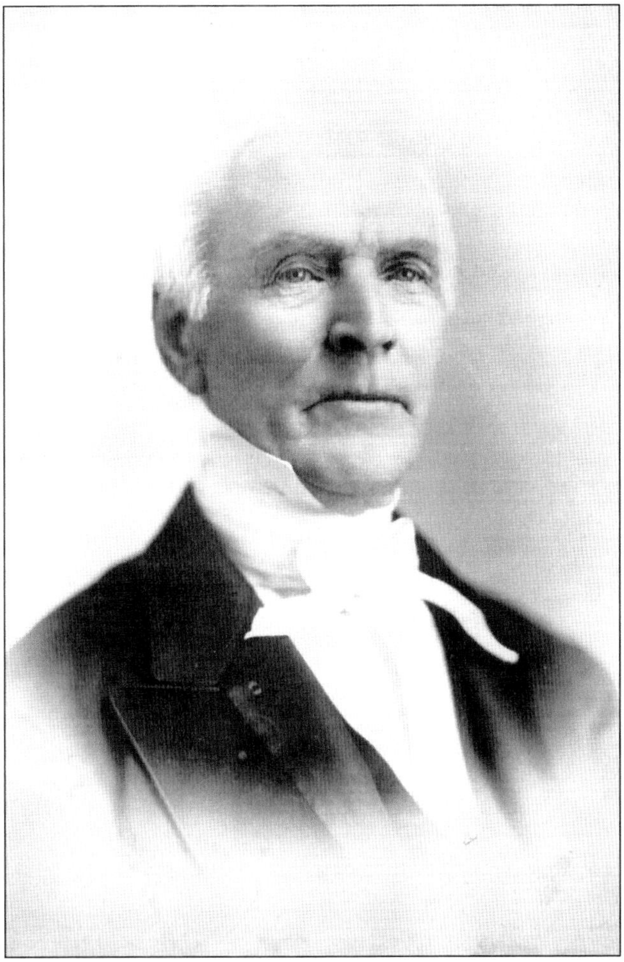

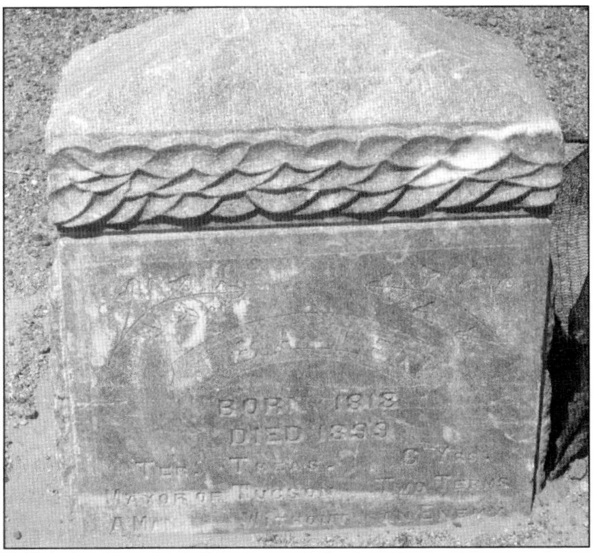

In the summer of 1879, Allen abandoned his store at Gird's Camp and moved to Tombstone, establishing a new store with an adjacent blacksmith and stable. He started a mercantile outlet at Bisbee in late 1880. In 1881, the 63-year-old Allen proposed marriage to Lola Tapia. The girl's mother agreed to the union on the condition that Lola remain in a convent. The marriage took place, and Lola remained at the convent until she gave birth to a daughter. In 1891, Allen was granted a divorce. Allen sank into poverty in Tucson, where he died on June 13, 1899, after surgery for facial cancer.

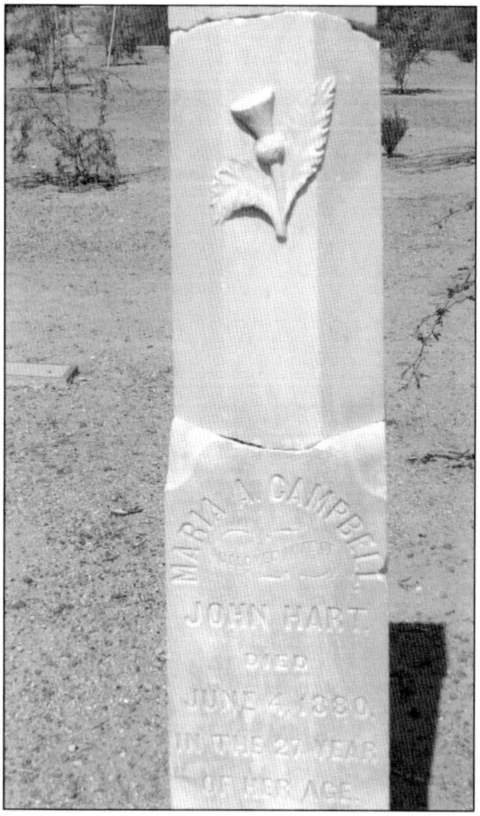

Maria Campbell, wife of John Hart, died in Tucson on June 4, 1880. Her birthday is not known, but she was only 27 years old. Her tall, obelisk-like grave marker is decorated with a thistle. The thistle is a favorite among those from Scotland, befitting a lass with the name of Campbell.

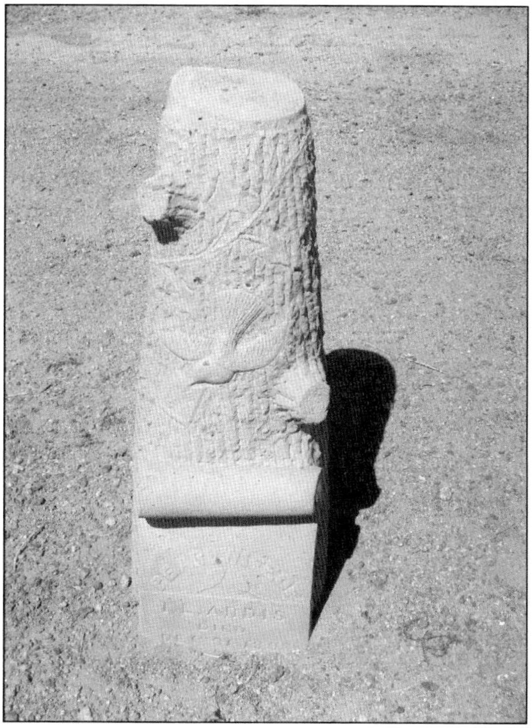

Neither the birthday nor the death date of Pearl Ardis is known. Her husband, I.L. Ardis, would have been a member of the Woodmen of the World, as reflected in her treestone. Pearl's grave is adorned with a flying dove and an invitation saying: "Come."

Art C. Gilbert's treestone is inscribed with the Latin words "*dum tacet clamat*," meaning, "Though silent, he speaks." Gilbert was born April 16, 1876, in Oregon and died in Tucson on September 3, 1906, of tuberculosis. At the time of his death, he was married and had worked as a blacksmith. There appears to be a faint image of an anvil on his stone.

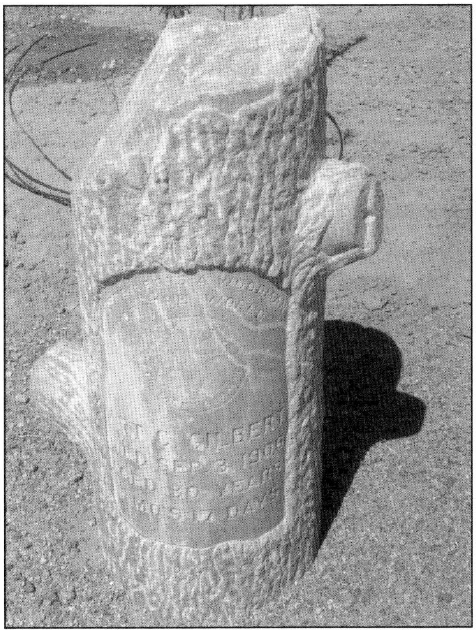

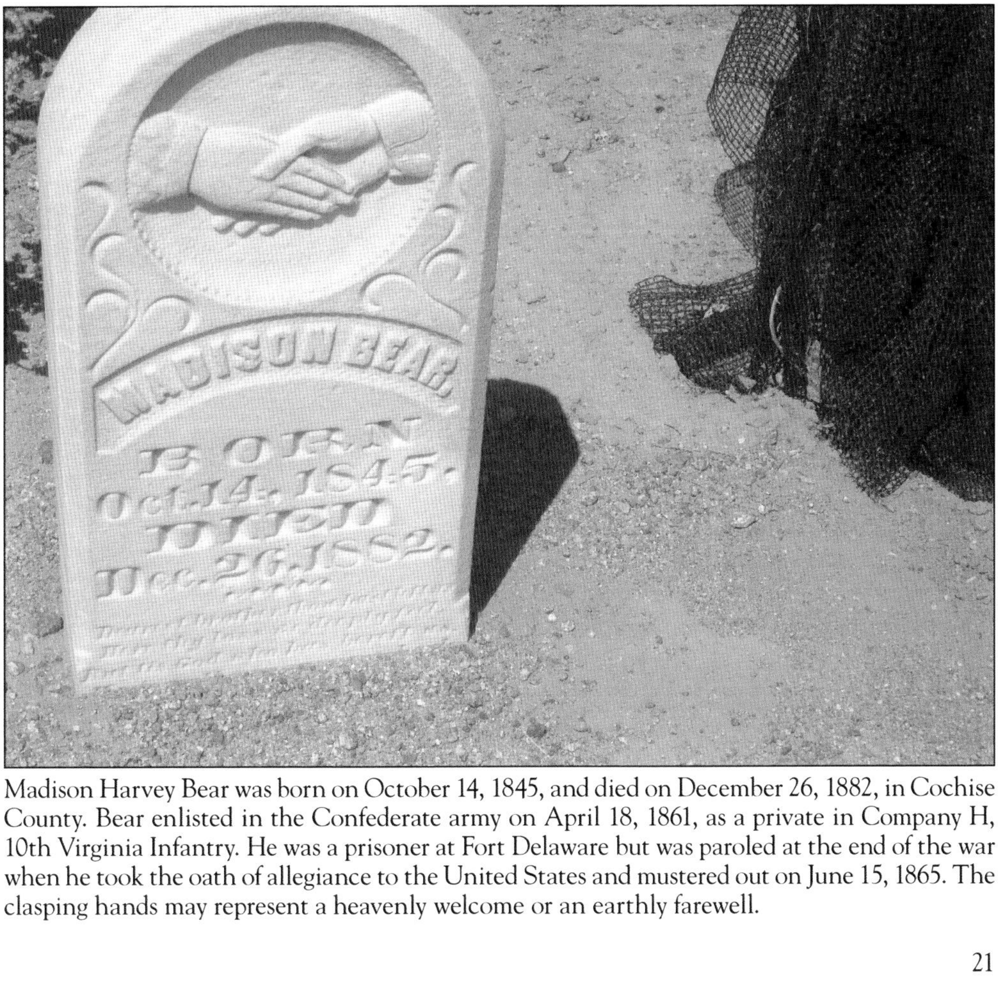

Madison Harvey Bear was born on October 14, 1845, and died on December 26, 1882, in Cochise County. Bear enlisted in the Confederate army on April 18, 1861, as a private in Company H, 10th Virginia Infantry. He was a prisoner at Fort Delaware but was paroled at the end of the war when he took the oath of allegiance to the United States and mustered out on June 15, 1865. The clasping hands may represent a heavenly welcome or an earthly farewell.

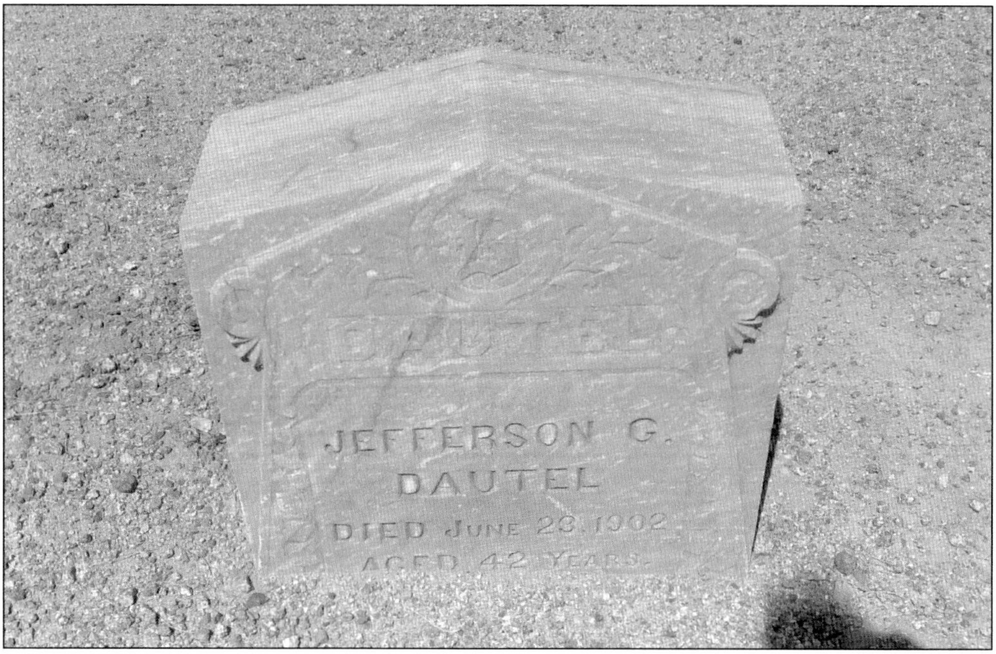

Jefferson G. Dautel was born in Kentucky on July 7, 1860, and died of tuberculosis in Tucson on June 23, 1902. He was living in Colorado and working as a bartender when he contracted tuberculosis in 1899. He sought help for the disease by moving to the warm, dry Arizona Territory. He settled in Tucson, where he continued to work in the saloon business. Dautel died on June 23, 1902, at his home at 77 East Alameda Street in Tucson. He was 42 years old when he died.

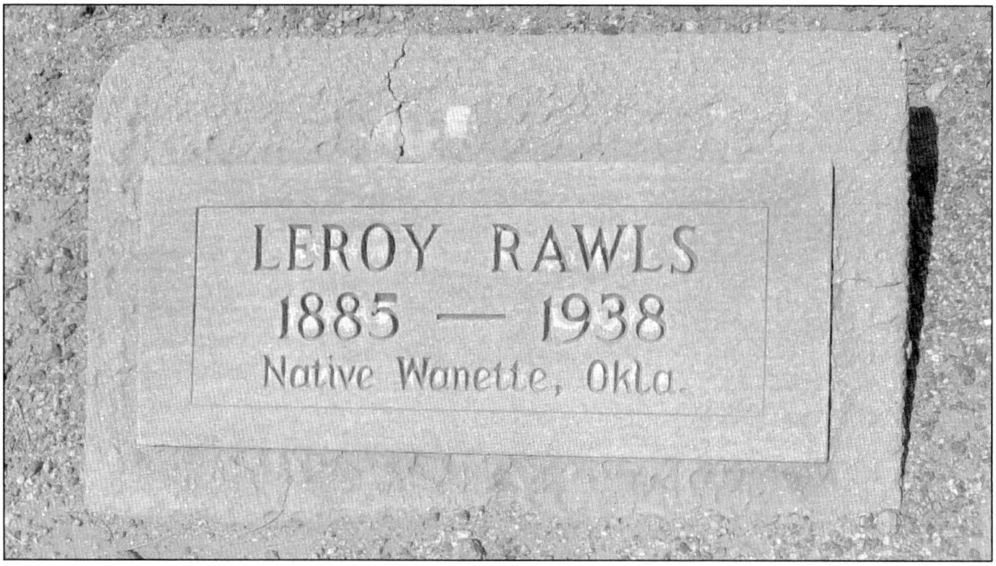

John Leroy Rawls was born on November 21, 1885, in Wanette, Oklahoma. Most of his time in Arizona was spent as a farmhand in the Phoenix area. On Tuesday evening, November 29, 1938, while attempting to hop a train traveling along the tracks in Tucson, Rawls fell and was killed. He was survived by his wife, Hattie. He died during the Great Depression, and the Rawls family was going through hard times. Leroy rode the rails looking for work so that his family could eat and lost his life in the process.

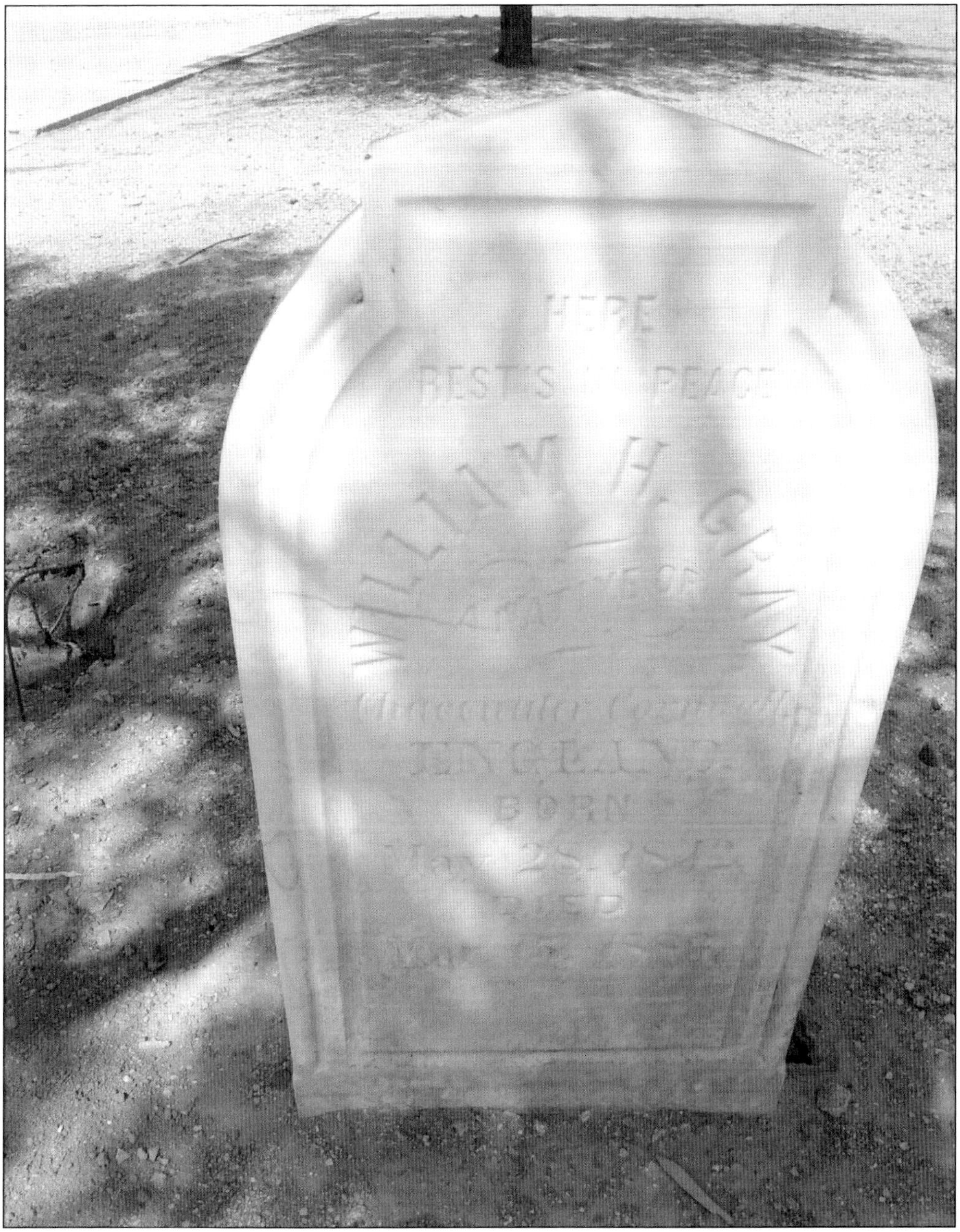

William H. Gray, a native of Chacewater, Cornwall, England, was born on May 28, 1842. He died in Tucson on March 15, 1883.

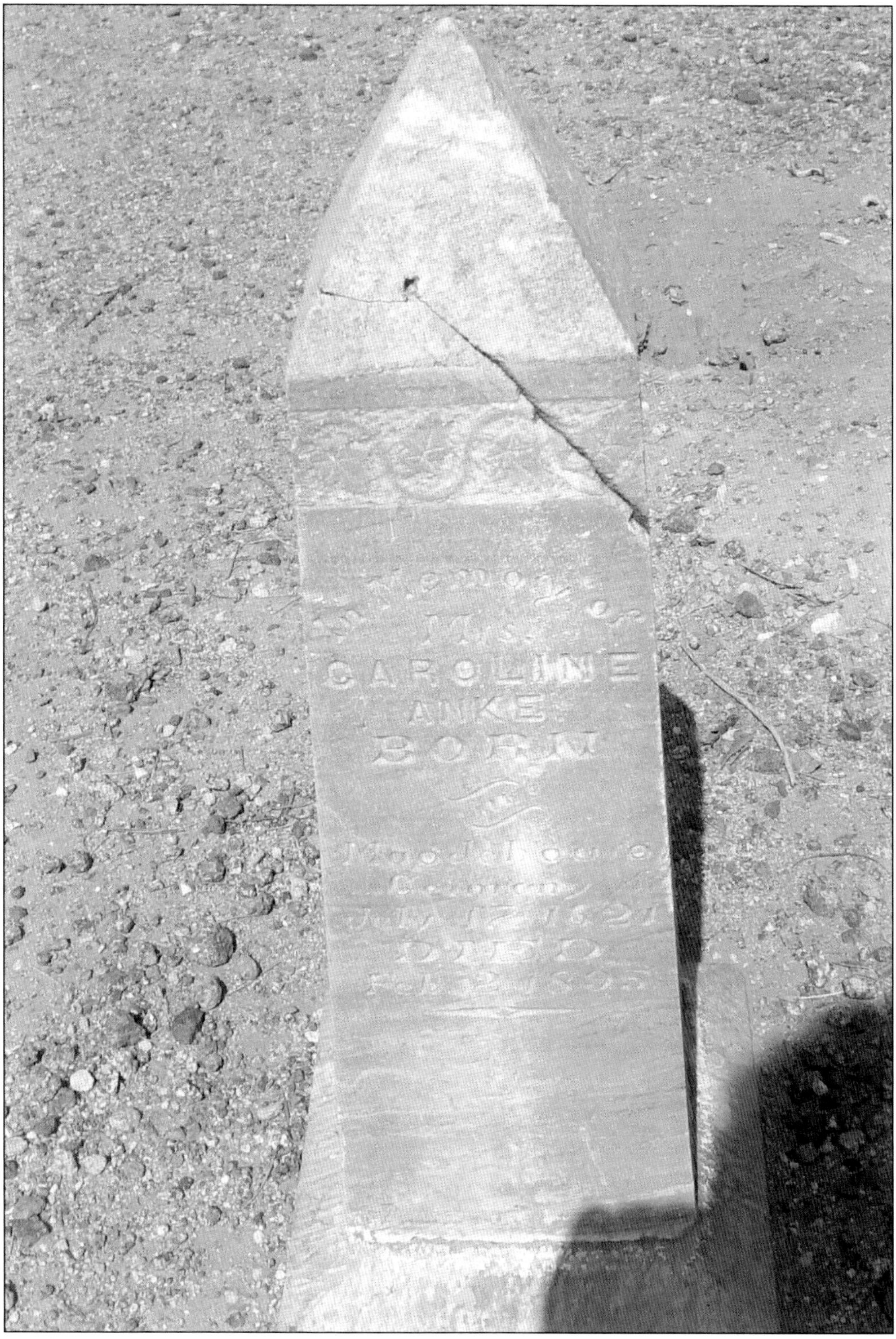

Caroline Anke was born on July 17, 1821, in Germany. She died on February 2, 1895, at age 74. The varied nationalities of the deceased reflect the diversity of immigrants to Southern Arizona.

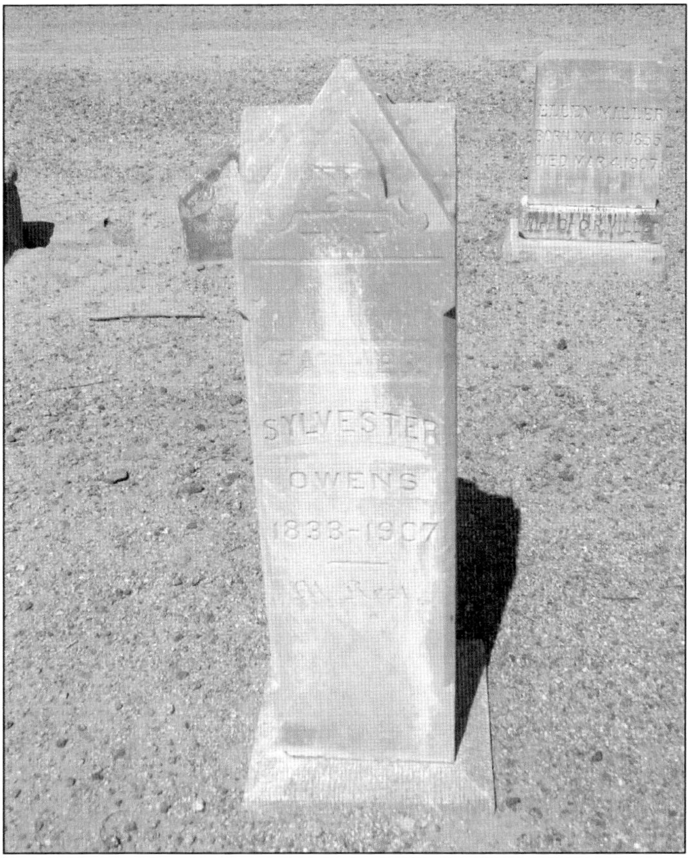

Sylvester Owens was born on January 24, 1833, in New York City. He died on April 14, 1907, in Tucson. Owens, a liquor dealer, died of gangrene in St. Mary's Hospital.

This tombstone has sunk into the soil so deeply that nothing more than the names and birth and death dates of Mabel and Brownie, presumably siblings, are visible.

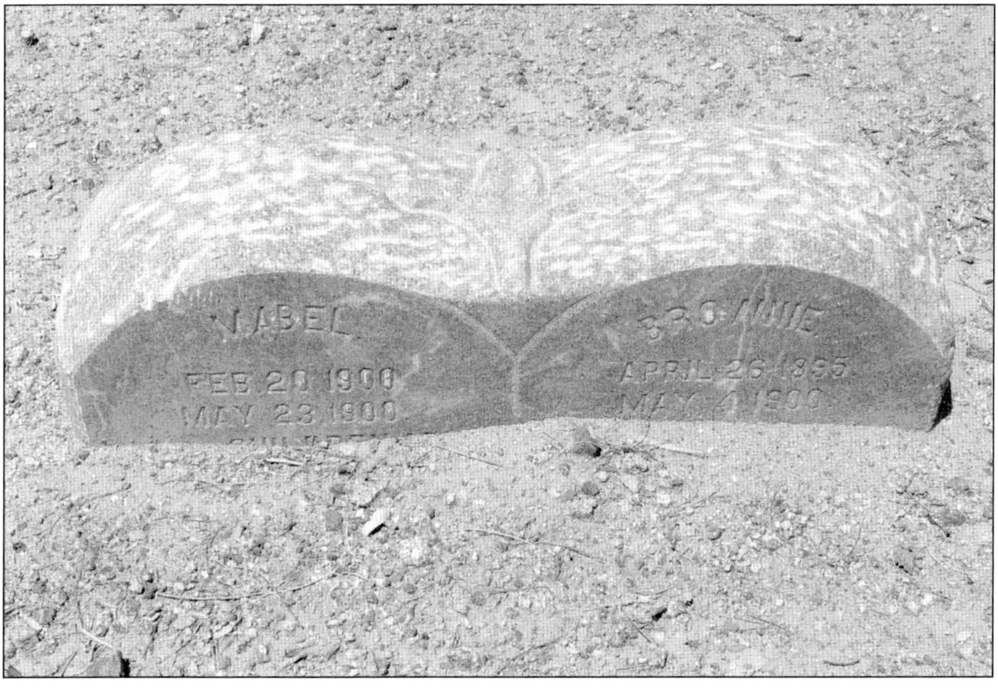

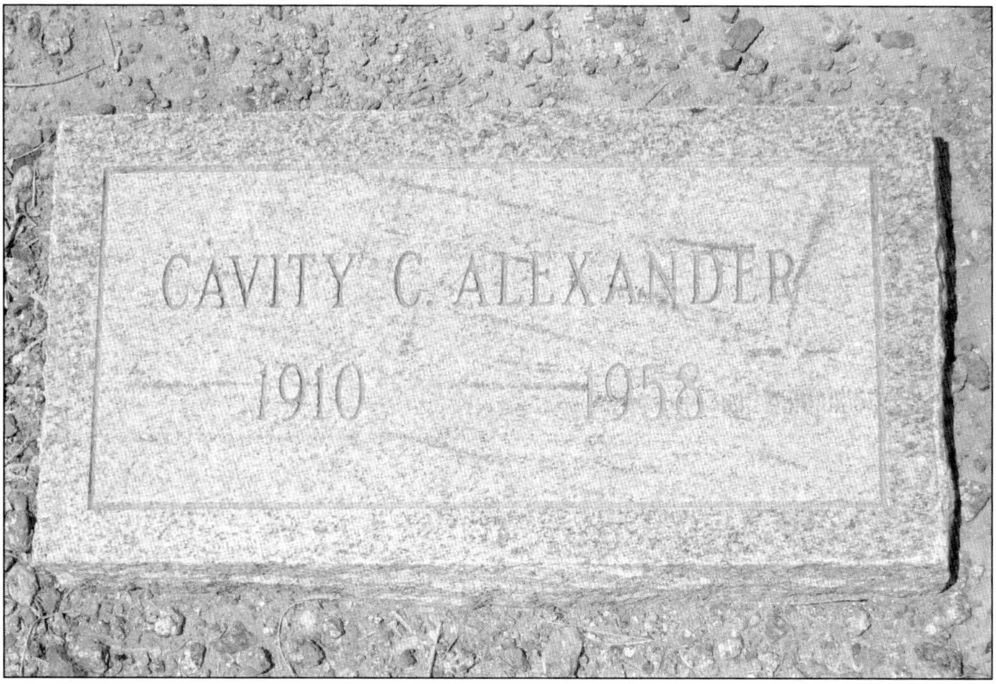

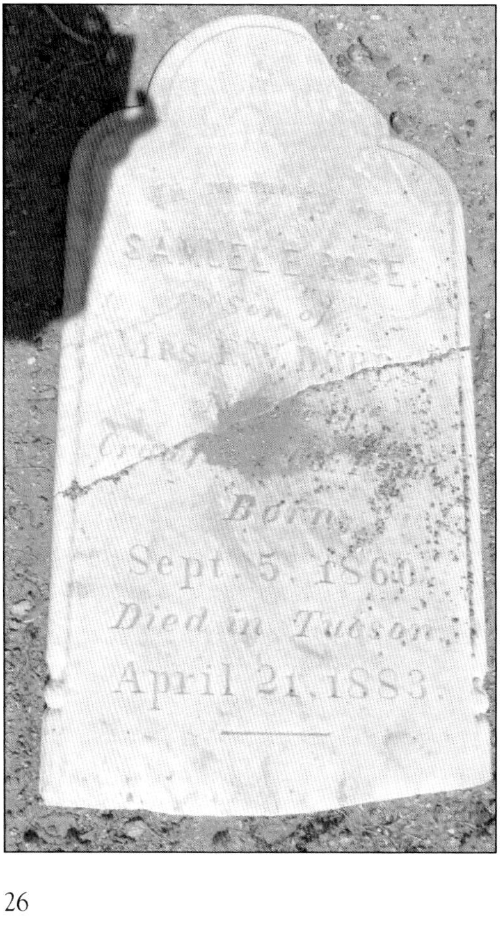

Cavity Alexander was born in 1910. He spent the most of his life in Tucson and gained a reputation as a local drunk who had numerous run-ins with the police. When he was sober, Alexander worked as a laborer. On March 10, 1958, his body was discovered in the 4200 Block of North Oracle Road in Tucson. An autopsy revealed that he had died of acute alcoholism and exposure to the elements.

Samuel E. Rose's gravestone is falling into terrible disrepair. He was born on September 5, 1860, to Mrs. E.W. Dobbs in Crawford County, Pennsylvania. He died in Tucson on April 21, 1883.

John Burt was 56 years old when he died in Tucson on November 17, 1880.

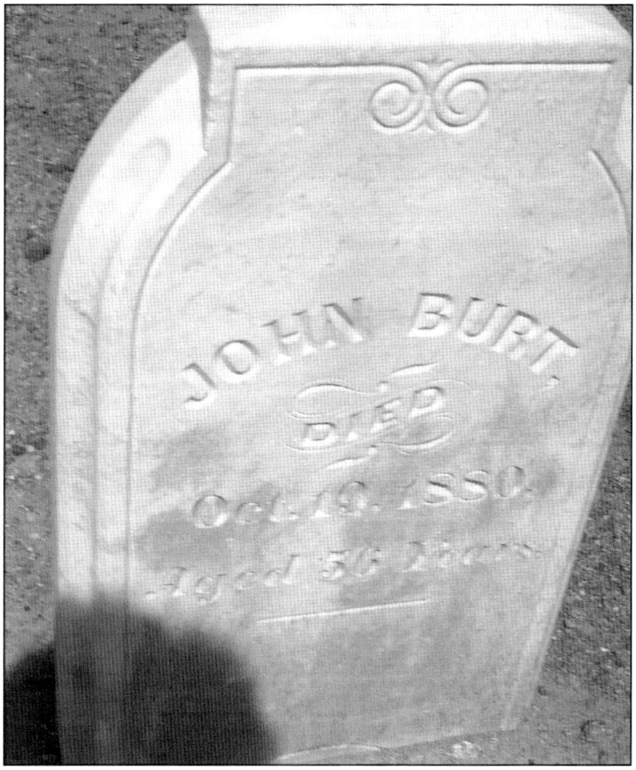

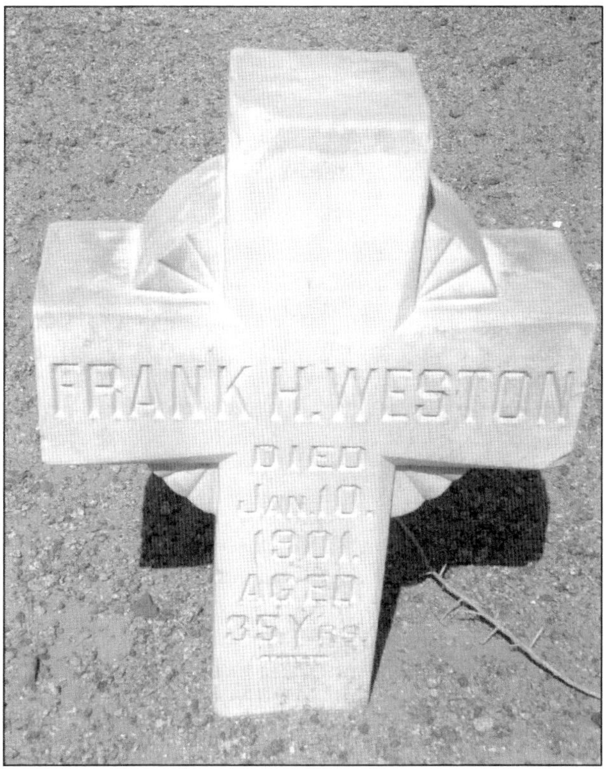

Frank H. Weston was 35 years old and had lived in Tucson for about one year when he contracted typhoid fever and died in St. Mary's Hospital on January 10, 1901. He was single and listed his occupation as "draughtsman" and his birthplace as San Francisco.

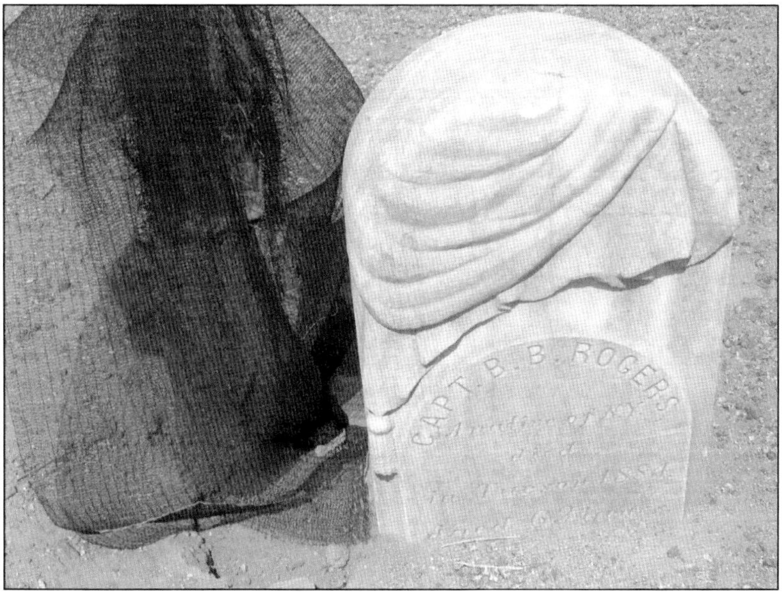

Capt. B.B. Rogers's birthday is unknown. However, he was a native of New York and had a military affiliation. He died in Tucson in 1884 at age 63.

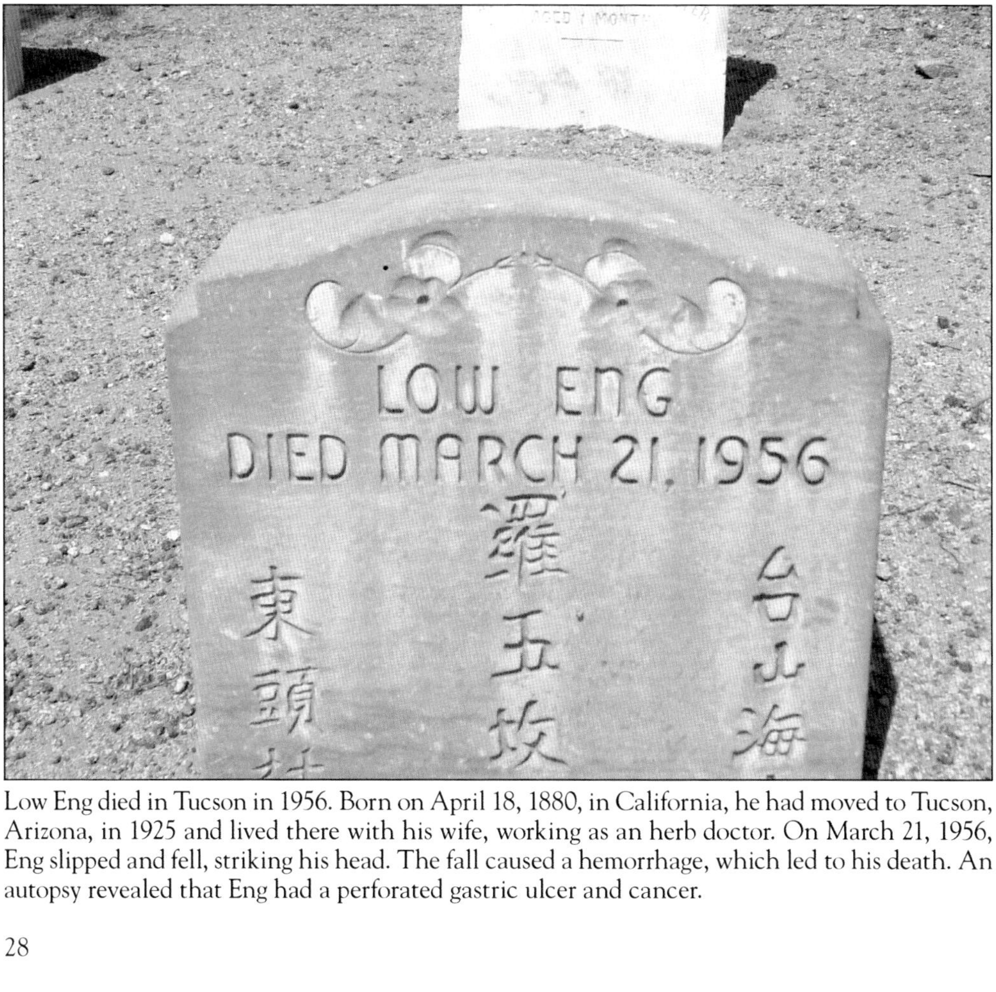

Low Eng died in Tucson in 1956. Born on April 18, 1880, in California, he had moved to Tucson, Arizona, in 1925 and lived there with his wife, working as an herb doctor. On March 21, 1956, Eng slipped and fell, striking his head. The fall caused a hemorrhage, which led to his death. An autopsy revealed that Eng had a perforated gastric ulcer and cancer.

This marker is a flat piece of marble with only Chinese characters. The man's surname is Gee or Jee, and he is from the district of Tai Shan or Toi San in the Pearl River Delta area of southern China; in the early days of Chinese immigration to the United States, about 70 percent of the arriving Chinese came from that area. The Chinese put the word "grave" on tombstones.

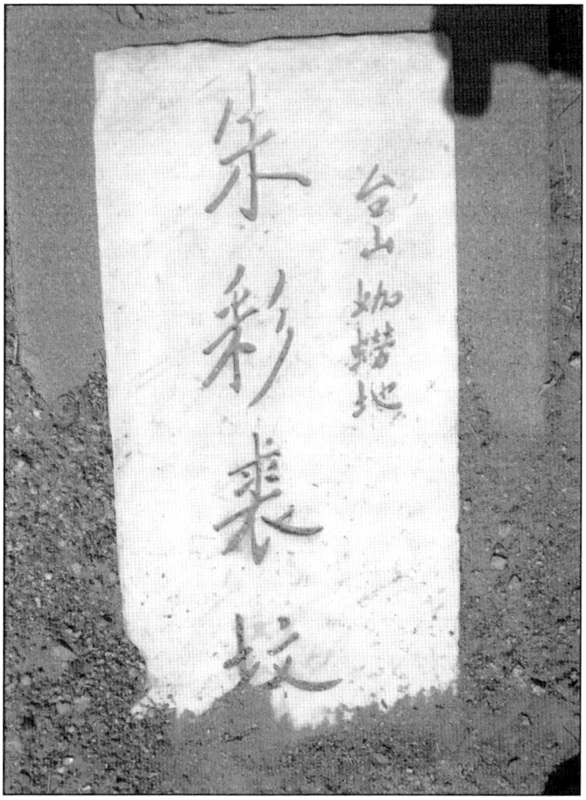

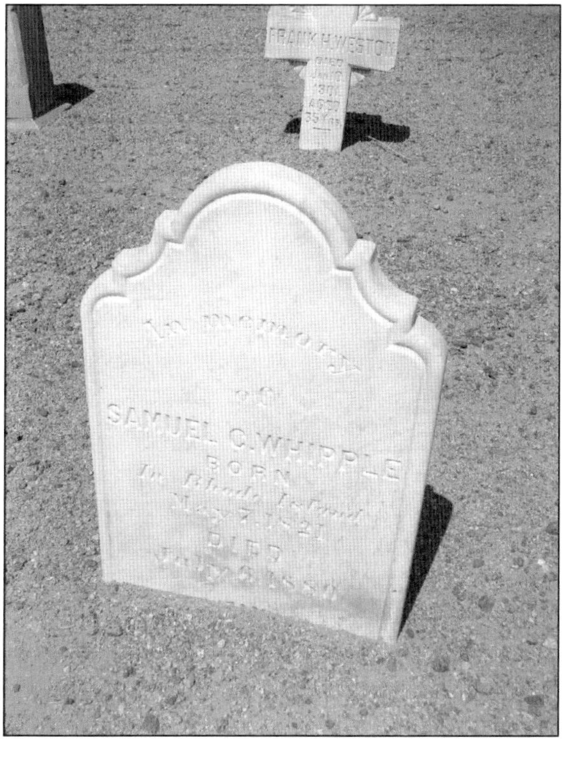

Samuel C. Whipple was born on May 7, 1821, in Rhode Island and died on July 6, 1880, in Tucson. He enlisted as a private at Downieville, California, on November 9, 1864, and was mustered into Company K, 7th California Infantry on November 21. He was posted to Fort McDowell, Arizona Territory, where he was mustered out on March 19, 1866, by special order no. 18.

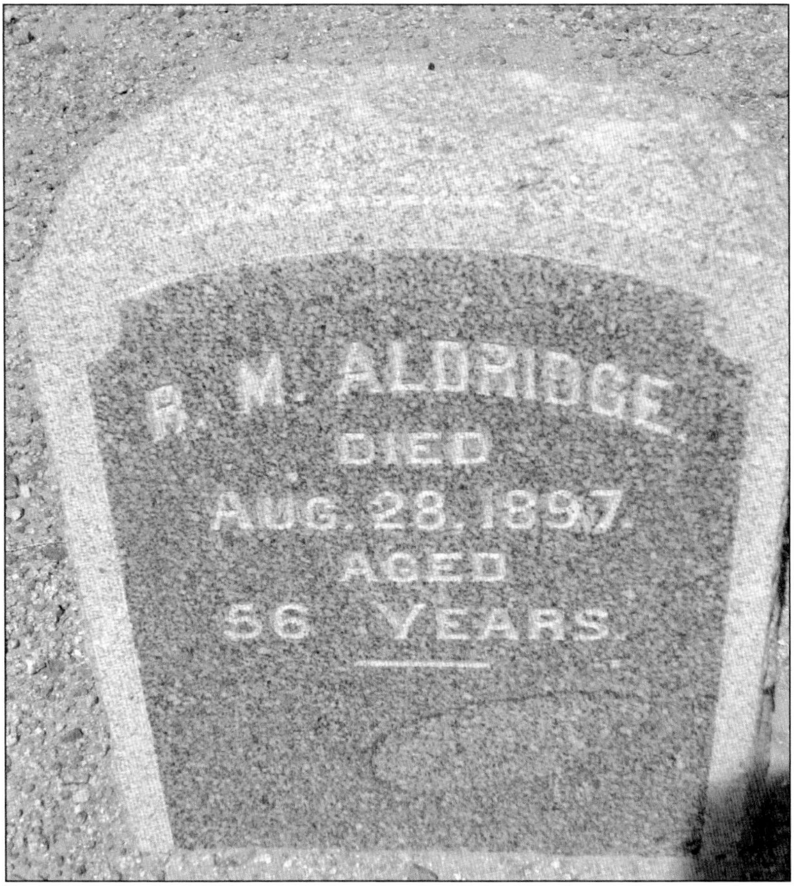

We do not know R.M. Aldridge's birth date, but according to the gravestone, he was 56 years old when he died on August 28, 1897.

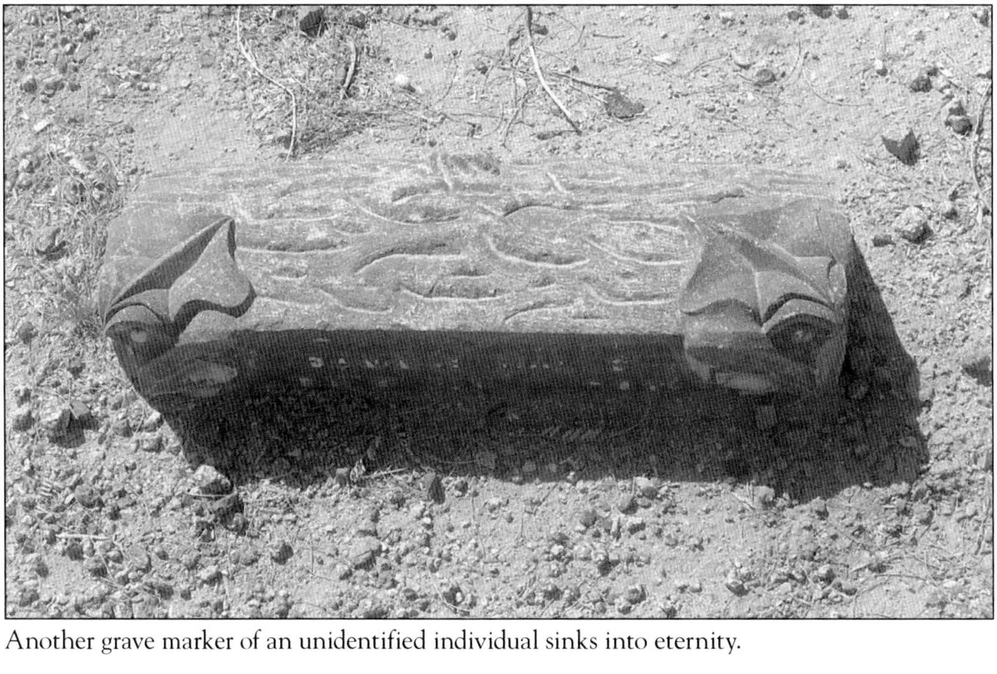

Another grave marker of an unidentified individual sinks into eternity.

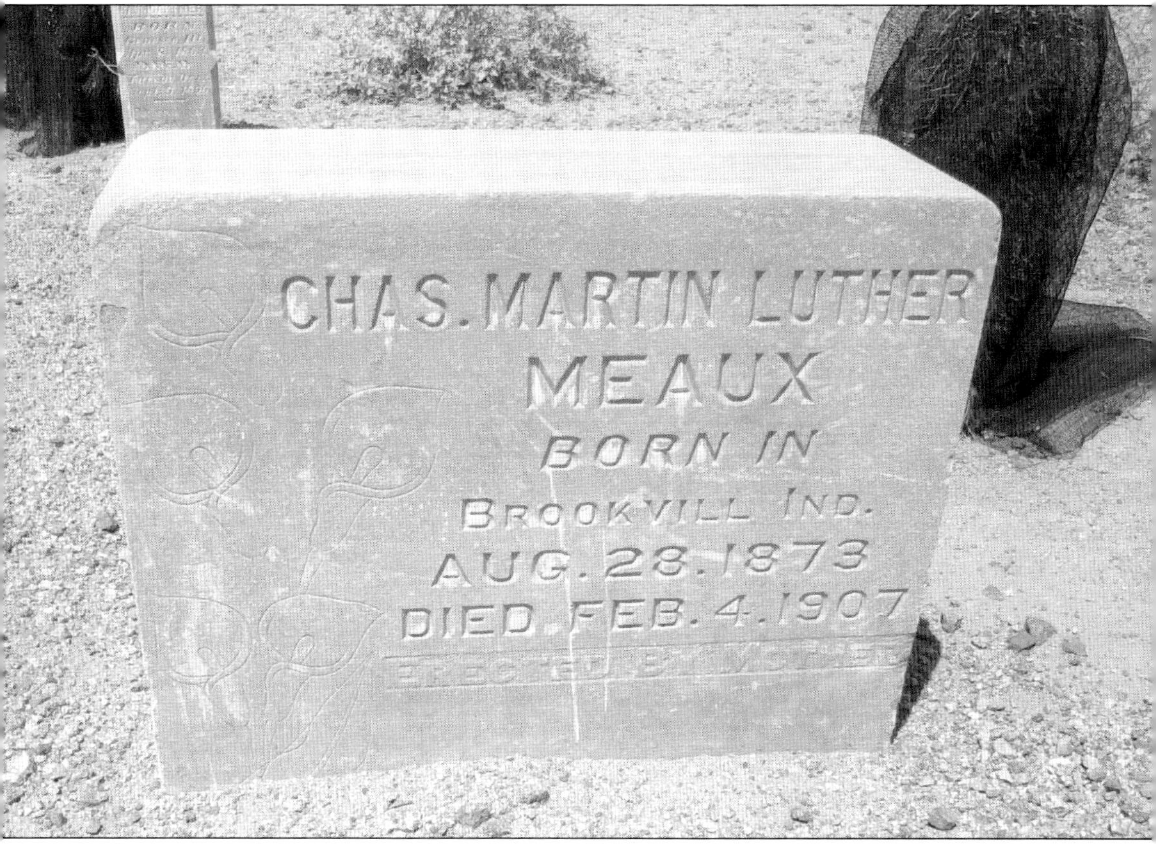

Charles Martin Luther Meaux's tombstone, decorated with lovely lilies of the valley, was provided by his mother. Meaux was born on August 28, 1873, in Brookville, Indiana, and died on February 4, 1907. When he contracted tuberculosis in 1904, he came to the Arizona Territory in hopes that the warm, dry climate would be good for his condition. His health deteriorated rapidly, and he checked into St. Mary's Hospital on February 2, 1907, and died two days later.

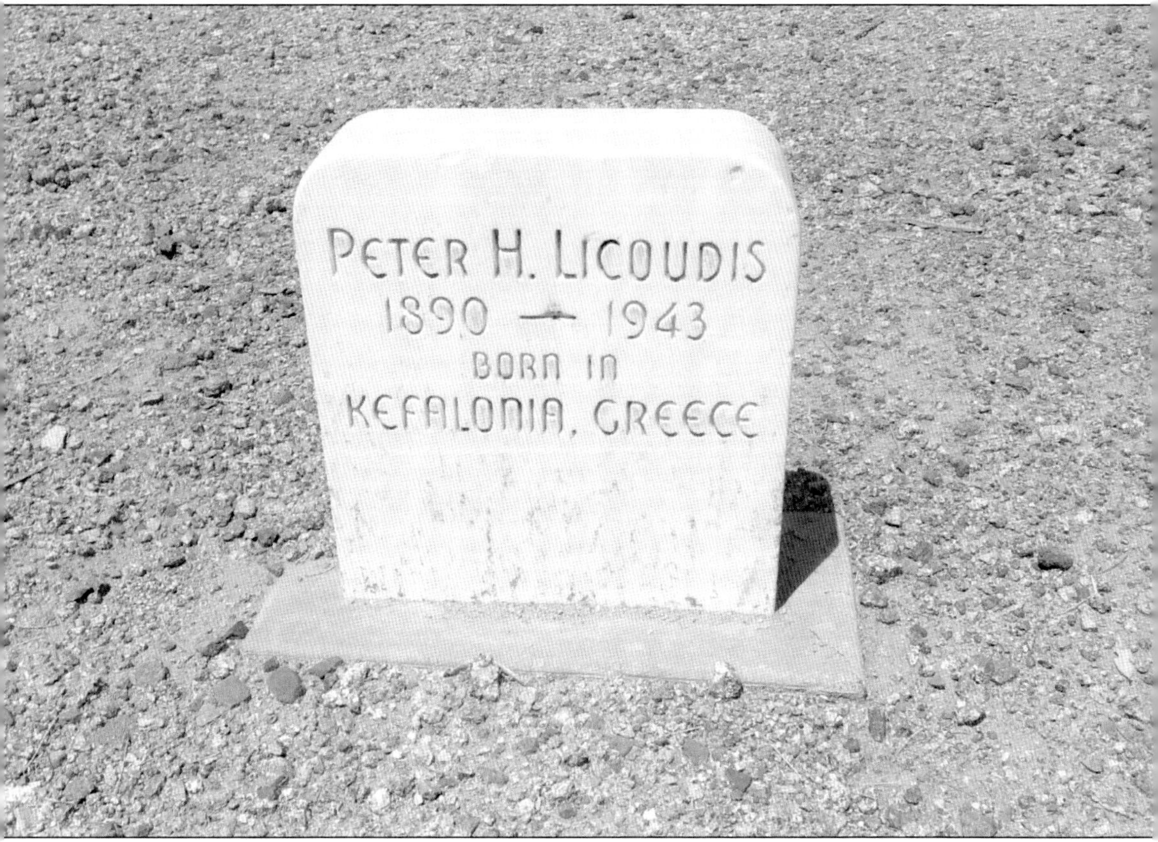

Peter H. Licoudis was born in Kefalonia, Greece, in 1890 and died in Tucson in 1943.

Three

Cochise County Graves and Cemeteries

Cochise County, created from Pima County in 1881, was named for Apache chief Cochise, who, along with a band of Chiricahua Apaches, made his stronghold in the Dragoon Mountains. The area boomed in 1878 when Ed Schieffelin, a prospector, located several silver claims in the area and founded Tombstone. Tombstone served as the county seat until 1929, when it was moved to Bisbee. The town of Tombstone is famous for the 1881 Gunfight at the O.K. Corral, which involved the Earp brothers and Doc Holliday versus Billy Clanton and the McLaury brothers. A number of Western movies, including the original 1957 version of *3:10 to Yuma*, have been made in the county. Cochise County's towns and rural areas contain a number of interesting cemeteries.

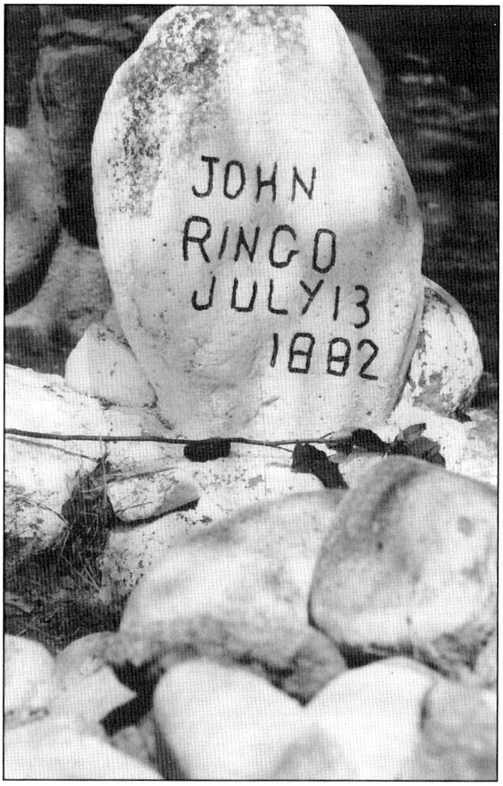

This is Johnny Ringo's grave. The outlaw, supposedly born John Peters Ringgold (although this is disputed by some) in Indiana on May 3, 1850, died on July 13, 1882. His family moved to Missouri when he was six. When Johnny's father, Martin Ringgold, came down with tuberculosis, he decided to move his family to San Jose, California, in search of a drier climate. During the five-month journey, John sustained a serious foot injury, Indians attacked the family wagon, and John witnessed a murder. An accidentally misfired shotgun took the life of his father, forcing the family to bury him along the trail. By age 19, John had developed a taste for alcohol, and he left home for Texas, where he became involved in the Mason County (or Hoodoo) War over cattle ownership. During this time, he shortened his surname to Ringo. (Courtesy of Richard Lapidus.)

Ringo moved to the Arizona Territory, where his profession was listed as "speculator" in the 1882 Great Register of Cochise County. He rustled cattle and committed robbery, and one day his body was found in West Turkey Creek near Tombstone—he was sitting in a tree with a gunshot wound to the head. The coroner declared the act a suicide and ordered him buried a few feet from his place of death. Among the suspects rumored to have possibly killed Ringo were Wyatt Earp, Lou Cooley, and Buckskin Frank Leslie. The tree is still there, and the grave now has a designated Arizona Historical Society marker. The site is located on private property, about 100 yards from the owner's house, and visitors must check with the owner before going to see the grave.

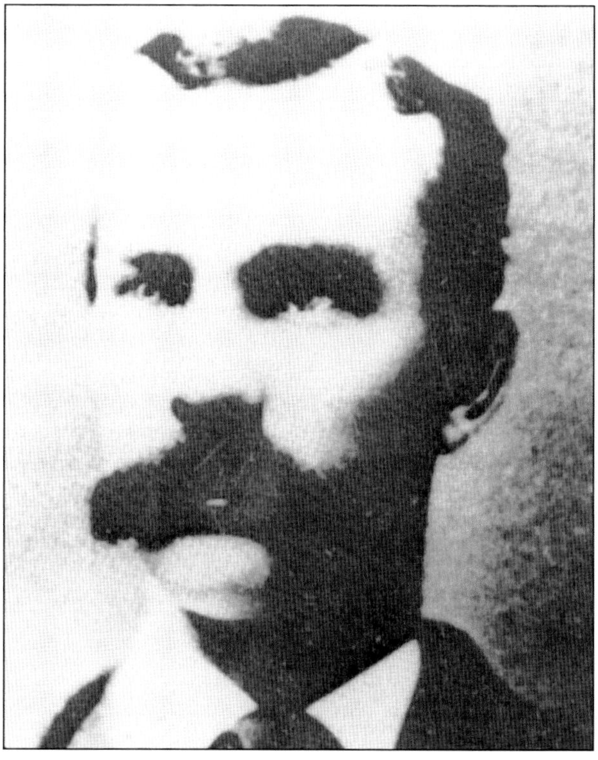

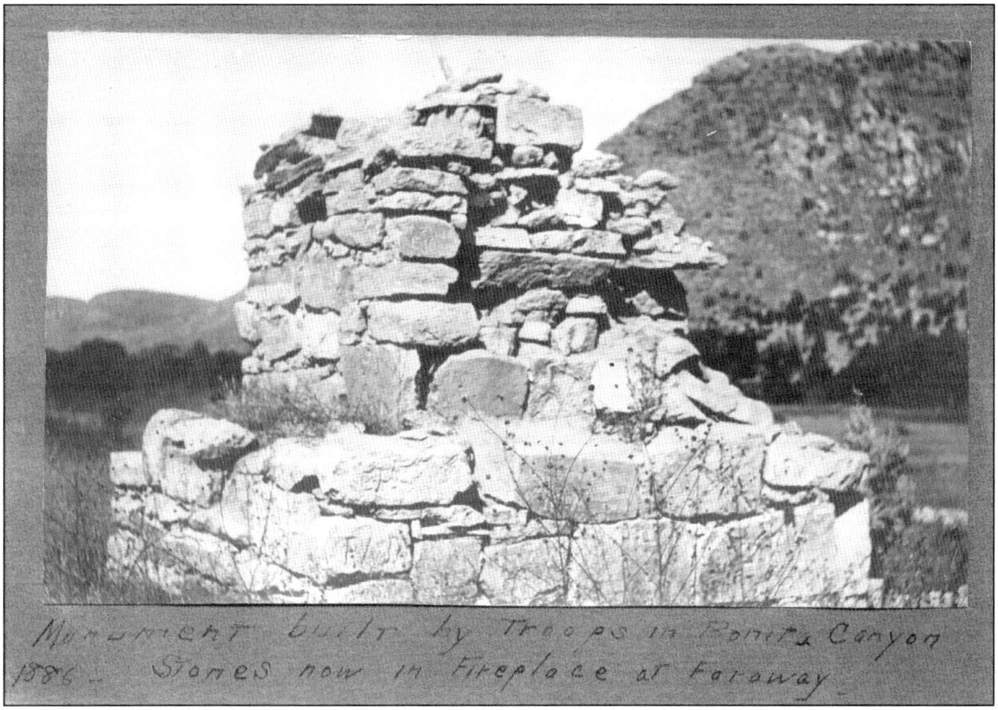

The Pres. James A. Garfield Memorial and its inscribed bricks are part of the fireplace of the Faraway Ranch, which is under the aegis of the Chiricahua National Monument. The stones, inscribed with the names and ranks of soldiers stationed at the Bonita Canyon camp, were carved by the black Buffalo soldiers of the 10th Cavalry as a tribute after Garfield's assassination. As they were redeployed, people took pieces of the memorial. To preserve it, rancher Ed Riggs dismantled it and remade it as a fireplace. As a Civil War officer, Garfield commanded black troops, and as president, he was sympathetic to the plight of black Americans. The Bonita Canyon camp was established as part of the US military's Geronimo Campaign, which began in September 1885 and ended in September 1886 with the surrender of Geronimo. (Courtesy of WACC.)

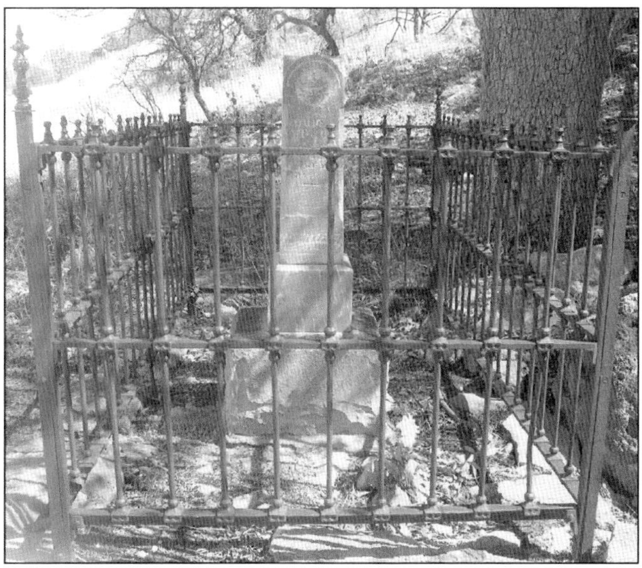

Louis Prue was born in June 1843 in Canada. He enlisted on October 15, 1861, as a private in Battery H, 2nd New York Heavy Artillery. He transferred to Company F, 14th Veteran Reserve Corps, as a private on September 9, 1865. He settled in the Sulphur Springs area in 1879 and was reportedly the first white settler in that locale. Prue got married and established a cattle ranch. The Erickson family laid him to rest under the oak on the hillside at the mouth of Bonita Canyon after he died from a fall off a horse on December 16, 1892.

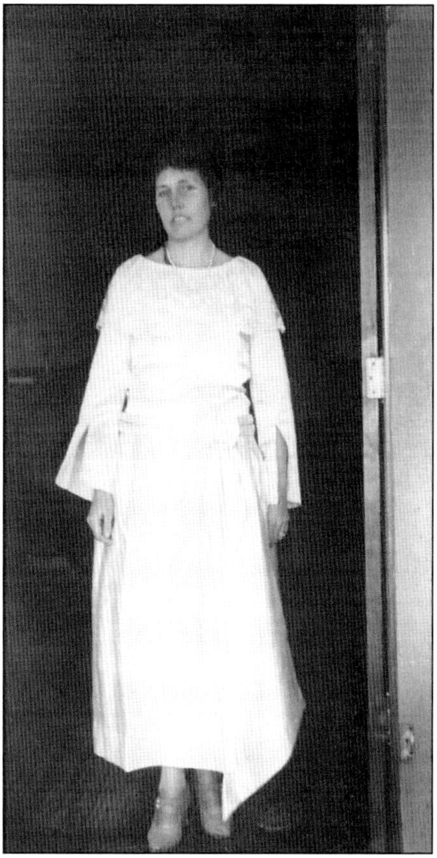

Lillian Erickson Riggs is pictured at left in her wedding dress. Lillian's story, which is central to the Faraway homestead in the Chiricahua Mountains, began when she was born on February 9, 1888. An aggressive, liberated woman, she was known in her later years as the "lady boss." On April 22, 1918, she and her sister Hildegard purchased the Stafford homestead for $5,000. They paid for the land with Lillian's teaching wages, a bank loan, money from guests, and income from their cattle. The sisters began hosting visitors for a week or more, feeding them and offering them horseback trips into the Chiricahua Mountains; they named the site Faraway Ranch. (Courtesy of WACC.)

The Erickson-Riggs cemetery is located on Route 186, and its earliest burials occurred in 1885. When Hildegard married and left, Lillian operated Faraway Ranch by herself until she married Edward Riggs in 1923, a year that marked the beginning of major development of the ranch. Lillian and Ed operated the ranch for vacationers, and Lillian ran it by herself for over 20 years after Ed died in 1950. Even after losing her eyesight, she loved riding on the property. In 1973, Lillian entered a rest home in Willcox, and the family let longtime foreman Andy Anderson take care of the ranch. She died on April 26, 1977, at age 89.

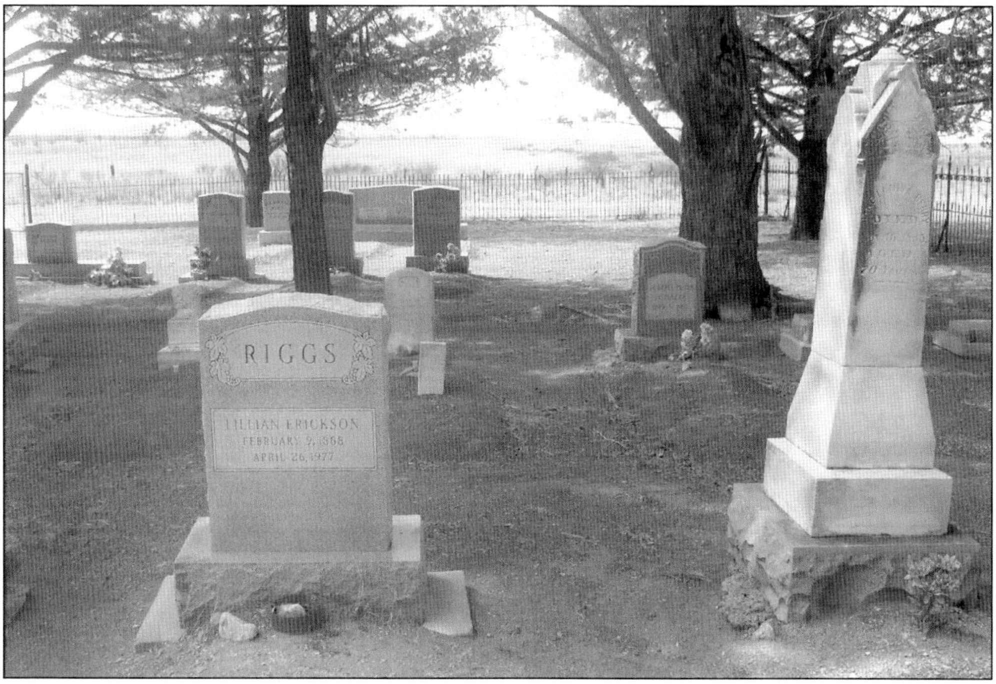

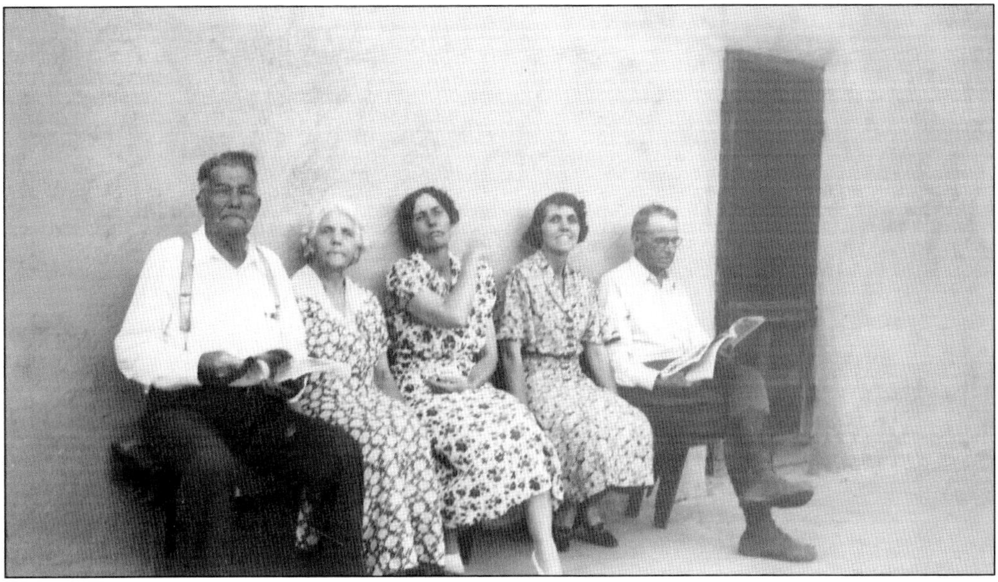

Pictured here are, from left to right, Neil (Nels) Erickson; his wife, Emma; their children Hildegard and Lillian; and Lillian's husband, Ed Riggs. Neil was born in Sweden in 1859 and died in 1937. Neil served as an Indian fighter in the US army and traveled the mountains of Cochise County on maneuvers. In 1887, after Geronimo surrendered, Neil settled down to ranching and a career with the newly formed Division of Forestry. Edward Murray ("Ed") Riggs was born on September 22, 1885, and died on June 29, 1950. (Courtesy of WACC.)

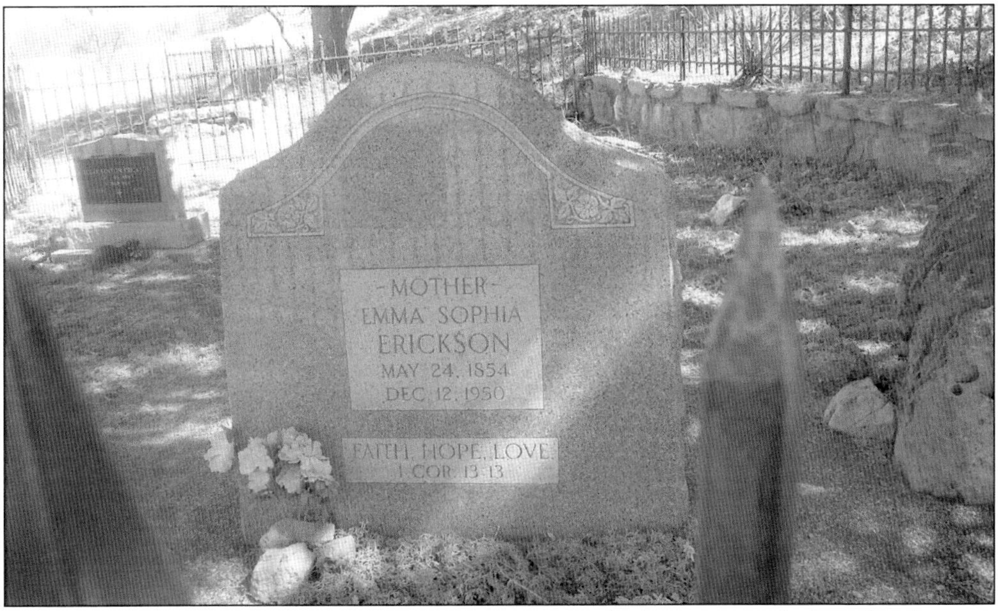

Emma Sophia Peterson, born in Sweden on May 24, 1854, died at age 96 in the Douglas, Arizona, hospital on December 12, 1950. When her mother died giving birth to her seventh child, Emma's father married the family housekeeper. Emma did not get along well with her stepmother, and by the time she was a teenager, she decided that it was time to leave home. She immigrated to the United States, where her brother and sister were living. In the 1880s, she met Neil Erickson, worked as a domestic at Fort Bowie, Arizona; and opened a boardinghouse at Fort Bowie.

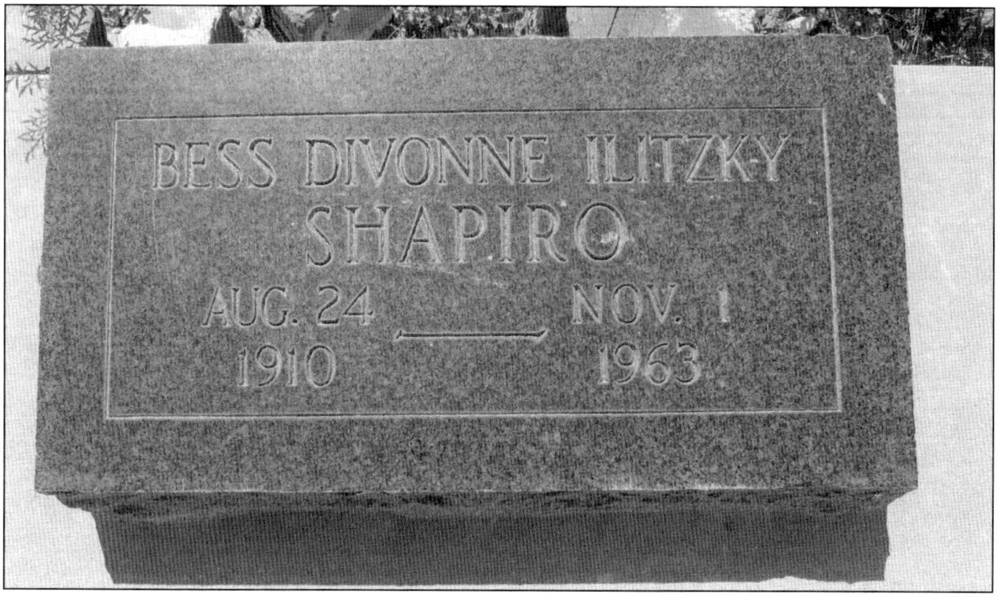

The old Jewish cemetery in Douglas, which was founded in 1904, was restored in 1992; it appears to be the first Jewish cemetery in Arizona. It contains 30 identifiable graves—early Douglas and nearby Bisbee were prosperous towns with many Jewish merchants. The cemetery is located on the eastern limits of Douglas, about two blocks north of the international border. Bess Shapiro was born on August 24, 1910, in El Paso and died November 1, 1963, in Los Angeles. She resided in Douglas for most of her life until her family moved to California in 1950.

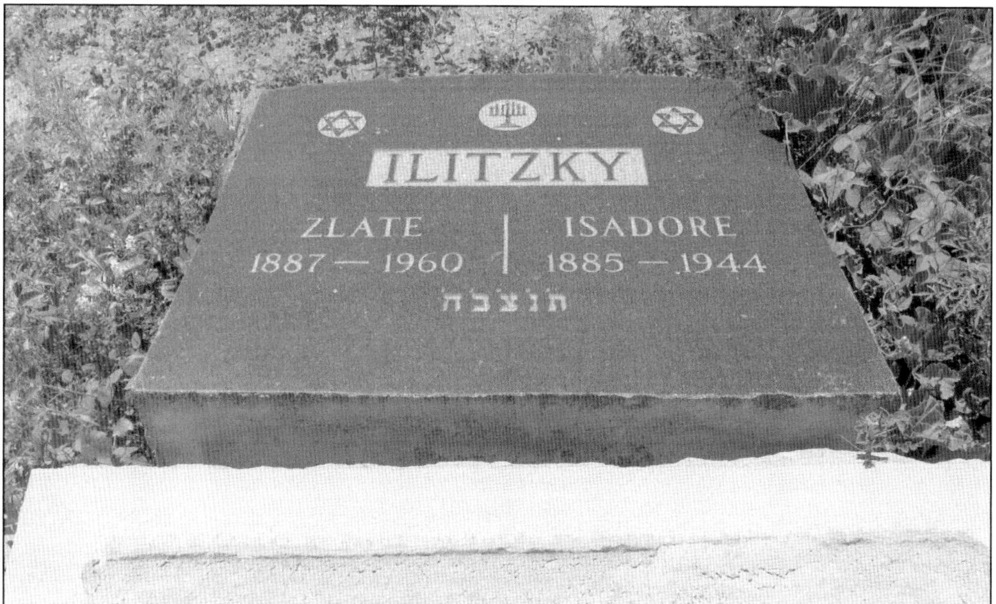

Both Isadore Ilitzky and his wife, Zlate, were born in Russia. Isadore was born March 9, 1885. He arrived in Douglas around 1912 and ran a furniture store and a junkyard. The Ilitzky remains were reinterred in the Calvary Cemetery in Douglas, so all that is left in the Jewish cemetery is their headstone decorated with the Star of David and a seven-branched menorah, which dates back to the Temple of Solomon. Isadore died on February 2, 1944, of heart trouble and asthma.

Little is known of Daniel Silver, who was born in 1926 and died in 1957, except that he was Jewish. The symbols on each side of the Star of David are Hebrew for "Here Lies."

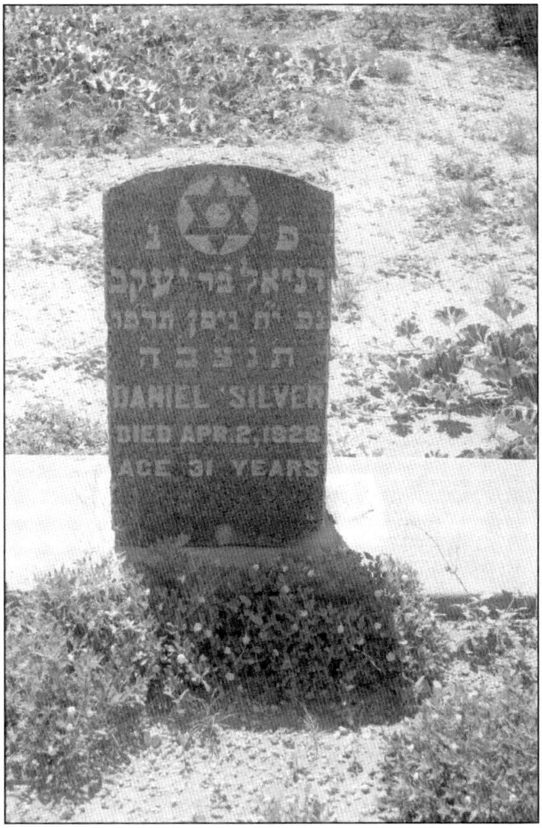

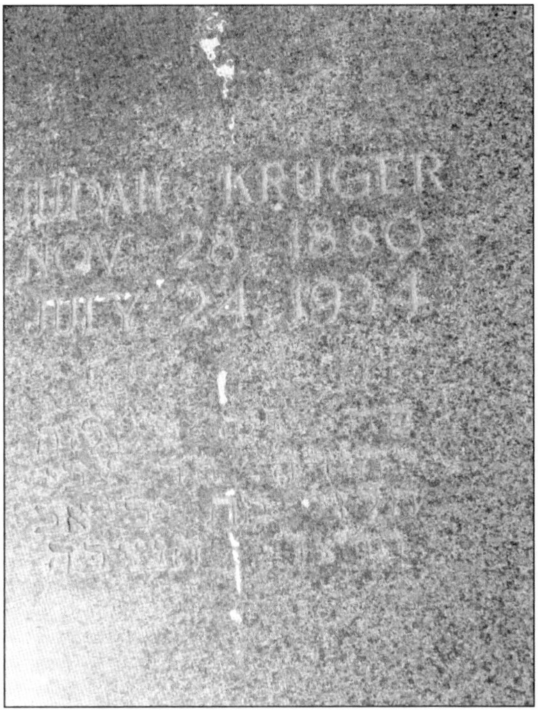

Judah Kruger, a Bisbee merchant with a store on Brewery Gulch, was born on November 28, 1880, and committed suicide on July 24, 1934. His remains were taken to Houston in 1947. He left three notes, all written in Yiddish. To his wife living in Tucson, he said he was "ending 30 years of suffering." In another note, addressed to I. Jacobson, Kruger asked that he be buried in Douglas in a suit of clothes from his store and that the funeral be inexpensive. Charles Fruitman, a longtime friend, told police he had visited Kruger the day before and that he appeared to be in a nervous state. Fruitman returned to Kruger's store and, finding it locked from the inside, notified police. Chief J.L. Ramsower broke the lock on the door, and in the back part of the store, they found Kruger lying dead in a pool of blood next to a .38-caliber revolver. Kruger was survived by his widow and five children and a brother in Dallas.

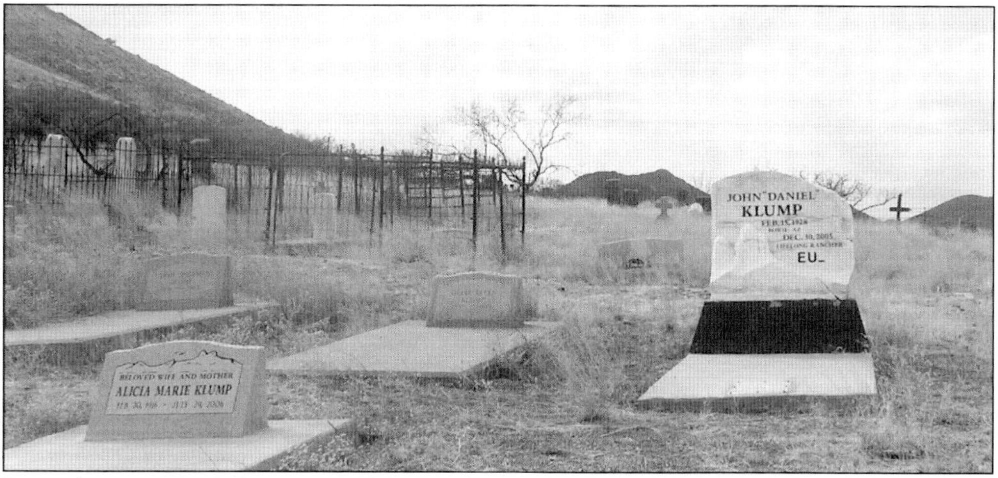

Dos Cabezas was settled in 1878, and the town soon had a barbershop, a general store, a brickyard, a hotel, a blacksmith, a post office, and a population of about 300 people. Dos Cabezas thrived for decades as a transportation center and mining town, but after the mines closed and most of the residents left the area, the town lost its post office in 1960. Today, the ruins are visible off the highway on Arizona State Route 186 south of Willcox. The Dos Cabezas Pioneer Cemetery is the final resting place of many Southern Arizona ranching families, including the Klumps. Their graves display icons, including horses and brands, related to their profession. John Daniel "Dan" Klump of Willcox died on December 30, 2005, in Tucson at age 77. Born in Bowie on February 15, 1928, he had been a longtime rancher in Cochise County and an avid Willcox livestock-auction observer and participant.

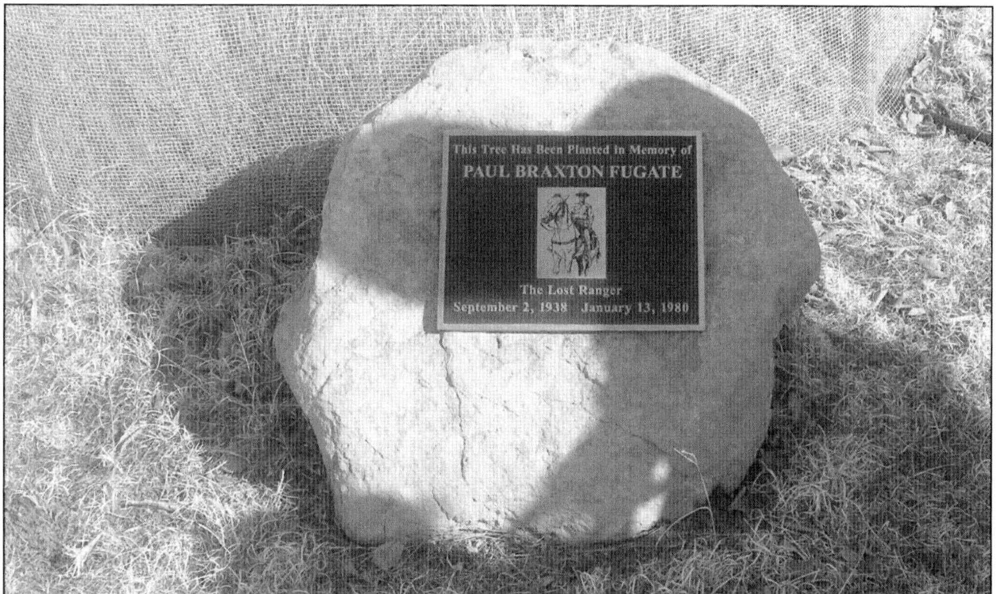

In January 1980, Chiricahua National Monument ranger Paul Fugate disappeared while on foot patrol in the Chiricahua backcountry, and what happened to him remains a mystery. When he did not return, the National Park Service and the Cochise County Sheriff's Department mounted extensive efforts to find him, but turned up nothing. Fugate's remains have never been recovered, but the park contains this monument marking his disappearance.

If ghosts get lost, Bisbee's Evergreen Cemetery has street signs to help guide them back home. This pioneer cemetery, located in the Lowell suburb of Bisbee, was established in 1912 as a result of concerns that water contamination was the cause of a series of typhoid outbreaks. The cemetery reflects the multicultural flavor of this community. Mine, mill, and smelter employees and vendors came to Bisbee from all over the United States, Mexico, Canada, and Europe.

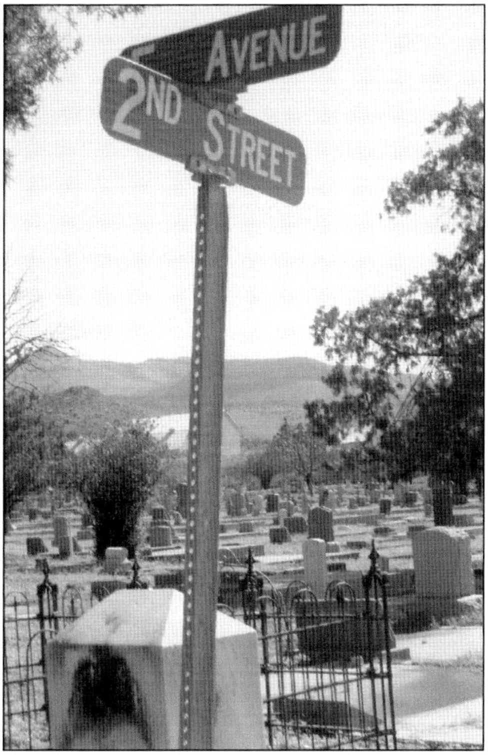

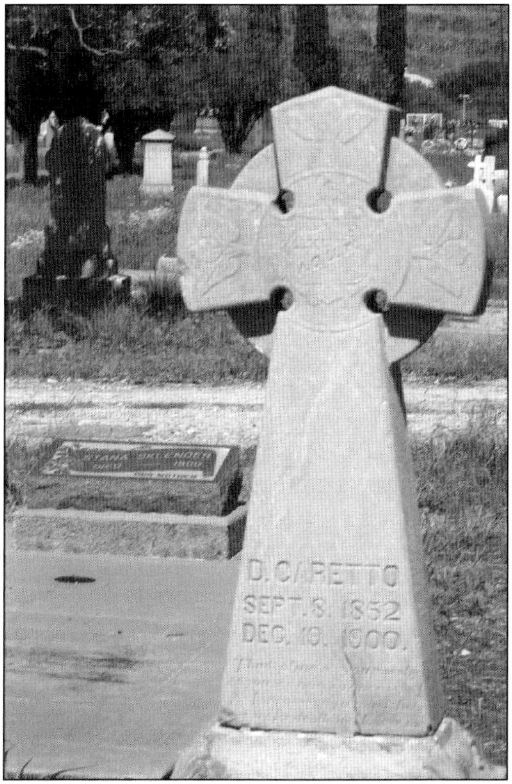

The Ancient Order of United Workmen (AOUW) was formed by John Jordan Upchurch in 1868 in Meadsville, Pennsylvania. Upchurch, a mechanic, organized the AOUW in hopes of forming a group that would unite the conflicting interests of labor and management. This organization provided benevolent insurance for its members' widows and orphans. Through Upchurch, a Freemason, the AOUW took on a number of Masonic features. It held secret rituals, and the square and compass and all-seeing eye were organizational symbols. Dominic Caretto's lovely Celtic tombstone, with lilies on its cross, marks him as a member of the AOUW. Caretto was born on September 8, 1852, and died in Bisbee on December 19, 1900.

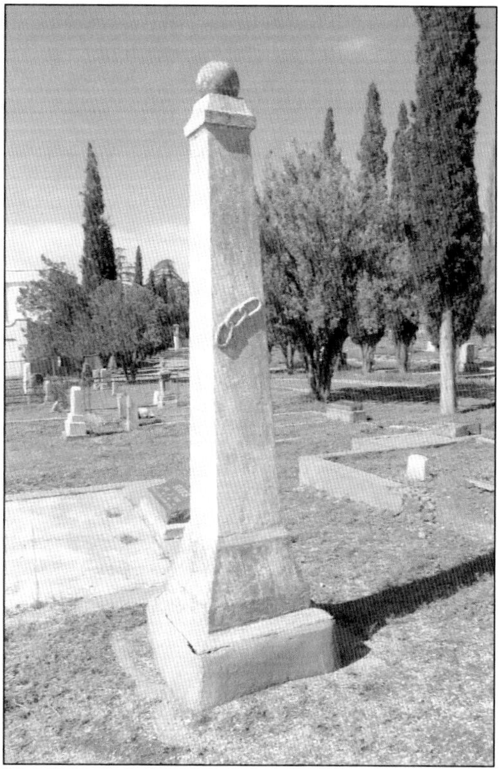

The symbol of the Independent Order of Odd Fellows (IOOF) is the three-link chain. The links represent friendship, love, and truth. This organization has its roots in England, where it was formed in the 1700s. The IOOF was founded in North America in Baltimore, Maryland, on April 26, 1819, and became the first fraternity in the United States to include both men and women when it adopted the Beautiful Rebekah Degree on September 20, 1851. This stone marks the area of the Bisbee Pioneer Cemetery where IOOF members are buried.

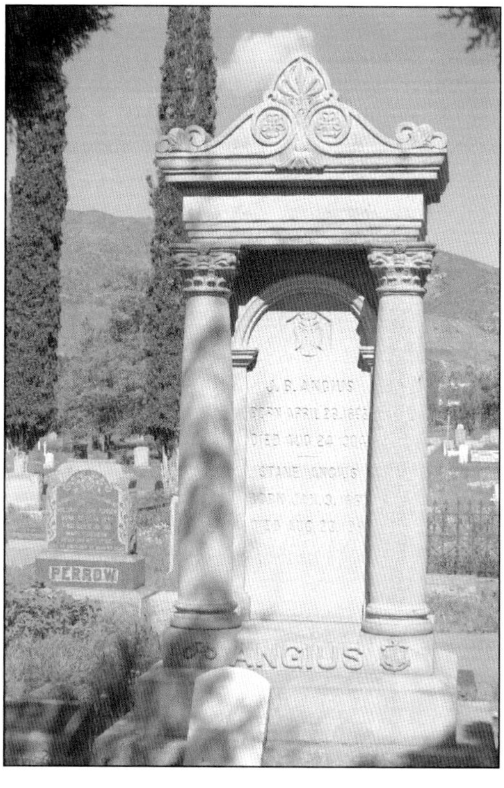

Hotel keeper John B. Angius was born on April 28, 1858, in Austria, and died on August 24, 1904, in Bisbee. Angius came to America when he was 20 years old and established a grocery business in Virginia City. When he came to Arizona, he opened a grocery in Tombstone, where he remained until 1887 before returning to Europe and marrying Stana Medigovich. In 1887, he went to Bisbee, where he was in the grocery business until his death. His tombstone has a classical architectural motif with Corinthian columns. The double eagle is an ancient Hittite symbol of power and respect.

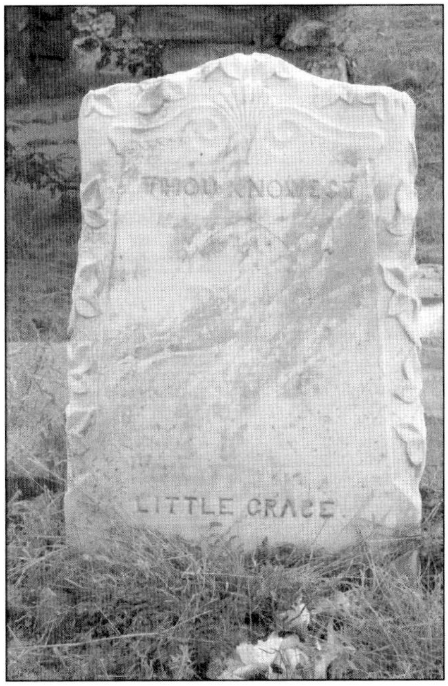

There is something beautifully mysterious about this Bisbee tombstone with its words, "Thou Knowest." It may have come from the poem that says: "Thou knowest, Lord, the weariness and sorrow/Of the sad heart that comes to Thee for rest;/Cares of today, and burdens for tomorrow,/ Blessings implored, and sins to be confessed;/I come before Thee at Thy gracious word,/And lay them at Thy feet: Thou knowest, Lord." A single hand is etched in the stone above the inscription "Little Grace."

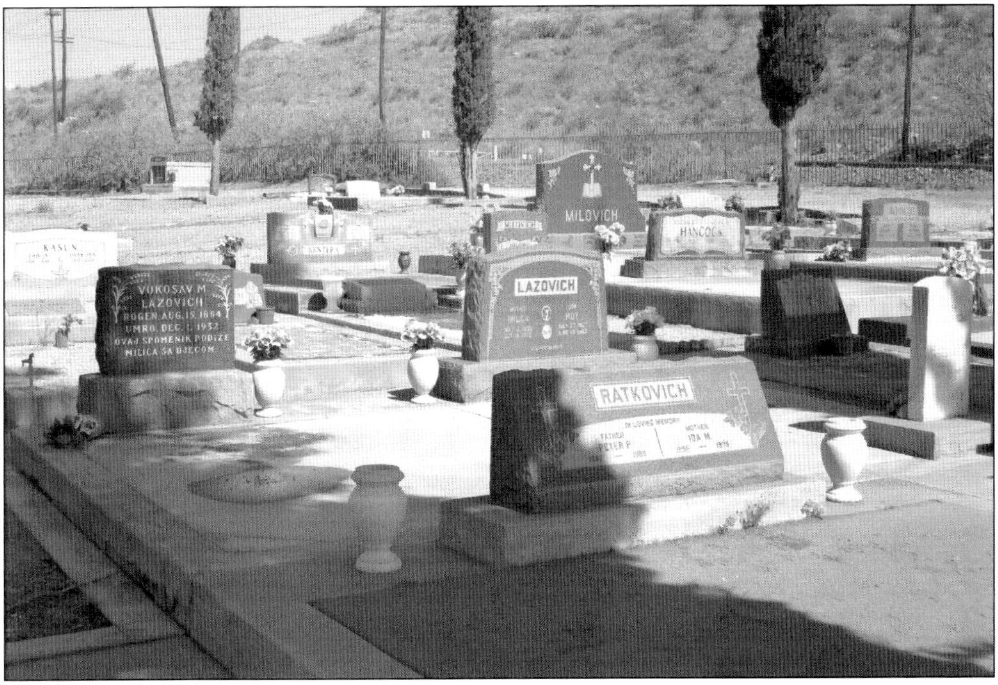

Bisbee had a large population of Serbs working its copper mines. Vukosav Lazovich was born in Morasca, Yugoslavia, on August 15, 1884, and died on December 1, 1932, in Bisbee. He was the son of Mihailo Lazovich and Stoja Grdich, both born in Morasca, Yugoslavia. He died at the Copper Queen Hospital of pneumonia and influenza. Olga Milovich died on June 30, 2010. Prior to retirement, she worked for many years in an administrative support role in the state capital for Wesley Bolin, then secretary of state, as well as for Gov. Rose Mofford and other political leaders.

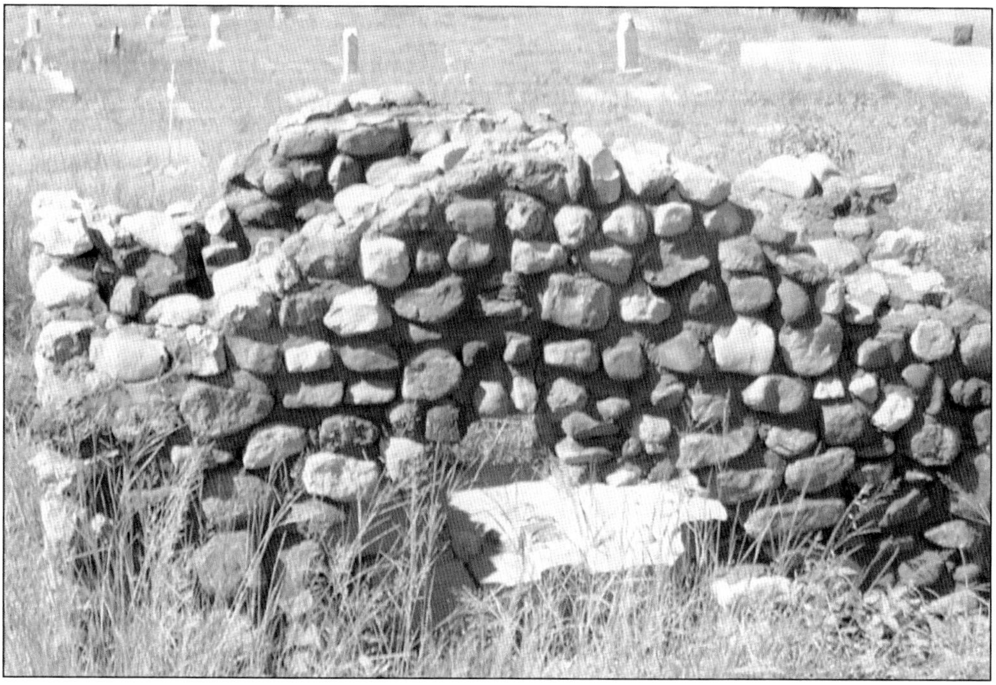

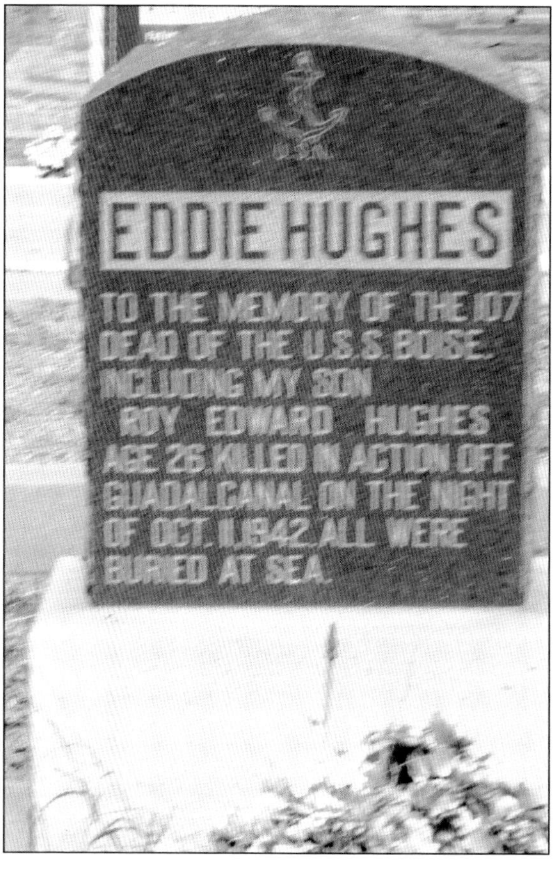

This ornate rock-bridge tombstone, reminiscent of ancient stone cairns or piled rocks, holds a secret as to who may be buried underneath. In most cultures, rocks represent stability and strength. Although there is no name on this gravestone, Bisbee records indicate that Manuel Figuroa was buried here in 1925.

One can only imagine the grief of a Bisbee father who lost a son at sea during World War II. The inscription on this tombstone reads: "To the memory of the 107 dead of the USS *Boise*. Including my son Roy Edward Hughes age 26, killed in action off Guadalcanal on the night of Oct 11, 1942. All were buried at sea."

Joseph Cullen Root founded the Modern Woodmen of America (MWA) because he wanted to create a fraternal benefit society that would bind people of all religions and races. Root chose the name "woodmen" after being inspired by a sermon that talked about "woodmen clearing the forest to provide for their families." After being evicted from the MWA, Root formed Woodmen of the World (WOW), headquartered in Omaha, Nebraska, a group famous for its members' treestones. From 1890 to 1900, WOW's life insurance policies provided for grave markers, which were free of charge for members. The society still makes certain that "no Woodmen (or women) shall rest in an unmarked grave."

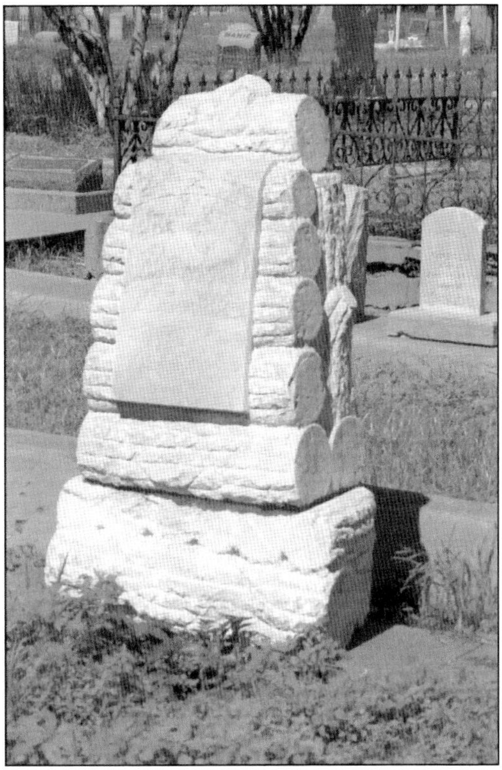

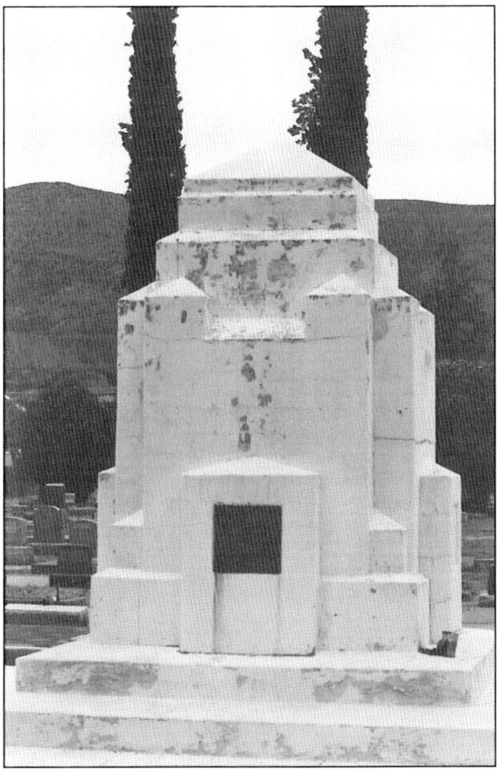

George Warren died on February 13, 1893, in Bisbee. Warren discovered the site of the Copper Queen Mine in Bisbee, but he never enjoyed the riches and died an alcoholic. In 1880, photographer Camillus Sidney (C.S.) Fly took a photograph of Warren; the image was used on the state seal of Arizona, possibly making Warren the only drunk on a state seal. His pauper's grave, originally marked by a wooden plank that said "G.W. 24," was later replaced with this monument. Warren owned an interest in the Copper Queen Mine, which—according to legend—he lost while betting on a footrace with a horse in 1879. He was judged to be insane by Cochise County Court probate judge J.H. Lucas, and his property was sold at public auction. Warren went to Mexico and sold himself into peonage, but Judge G.H. Berry paid off his debt so he could return to Bisbee. He did odd jobs around saloons in exchange for whiskey. A death certificate indicates that he died of pneumonia and heart failure.

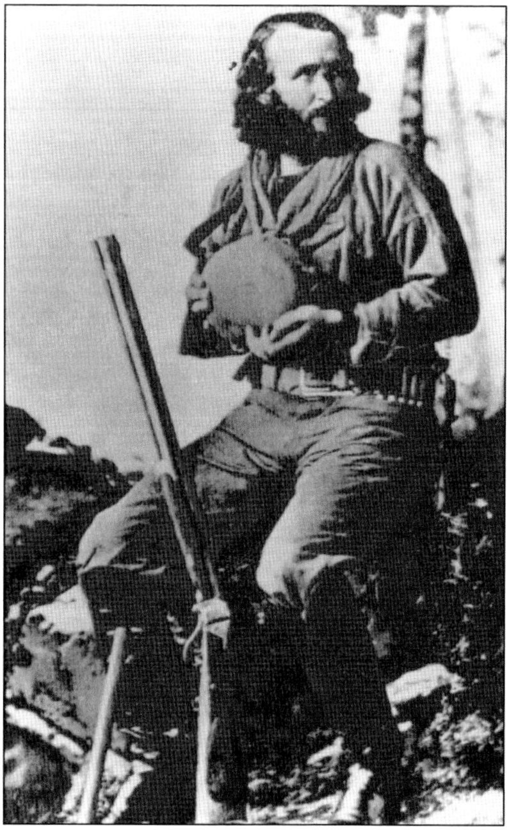

Prospector Edward Lawrence Schieffelin was born on September 27, 1847, in Pennsylvania and died on May 12, 1897, in Oregon. Schieffelin was employed by the Army as an Indian scout, but he prospected on the side. He followed the military to Fort Huachuca when they were chasing Geronimo. At the end of each day, the soldiers would ask him what he had found, and when he replied, "nothing," they said the only thing he would find was his tombstone. When Schieffelin made his way to Arizona and found his rich silver claim sometime around 1878, he called it Tombstone.

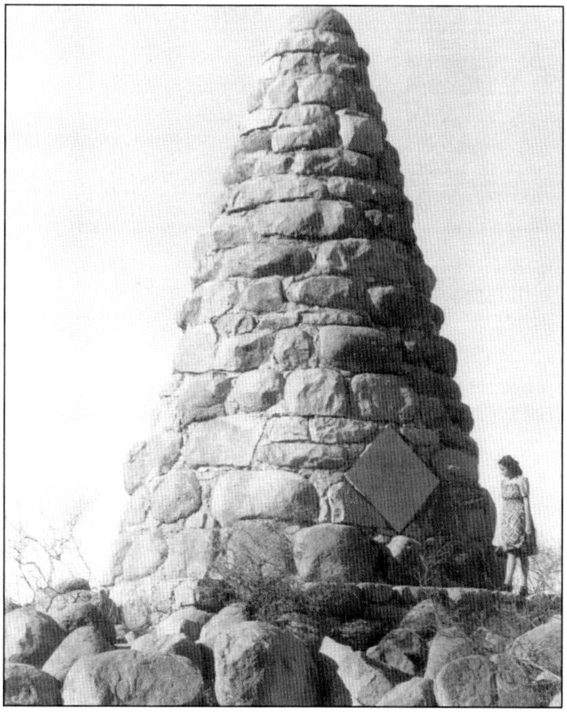

With the wealth he acquired after hitting a silver lode in Tombstone, Schieffelin went to San Francisco in 1883, where he met and married Mary Brown. They settled in Los Angeles, and he later headed out to Oregon to prospect again. In 1897, at age 49, he was found dead at the table in his cabin. He had rich gold ore with him, but no one knew where he had found it. In his will, he asked to be buried near Tombstone in his miner's clothing and with his pick and canteen. His remains are interred under this monument located just outside Tombstone.

The Jewish monument at Tombstone's Boothill Graveyard was erected after judge C. Lawrence Huerta and the Israel Rubin family were shown an adobe brick wall that was supposed to mark the Jewish cemetery. Rubin recited the traditional Kaddish prayer. In March 1983, the Tombstone City Council approved Huerta's restoration efforts, and his plans were endorsed by the Jewish Friendship Club of Green Valley, Arizona. The club erected a monument to commemorate Jewish pioneers and dedicated the site in October 1983. The Star of David is positioned on its east and west sides, and on the south side is a Hohokam Indian sun symbol. The monument contains Jewish and Indian religious items, including soil from Israel. The flames of the menorah atop the monument spell "Shalom," symbolizing the hope that all who share Mother Earth can dwell together in harmony. Although there were Jewish residents in Tombstone, there is no evidence that anyone is buried here. (Courtesy of Richard Lapidus.)

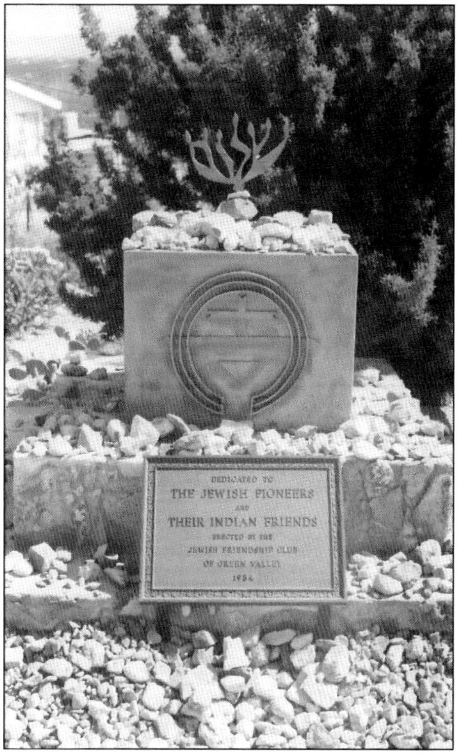

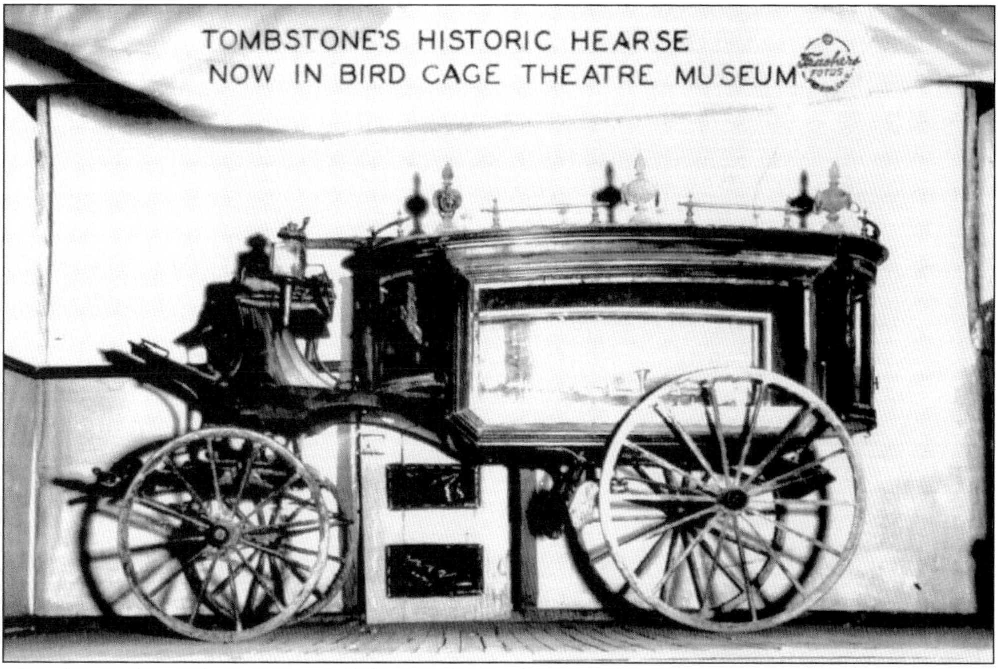

This horse-drawn hearse, on exhibit at the Bird Cage Theatre Museum in Tombstone, was owned by Watt & Tarbell Undertaking Parlor of Tombstone. The hearse took the dead to Boot Hill Cemetery from 1881 to 1906. Tarbell owned the Tarbell Undertaking Parlor on 418 Allen Street in 1887.

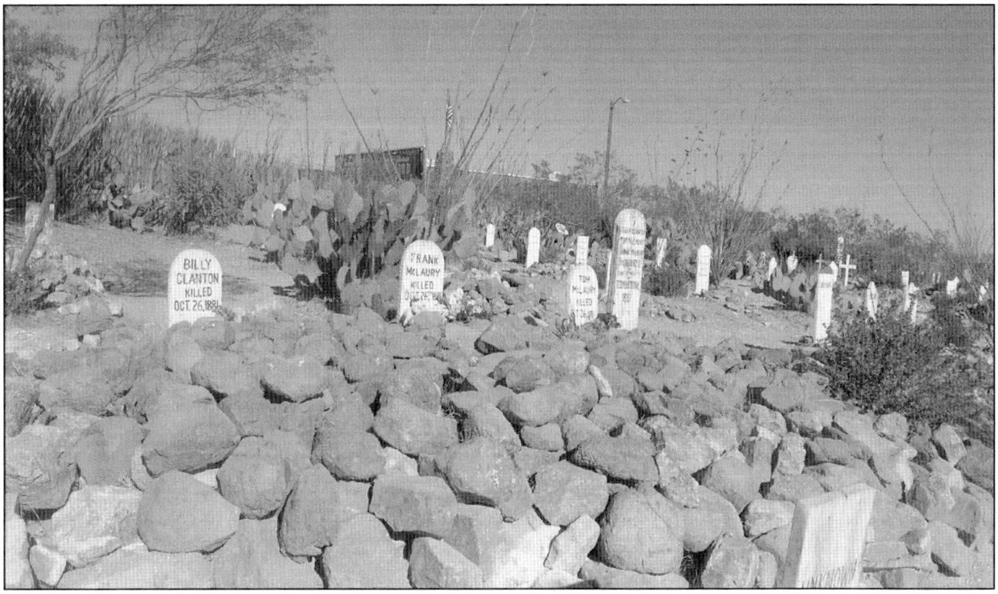

During the gunfight at the O.K. Corral, Tom and Frank McLaury and William Harrison "Billy" Clanton were killed. They were embalmed and placed on display in the window of a Tombstone hardware store, where they were photographed. Their funeral was a major event in Tombstone, and their interment in the town cemetery was attended by hundreds of sympathetic mourners.

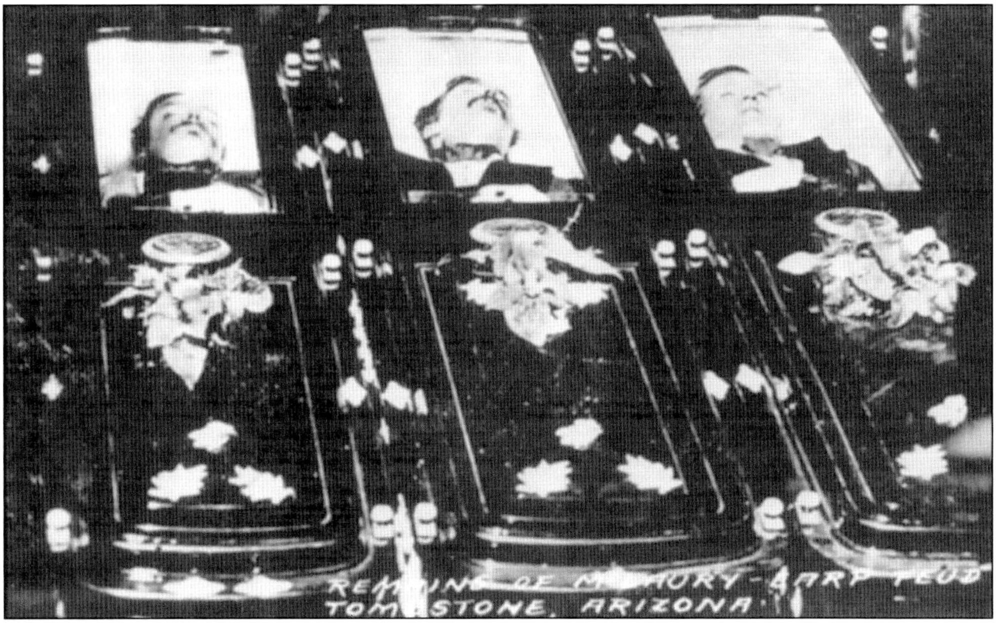

The *Tombstone Nugget* reported that the funeral of Billy Clanton and Tom and Frank McLaury was the largest ever witnessed in Tombstone. The bodies of the three men were neatly dressed and placed in handsome caskets with heavy silver trimmings. The silver plate on each casket was inscribed with the deceased's name, age, birthplace, and date of death. The procession was headed by the Tombstone brass band playing the "March of the Dead." The first wagon, which contained the body of Billy Clanton, was followed by a hearse carrying Tom and Frank McLaury. The two brothers were buried in one grave, and Clanton was placed nearby.

At Tombstone's Boothill Graveyard, humorous grave markers, such as the one pictured at right, have caused some to question the cemetery's authenticity. The cemetery itself is real; however, some markers were added much later, and the city of Tombstone replaces the wooden markers as they fade or become weathered. Lester Moore worked as a Wells Fargo station agent in the border town of Naco, Arizona. One day in 1880, Hank Dunstan arrived at the station to pick up a package. When Moore handed him a badly battered package, Dunstan became angry over its condition. The men argued, and both reached for their guns. Dunstan shot Moore four times, though Moore managed to fire off one shot of his own, mortally wounding Dunstan. Moore's body was transported to Tombstone, where he was buried in the Boothill Graveyard. He became famous for this epitaph: "Here lies Lester Moore, four slugs from a .44, no Les, no more."

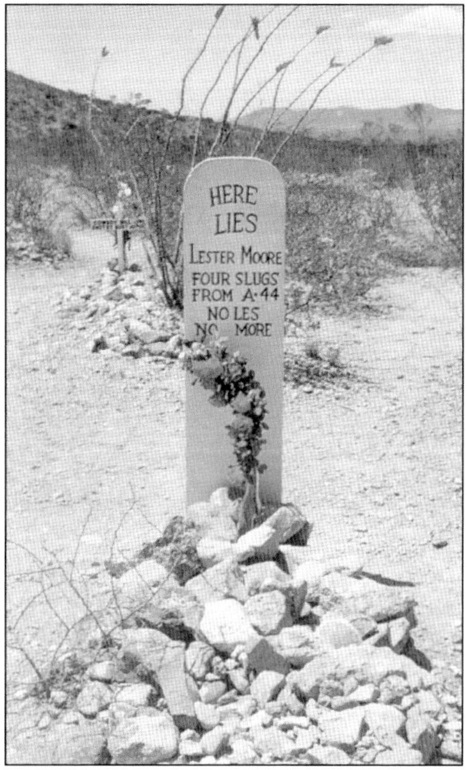

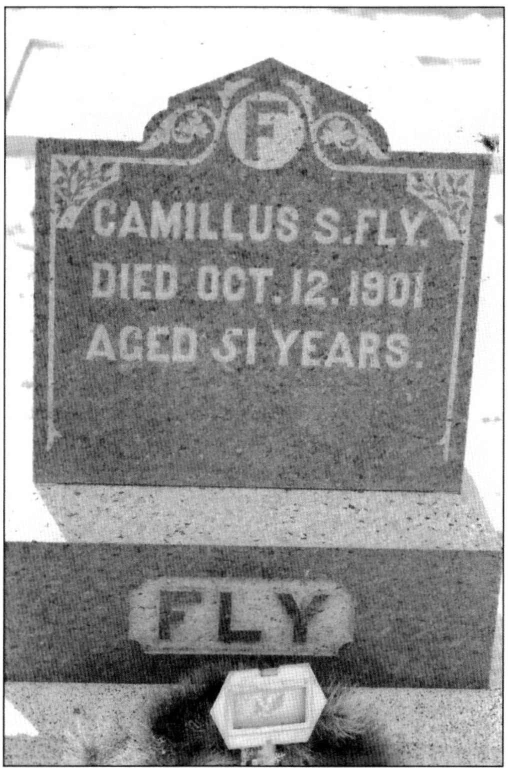

Camillus Sidney Fly is known for his photographs, but he was also a lawman. He was born on May 2, 1849, in Missouri. Fly married Mary Goodrich—also a photographer—on September 29, 1879, in San Francisco, and the couple moved to Tombstone in December 1879. In July 1880, they opened up a 12-room boardinghouse and a studio, which Mary ran while Camillus traveled around the area. In March 1886, Camillus accompanied Gen. George Crook to the Canyon de Los Embudos for negotiations with Geronimo; he later became famous for his photographs of Geronimo and other Apaches. Camillus had begun drinking heavily, and Mary took their child and left him. Fly was elected as Cochise County sheriff in 1895. He ranched in the Chiricahua Mountains until his death at Bisbee on October 12, 1901. Though Camillus and his wife had been separated for years, she was at his bedside when he died and made arrangements to have his body buried at the Tombstone Cemetery. (Courtesy of Richard Lapidus.)

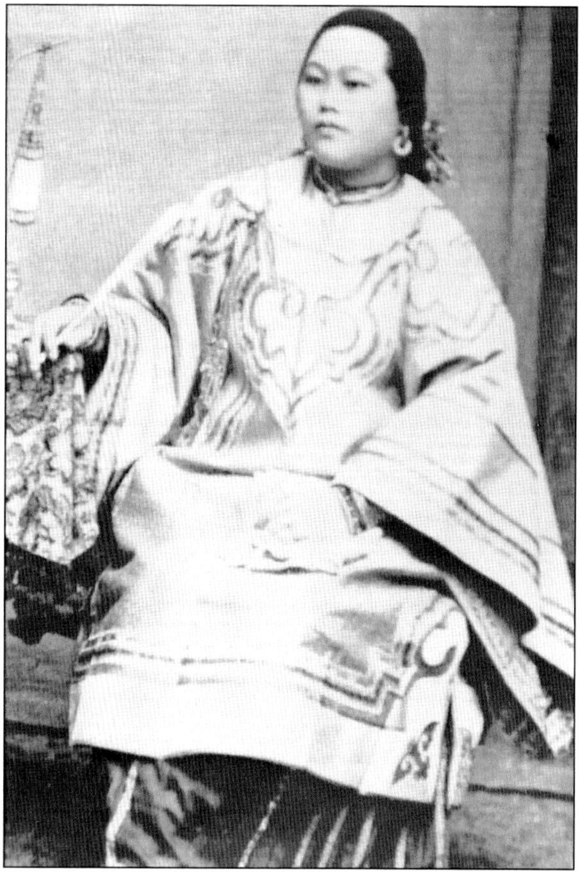

One of the most famous persons in Tombstone was China Mary Sing, who was born around 1840 in the province of Zhongshan in China. Clad in brocaded silks and jade jewelry, she was influential in the area. Those seeking Chinese domestic labor went to China Mary, and she also handled prostitutes, gardeners, and opium sources. She guaranteed a laborer's honesty and workmanship. Any work not done to the employer's satisfaction would be redone for free. Payment, however, was made to China Mary—not to the employee. China Mary managed a well-stocked general store that stocked both American and Chinese goods. White men and Asians were both allowed to play fan-tan in the gambling hall behind her store.

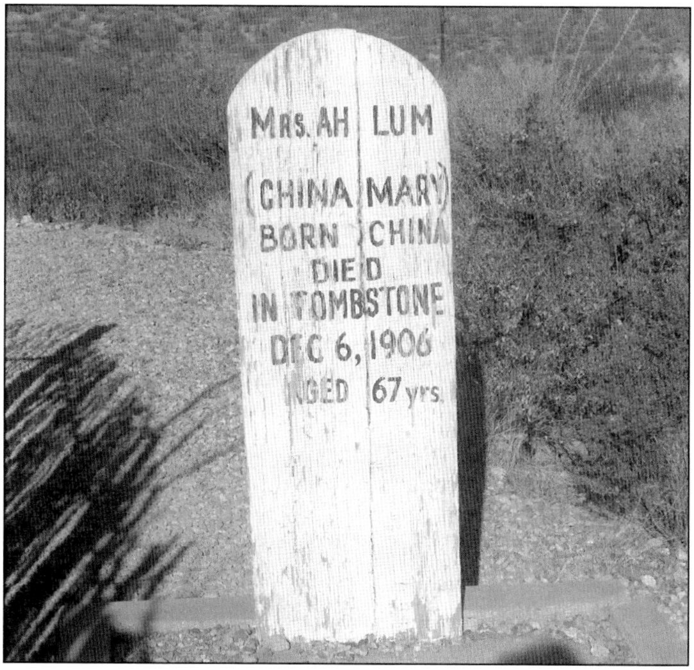

When China Mary died of heart failure on December 16, 1906, there was a large turnout for her service. China Mary was buried in Boothill Graveyard. Her husband, Ah Lum, born in December 1859 in China, died in Arizona of stomach cancer on May 3, 1931. He immigrated to the United States around 1874 and married China Mary on March 14, 1906. Mary died the same year they were married. Ah Lum is buried in the Tombstone Cemetery.

John Heath (or Heith), was born on March 30, 1851, in New Hope, Texas, and was lynched in Tombstone on February 22, 1884. Heath and five outlaws—Dan Dowd, Red Sample, Tex Howard, Bill Delaney, and Dan Kelly—planned the robbery of the mine payroll from the Goldwater & Castaneda Stores in Bisbee on the night of December 9, 1883. The Phelps Dodge Mining Company's payroll, however, had not arrived. Once they realized that their plan had been foiled, the scene turned deadly. The two outlaws in the store robbed customers of jewelry and cash. The three who were guarding the entrance outside began shooting wildly—one shot and killed J.C. Tappenier. Deputy Tom Smith came onto the street and was shot dead. Another bullet killed a pregnant woman named Annie Roberts. The outlaws rode off with Cochise County sheriff Jerome Ward and a posse following in pursuit. Heath, who had remained in a saloon, tried to misdirect the posse, and it turned out that he was the mastermind of the outlaws.

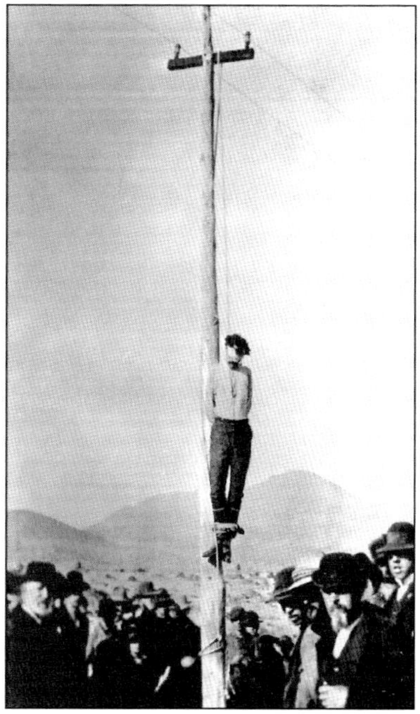

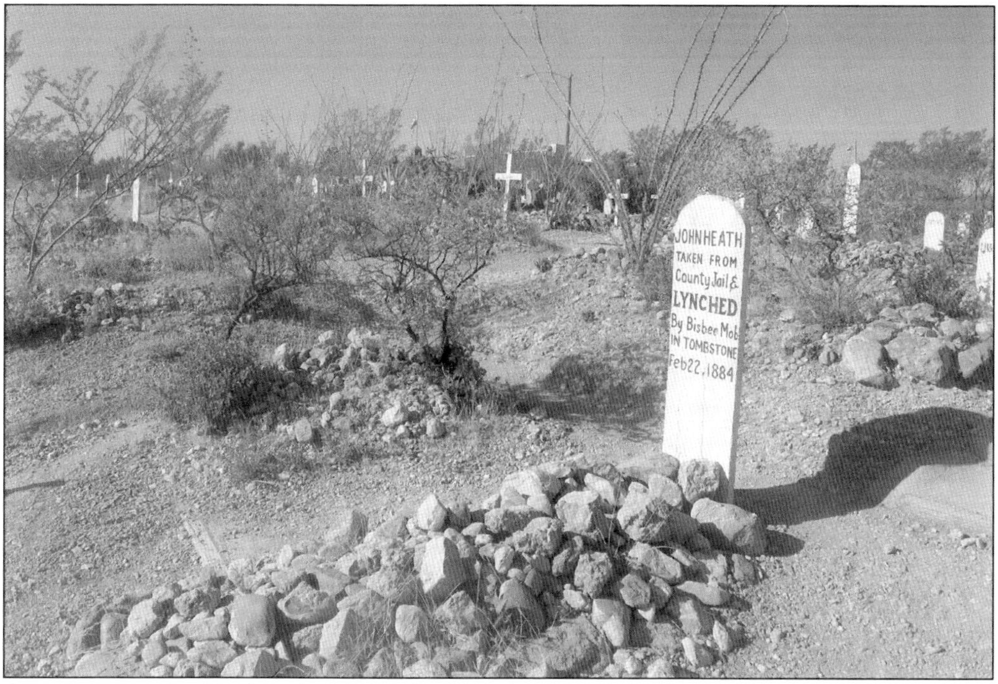

Over the next couple of weeks, the outlaws were captured and tried in Tombstone, where they were all sentenced to death. However, Heath—who helped plan the robbery but did not take part in the shootings—got a life term in prison. A Bisbee crowd felt that he was just as guilty as the rest, and they took over the jail, tied up the sheriff and the jailor, and hanged Heath from a nearby telegraph pole. The cause of death was listed as "Emphysema of the lungs or lack of oxygen self induced or otherwise, a common affliction at high altitudes." Heath is buried in the Boothill Graveyard.

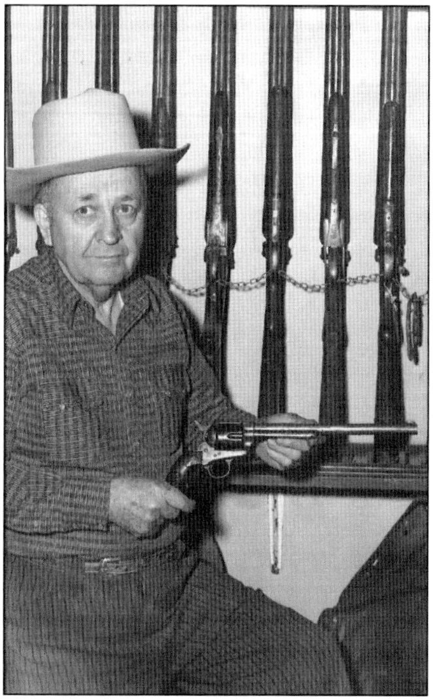

Attorney Harold O. Love was born in 1909 and died in 1986. His wife, Betty, was born on November 5, 1914, in Detroit, Michigan, and died on November 23, 2011, in Chevy Chase, Maryland. In 1964, a group of Detroit investors headed by Love purchased the *Tombstone Epitaph*, along with the O.K. Corral, the Crystal Palace, and Schieffelin Hall. Ten years later, Love and his colleagues announced that the *Epitaph* would begin to serve as a historical journal of the Old West. Meanwhile, through an agreement with the University of Arizona, Love and his fellow investors arranged to have journalism students at the college continue to produce and publish a biweekly local edition of the *Tombstone Epitaph*. In 1977, Betty and Harold moved to Tucson and worked to restore Tombstone.

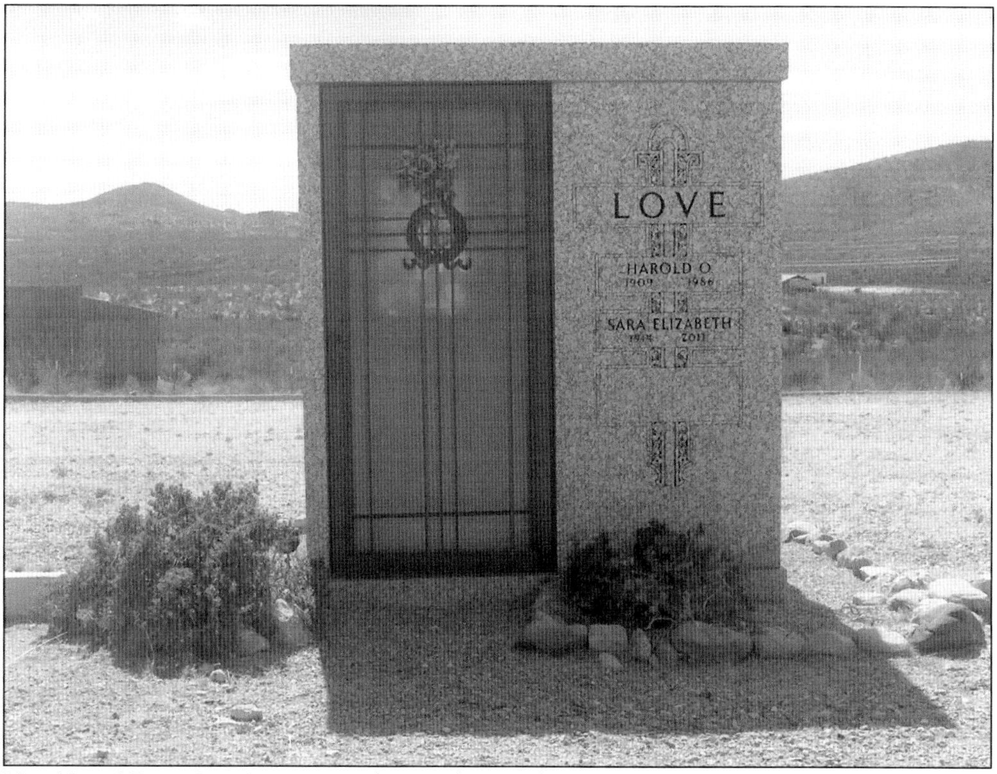

Harold and Betty Love's grave marker in the Tombstone Cemetery reflects modern classical architecture. The small, streamlined mausoleum displays a spartan but elegant use of decorative features that reflect the Art Deco style of the late 1920s.

Former Graham County sheriff and Cochise County deputy sheriff Arthur Wight was born on July 22, 1856, in Preston, Minnesota. He died during a gunfight on February 10, 1904, and is buried in the Tombstone Cemetery. Wight had arrested several striking laborers who were causing a public disturbance and placed them in jail. Friends of the arrested men went to the small holding pen, tipped it over, and freed them. Wight stepped outside and was shot. He was taken to the hospital but died before surgery. E. Eredia was to have been hanged for Wight's murder, but Wight's widow pleaded for his life, and Eredia was given a life sentence.

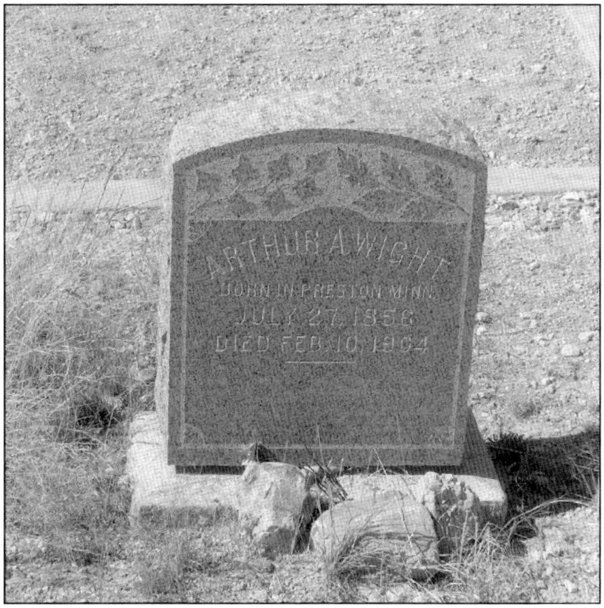

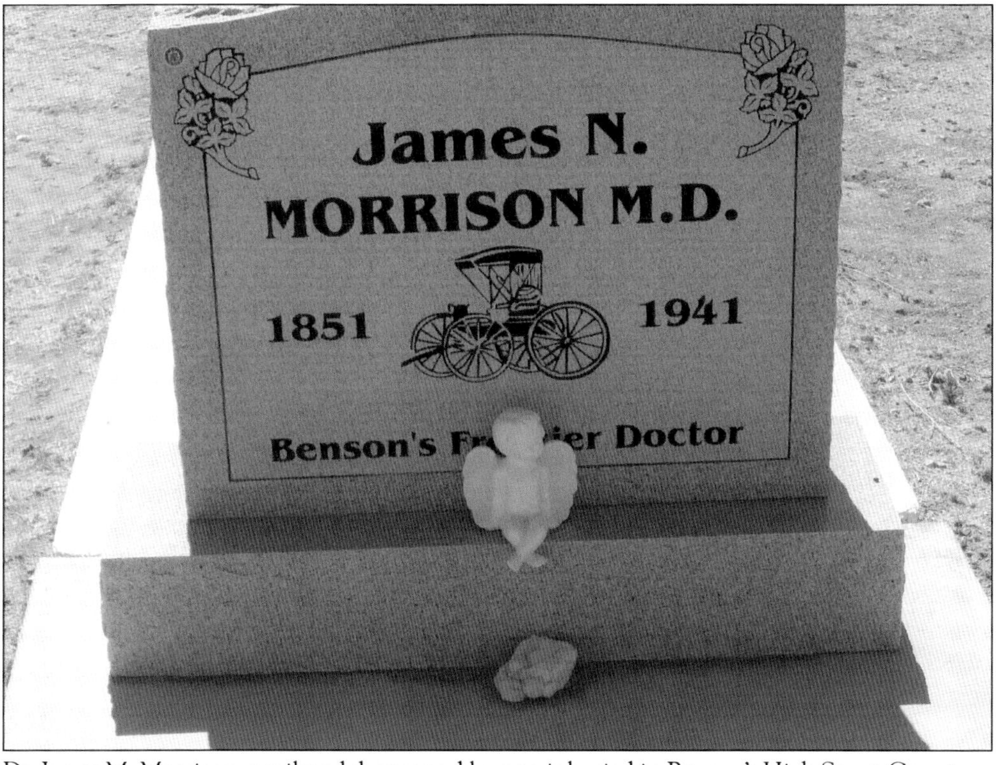

Dr. James M. Morrison, a railroad doctor and lawyer, is buried in Benson's High Street Cemetery. He was born in 1851 and died on February 5, 1941, with no heirs and very little money. In August 2007, the *Benson News-Sun* announced that Louise Larson had raised enough money to pay for Doctor Morrison's gravestone, with the inscription, "Benson's Frontier Doctor." It is decorated with an image of his carriage. Morrison practiced medicine for many years and treated patients during the Great Depression, a time when most people were struggling to make ends meet.

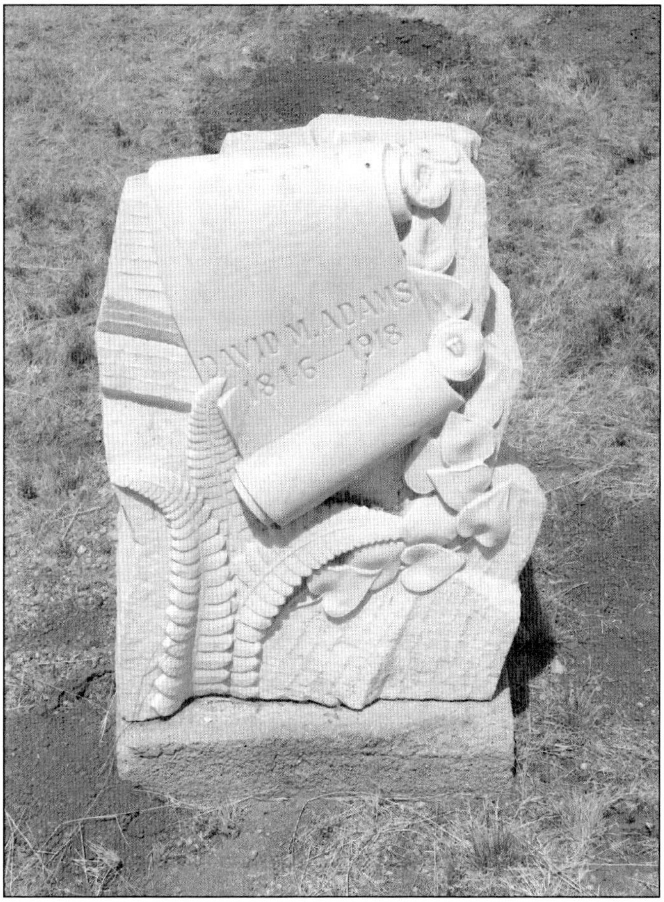

David M. Adams was born in Alabama in 1846 and served in the Confederacy, Company C, 24th Arkansas Infantry Regiment. He died of Bright's disease on February 18, 1918, and is buried in the Texas Canyon Pioneer Cemetery. Adams was engaged in the cattle business. His gravestone is decorated with a lovely scroll and ferns.

Francis Adams, born January 17, 1861, in Alabama, died of pneumonia and heart problems on June 16, 1938. He was also a rancher and was involved in mining. His elegant gravestone features a simple cross surrounded by primroses, harbingers of new beginnings.

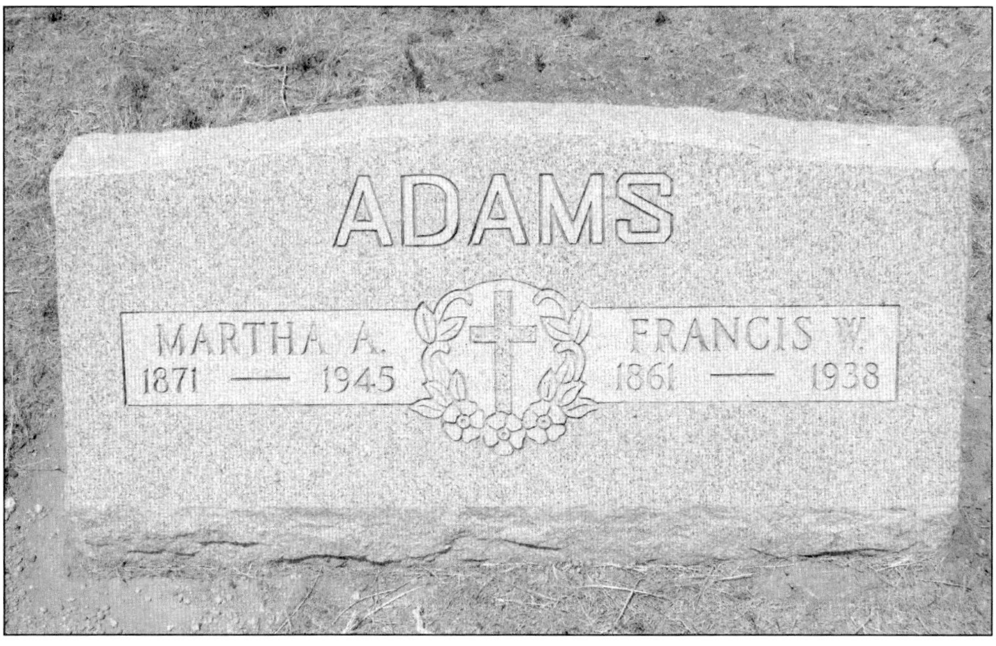

Prim Sebring was a Texas Canyon cattleman born August 13, 1855, in Bellbrook, Ohio. He died from cancer of the stomach on September 15, 1917, in Dragoon, Arizona. Prim, the son of John Sebring and Susan Hopkins, was the husband of Margaret Keintz Sebring (1861–1935). His grave marker is a stone, representing strength and stability.

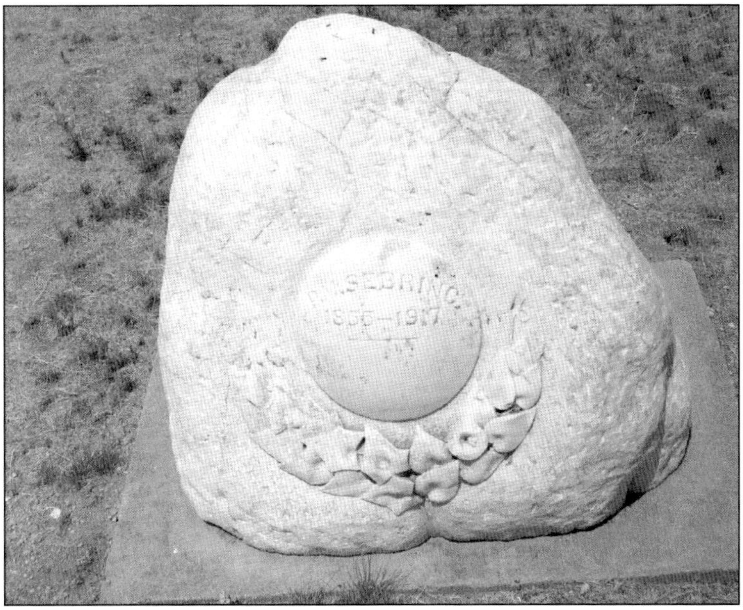

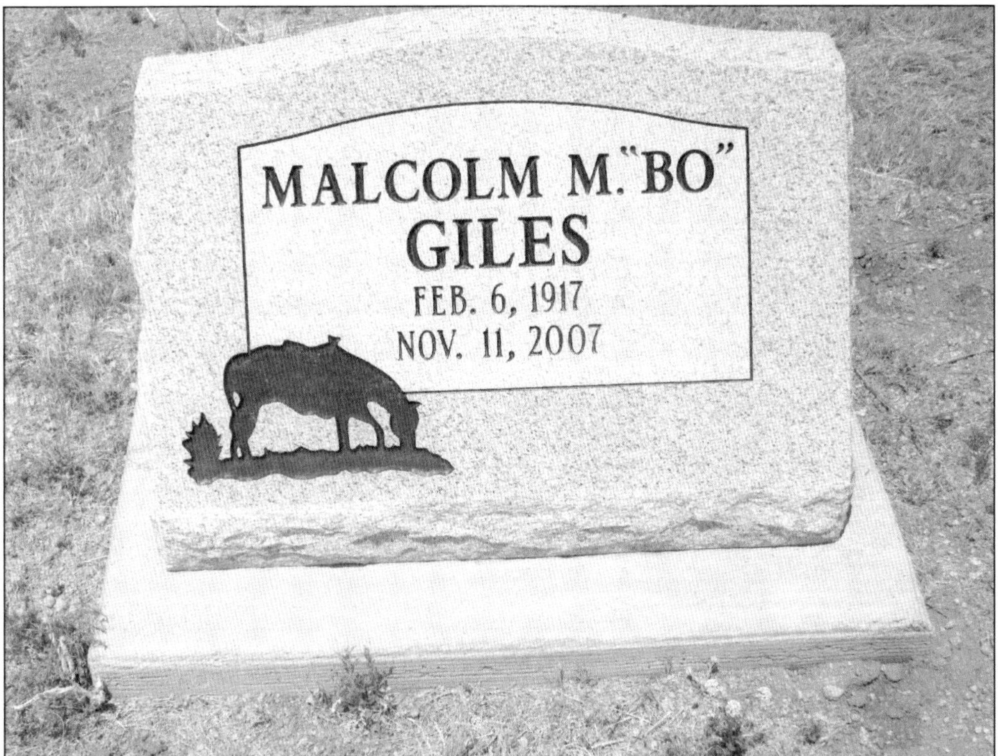

There is no doubt that Malcolm M. "Bo" Giles was a rancher—a riderless horse adorns his gravestone in the Texas Canyon Pioneer Cemetery. He was born on February 6, 1917, on the Fulton ranch in Dragoon, Arizona, and he died on November 11, 2007, in Pearce, Arizona. Giles farmed and ranched until his retirement in 1980. He was a past master of Willcox Lodge No. 10 F. & A.M. (Free and Accepted Masons).

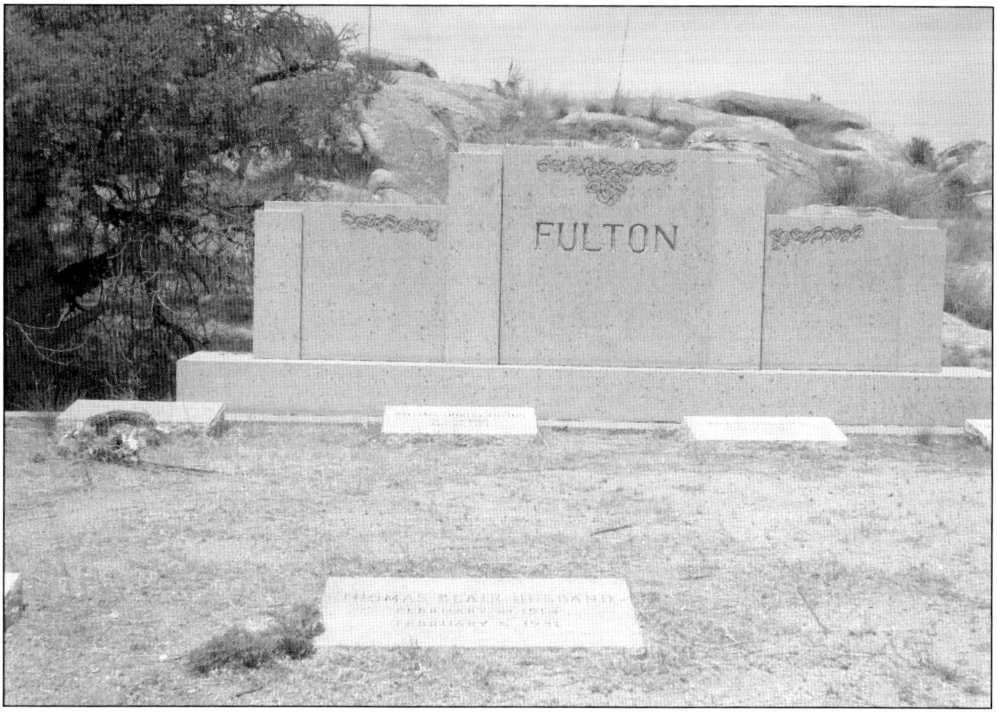

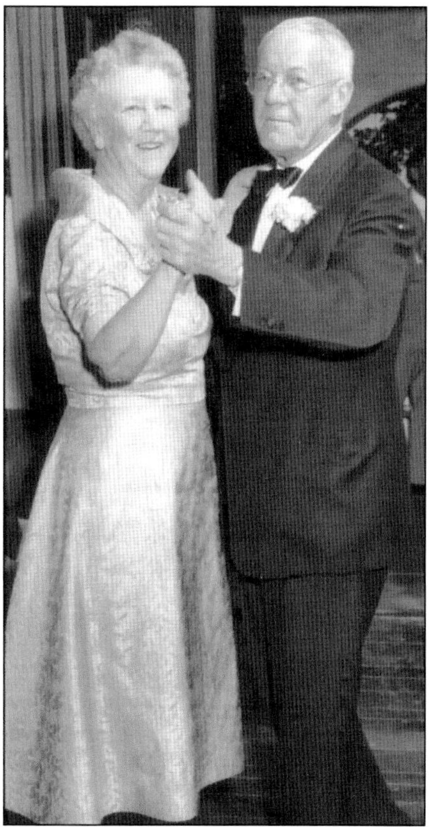

William Shirley Fulton was born on November 23, 1880, and died on November 20, 1964, in Waterbury, Connecticut. He received a degree from Yale University in 1903. In 1906, he married Rose Hinkley Hayden, and they had two children: William Hayden and Elizabeth. William S. Fulton worked as a machinist apprentice at and later served as president of the Waterbury Farrel Foundry & Machine Company. He began his encore career in 1930, when he established the FF Ranch near Dragoon, Arizona, and engaged in amateur archaeological excavations, publishing his research through the National Museum of the American Indian. In 1937, Fulton established the Amerind Foundation, a private, nonprofit archaeological research institution that continues the work of its founder to this day. (Courtesy of the Amerind Foundation, Inc.)

In the image at left, Rose and William Fulton dance on their 50th wedding anniversary. Rose was born in Waterbury, Connecticut, in 1881, and attended Rye Seminary in New York. When she traveled to Arizona and New Mexico, she acquired Southwest Indian arts and crafts. At the FF Ranch, she raised quarter horses that consistently won top honors at horse shows. She donated her art collection to the Amerind Foundation's museum. (Courtesy of the Amerind Foundation, Inc.)

Elizabeth Fulton Husband is pictured at right with her father, William S. Fulton. Elizabeth was born in Waterbury, Connecticut, on January 14, 1910. She owned the Four Spear Ranch and the Cochise Hotel and Gift Shop. She outlived two husbands (first, Kenneth E. Gunter, and second, Thomas B. Husband). She had a long history of service and philanthropy, serving on the board of directors for various clubs and on the board of directors of the Amerind Foundation. Elizabeth contributed many fine examples of Native American art to the foundation's museum. She died in November 2002 at her ranch. (Courtesy of the Amerind Foundation, Inc.)

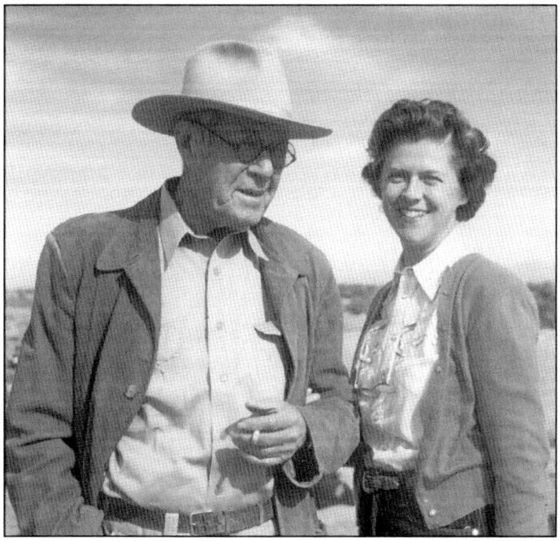

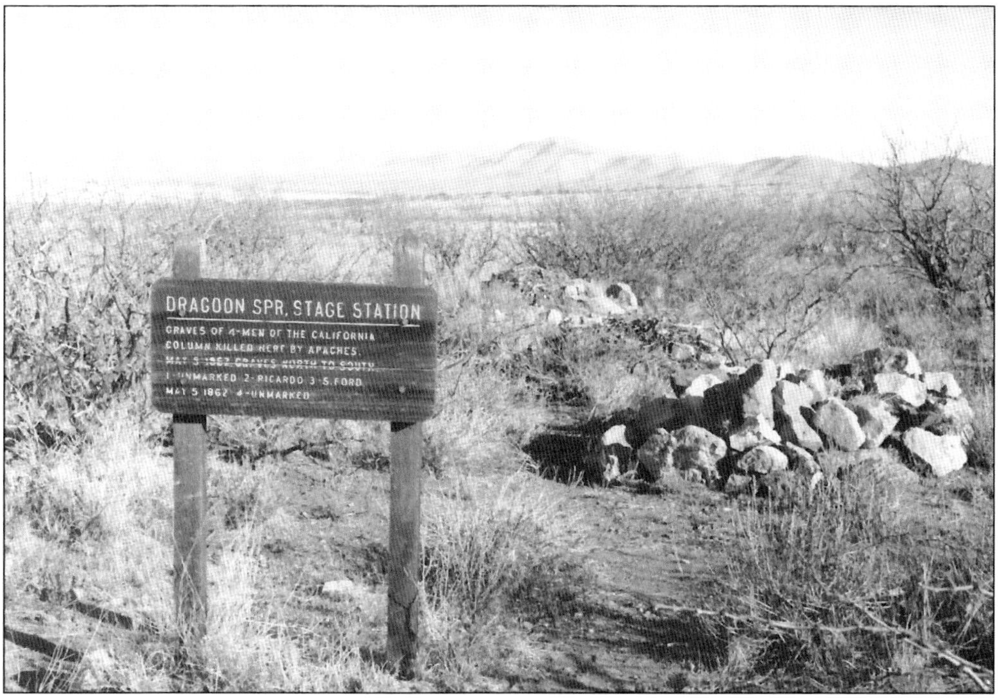

This cemetery is located at the Dragoon Springs stage station on the Butterfield-Overland stage route. It contains seven graves. James Hughes worked for the Overland Mail as a mechanic. William Cunningham and James Laing worked on the mail line and assisted Silas St. John with horses and mules. Cunningham, an Iowa native, shares a grave with Hughes. They, along with Laing, were murdered on September 9, 1858, by three members of their own crew during the construction of the station. St. John survived, but his left arm was severed by an axe during the attack.

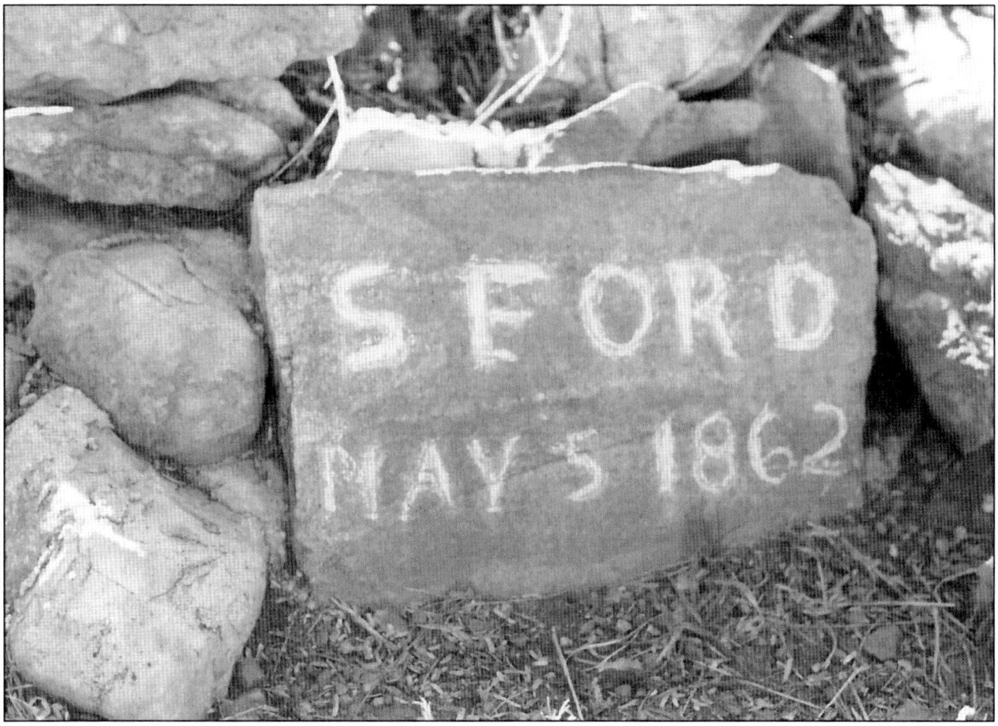

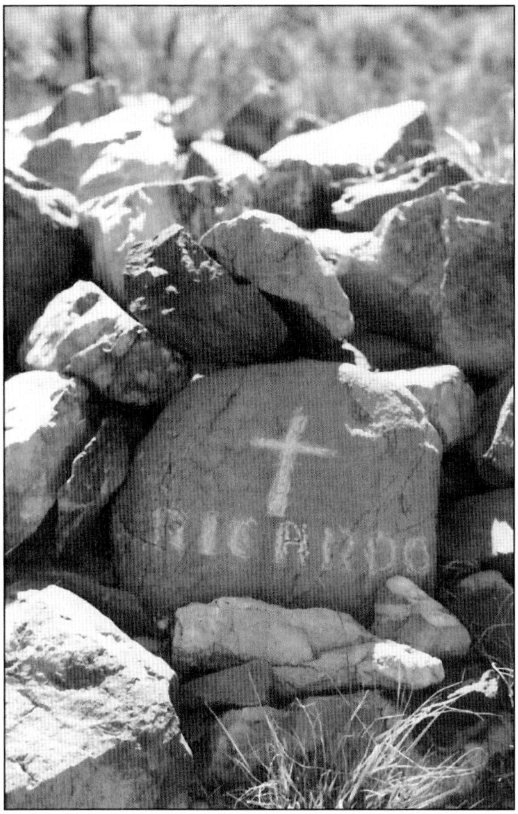

Samuel Ford's birthday is unknown, but he died on May 5, 1862, near the Dragoon Springs stage station. Ford, whose grave marker is pictured above, was a soldier in Confederate Company A, Baylor's Regiment. Ricardo, whose last name is not known and whose grave marker is pictured at left, was born in Mexico. When Confederates occupied Tucson from February 28 to May 14, 1862, they pressed several Mexican residents, including Ricardo, into service as cooks, launderers, and stock herders. When Capt. Sherrod Hunter left Tucson to escort Union prisoners and confiscated Tucson livestock back to Texas, Ricardo was taken along. Hunter's small command—including Ford—was ambushed by Apaches at Dragoon Springs on May 5, 1862, and both Ricardo and Ford were killed. Piling stones on a corpse was a means of keeping predators, such as coyotes, from feeding on the body.

This statue—*Mourning Hearts: A Soldier's Family*—was unveiled at the Fort Huachuca Cemetery in November 1996. Sculpted by Jessica McCain and funded by the Huachuca Museum Society, it is, according to a report from the fort, "the first monumental tribute on a US Army installation to a soldier's family." It acknowledges the fact that a soldier's calling often involves the ultimate sacrifice.

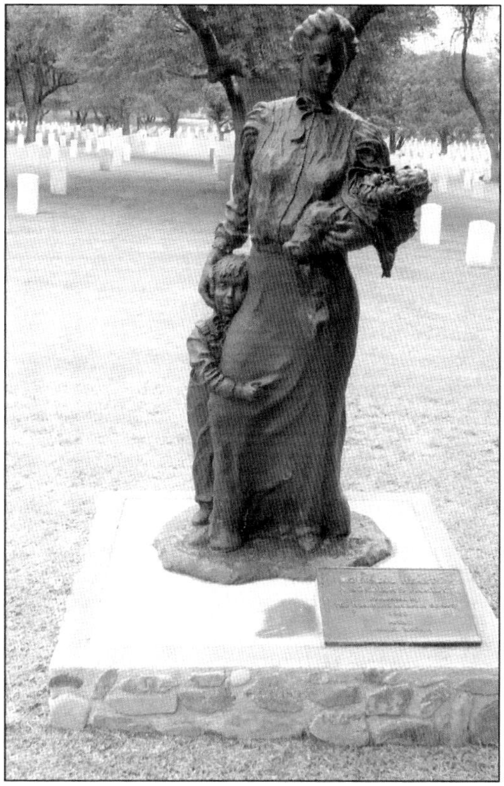

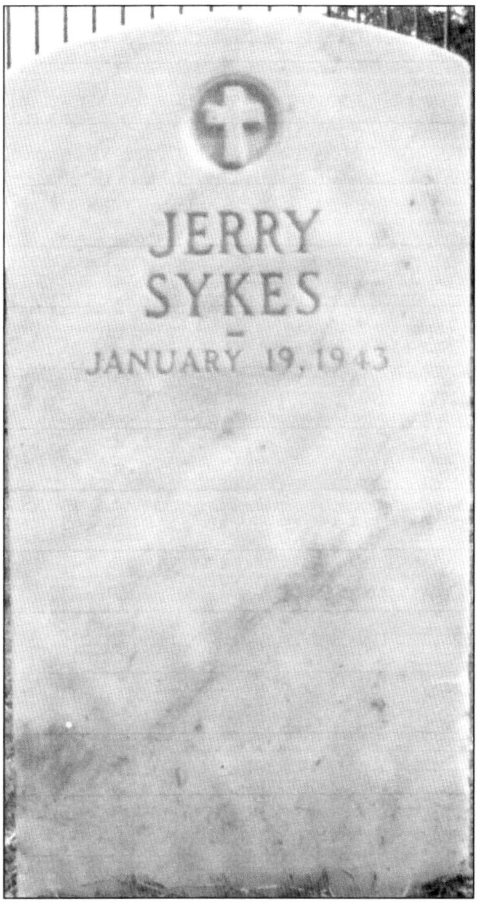

Pvt. James Rowe, a black soldier, was hanged at Fort Huachuca on November 6, 1942, by order of a general court martial for the stabbing of another black soldier, Pvt. Joseph Fields. The murder was over some cigarettes. S.Sgt. Jerry Sykes, another black soldier, was hanged on January 19, 1943, for stabbing Hazel Lee Craig, his former girlfriend, who is also buried at Fort Huachuca. The gravestones of both men include only their names and dates of death.

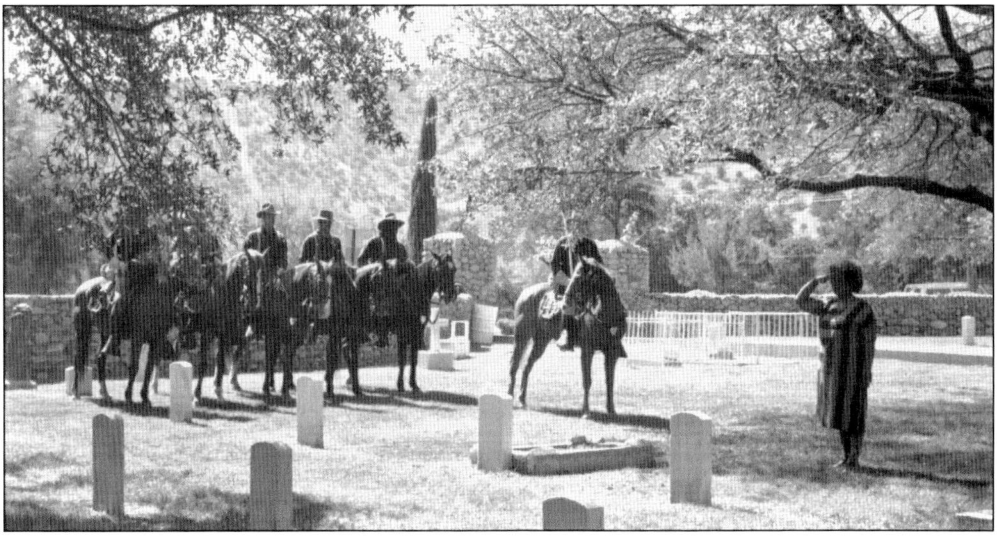

On August 28, 1984, 90-year-old M.Sgt. John P. Campbell died at a nursing home in Phoenix. He was one of the few remaining soldiers who had come to Fort Huachuca as a member of the 10th Cavalry, aka the buffalo soldiers. At Campbell's Fort Huachuca funeral service (pictured above) his grave was surrounded by soldiers on horseback in original buffalo soldier uniforms. Campbell was a veteran of World Wars I and II and served in four of the six major black combat units stationed at Fort Huachuca. Campbell came to the post as a bugler in 1912; his musical career included three years as a tenor saxophonist with the 10th Cavalry band. He also played semiprofessional baseball with both the cavalry and infantry teams. In 1977, he took part in the dedication of the bronze statue of the buffalo soldier at Fort Huachuca's main gate. (Courtesy of the Fort Huachuca Museum.)

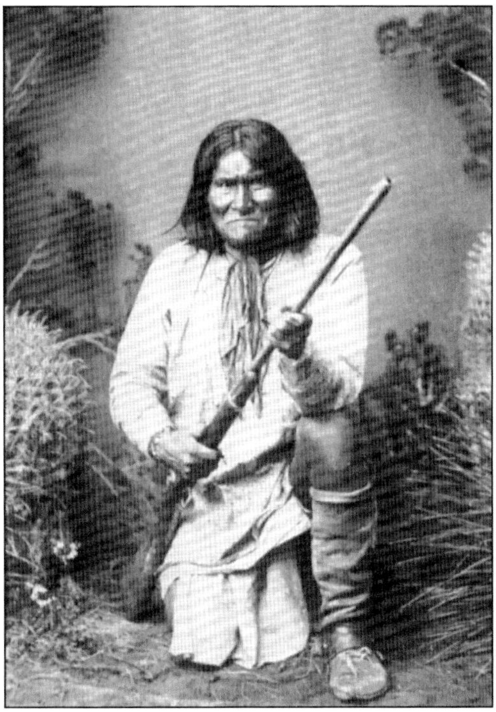

Geronimo (pictured) is buried in Oklahoma, but his son Little Robe is buried in the Fort Bowie Cemetery in Arizona. Geronimo, the spiritual leader of a group of Chiricahua Apaches, was settled on the San Carlos Reservation in Arizona but fled from the reservation several times. Geronimo, who finally surrendered on September 4, 1886, was the final Native American warrior to surrender to the federal government.

Little Robe—the son of Geronimo and his second wife, Ga-Ah—was born in 1883 and died on September 10, 1885, at Fort Bowie. Little Robe was part of a group of Apache prisoners captured near Nacori, Mexico, on August 7, 1885, and brought to Fort Bowie on September 1. Two of Geronimo's wives, Zi-yeh and She-gha, along with another of his sons, Fenton, were also in the group of prisoners. Little Robe, of whom the soldiers had become quite fond, probably died of dysentery. (Courtesy of Kristin Sanderson.)

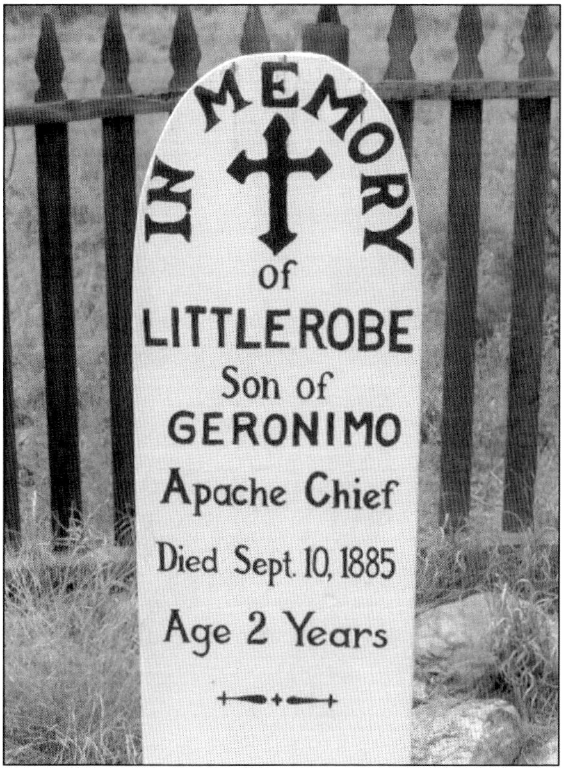

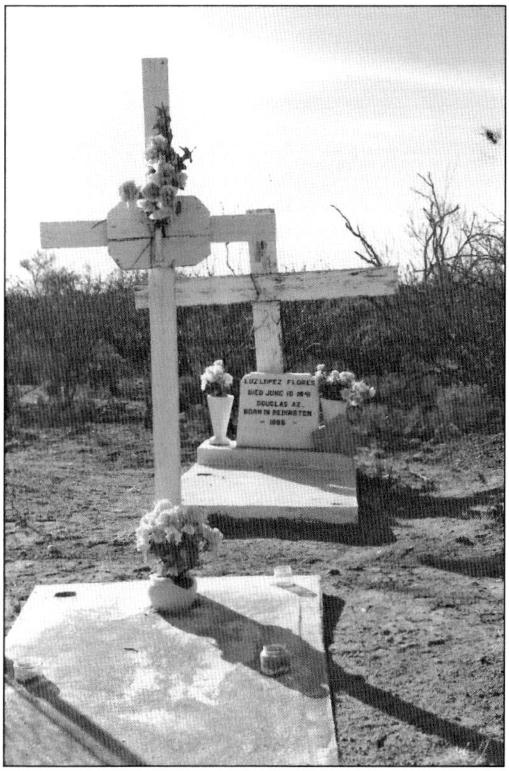

Gleeson is now a ghost town except for a few residents. In the 1880s, prospectors and miners moved in and took over the turquoise mines. Tiffany & Co. operated a turquoise mine here for a few years. Around 1900, John Gleeson found large copper deposits south of Turquoise and called his claim the Copper Belle. In October 1900, the Post Office Department opened a post office in Gleeson. From 1900 through the 1920s, Gleeson thrived. Between World Wars I and II, the price of copper fell, and by 1930, ranching became the primary occupation in the area. Luz Lopez Flores, whose grave is in the background of this image, was one of the last people buried in the Gleeson Cemetery. She was born in 1886 in Redington, Arizona, and died on June 10, 1942, near Douglas, where she had been visiting her daughter for two months.

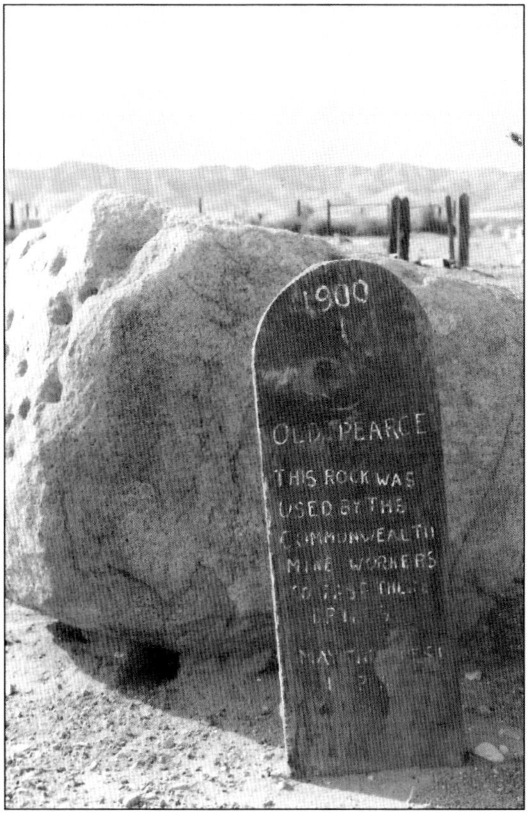

Even a mining drill stone finds a place to rest in peace at the Pearce Cemetery. The inscription reads, "1900 Old Pearce this rock was used by the Commonwealth Mine workers to test their drills." This competition is a timed event in which the driller with the fastest time wins. Large sums of money were waged on these contests, and contestants trained as if for the Olympics, since these events could bring them much more money than they could earn in the mines. (Courtesy of Susan and Bryan Ballard.)

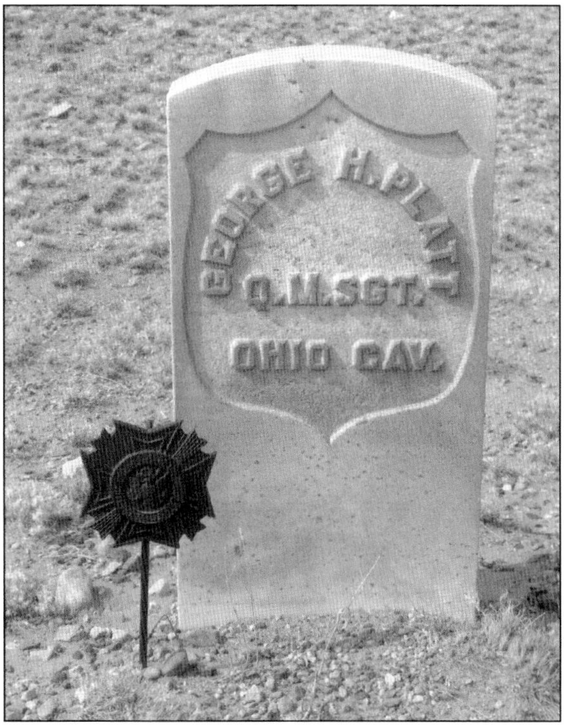

George Hart Platt, born in Ohio in 1832, was buried in the Pearce Cemetery on August 6, 1906. He enlisted on December 8, 1863, as a quartermaster sergeant in the Union Light Guard, Ohio Cavalry, and was discharged on December 9, 1865. Platt was a member of Tombstone's Burnside Post, Grand Army of the Republic, and served as post chaplain in 1891. He was a member of the Union Light Guard of Ohio, which was formed for the express purpose of acting as bodyguards to Pres. Abraham Lincoln. (Courtesy of Susan and Bryan Ballard.)

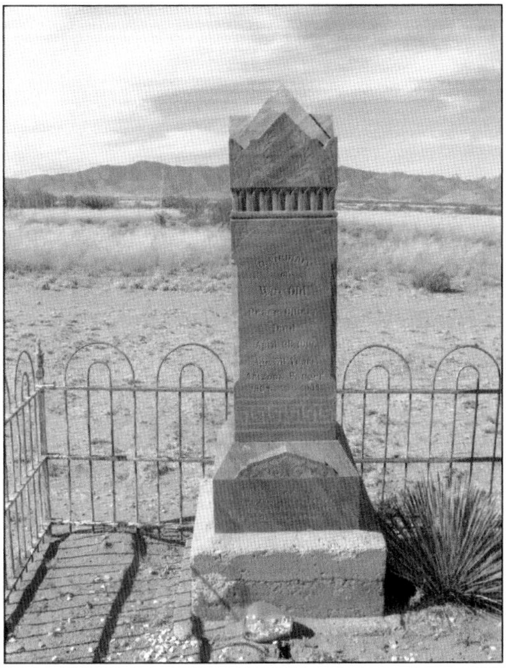

William "Billy" Old, born in 1870 in Morris County, Texas, died on April 28, 1914, at age 38. He served as an Arizona Ranger from 1904 until 1909. His grave is decorated with geometric designs, and the inscription at the bottom of the marker is inscribed: "This Monument is erected by the Citizens of Pearce as a tribute to his sterling worth in the discharge of his duty." Old worked as a cowboy and joined the Texas Rangers at age 27. He moved to Arizona and joined the Arizona Rangers in 1903. When a judge appeared to be in cahoots with the cattle thieves, Old sent for Capt. Tom Rynning. When Rynning got there, he found Old talking to the judge about the errors of his ways. The honorable judge, anchored to a mesquite bush with a chain, swore he would act square when horse thieves and rustlers came before him for hearings. (Courtesy of Susan Ballard.)

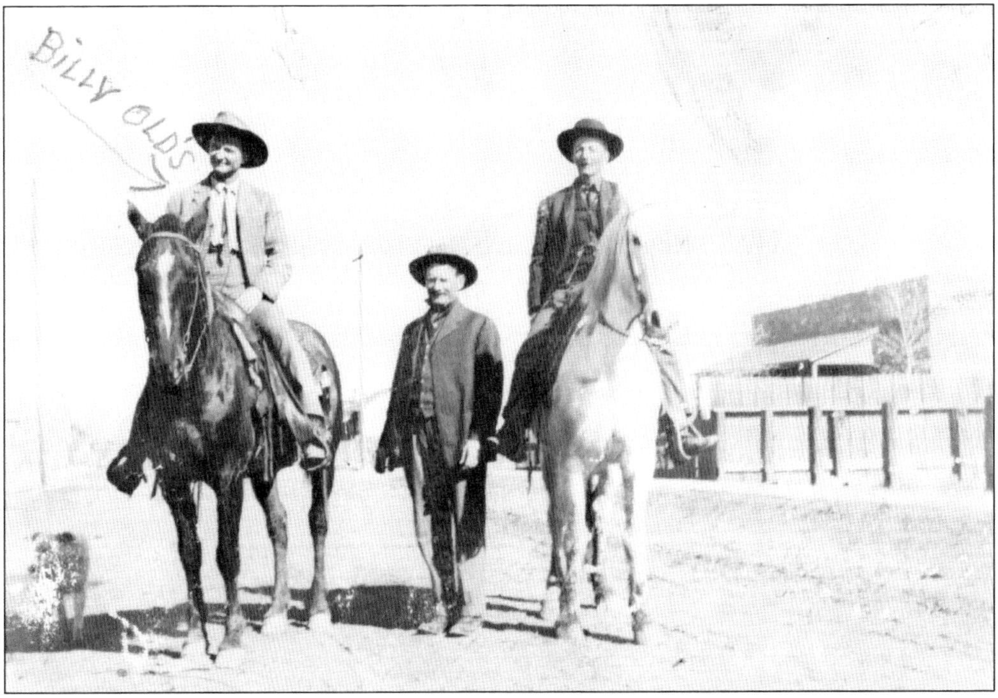

On November 6, 1906, in Kelvin, Arizona, William "Billy" Old (left) married 19-year-old Anna B. Beck; they had two sons. When the Arizona Rangers were discontinued in 1909, Old went to work as a special agent for the Southern Pacific. He served as a town constable in Pearce and moved his family there. When it came to women, William had a roving eye, and Anna became jealous, so on April 28, Anna shot and killed Billy. She appeared at his funeral in handcuffs. She went to trial two years later and was acquitted and later remarried. She died in 1981 at age 94.

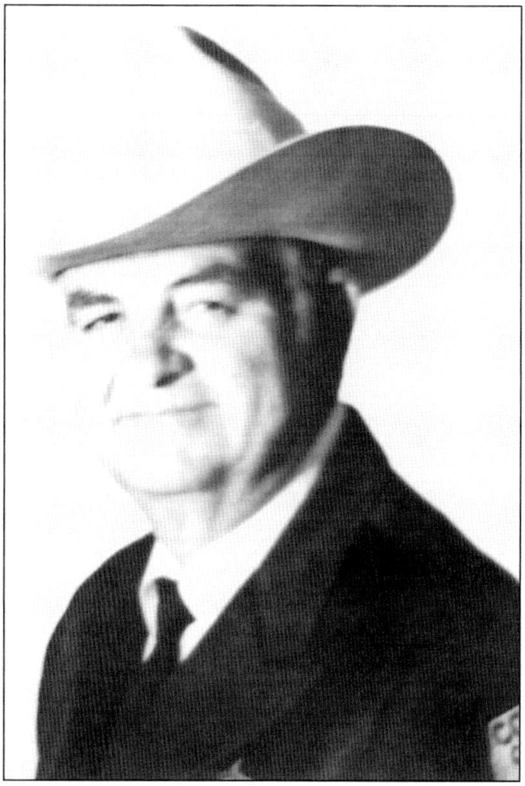

Cochise County sheriff Jimmy Judd was born on March 25, 1933, in Benson, Arizona. He died of cancer on December 2, 2005, and approximately 900 mourners attended his services at the Church of Jesus Christ of Latter-day Saints in Benson. Judd served an unprecedented four terms as Cochise County sheriff, starting in 1976. In 1994, he was on the judicial bench as city magistrate in Benson. The defining moment in his career came after the October 23, 1982, shoot-out between Cochise County sheriff's deputies and members of a fundamentalist religious sect in Miracle Valley. The melee resulted in the deaths of two church members, and several deputies were injured.

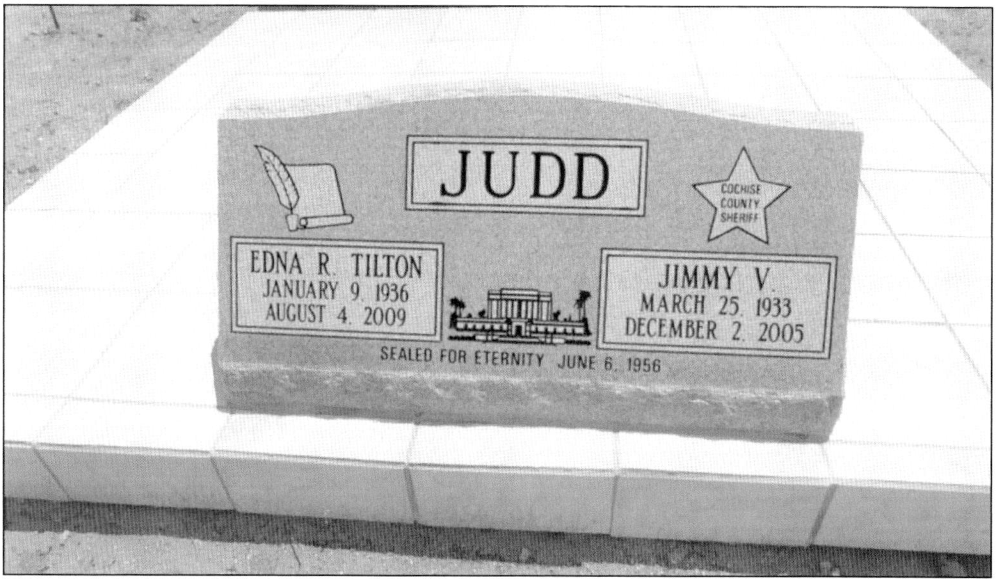

Sam Sanders, a counselor in the bishopric for the Church of Jesus Christ of Latter-day Saints, conducted Judd's funeral services. Judd, a Korean War veteran, was honored with the release of white doves as Sgt. Bob Saunders, of the Tucson Police Department Bagpipe Unit, sang "Amazing Grace." Judd was laid to rest with his trademark cowboy hat and boots perched atop the casket. His tombstone is inscribed with a "sealed for eternity" date; a drawing of the Mesa, Arizona, LDS temple; and his badge.

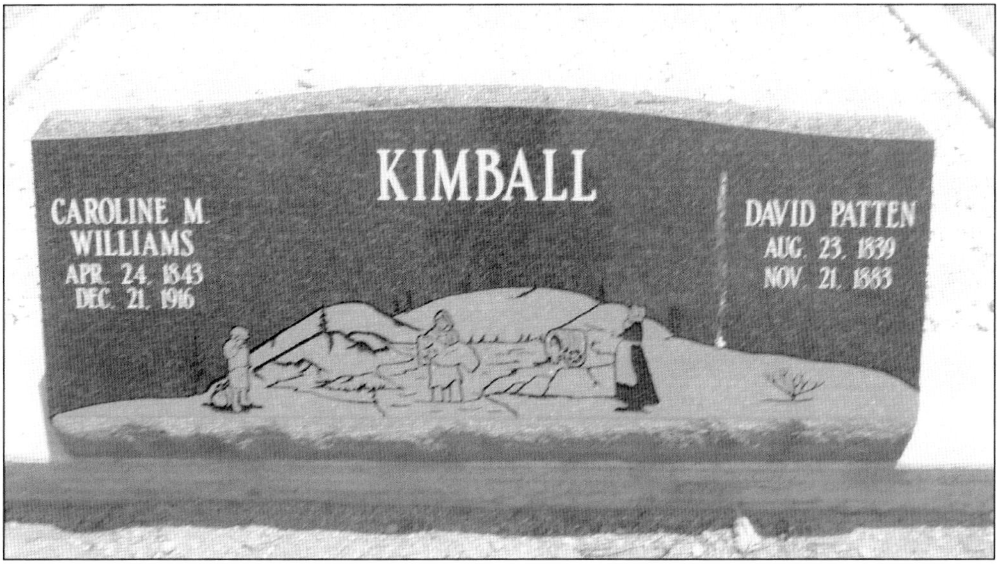

David Patten Kimball served as a bishop of the St. David Ward of the Church of Jesus Christ of the Latter-day Saints from 1882 to 1883. He was born on August 23, 1839, in Nauvoo, Illinois. In the winter of 1856, in response to a request from Brigham Young, Kimball helped a company of handcart pioneers stranded near the Sweetwater River. The handcart company, carrying all their possessions, had left Iowa and headed for Salt Lake Valley on July 28. By October, cold weather and snow trapped them in the mountains in Wyoming. Young promised Kimball and others a guaranteed place in heaven for their efforts. Kimball died at age 44 on November 21, 1883, in St. David, Arizona.

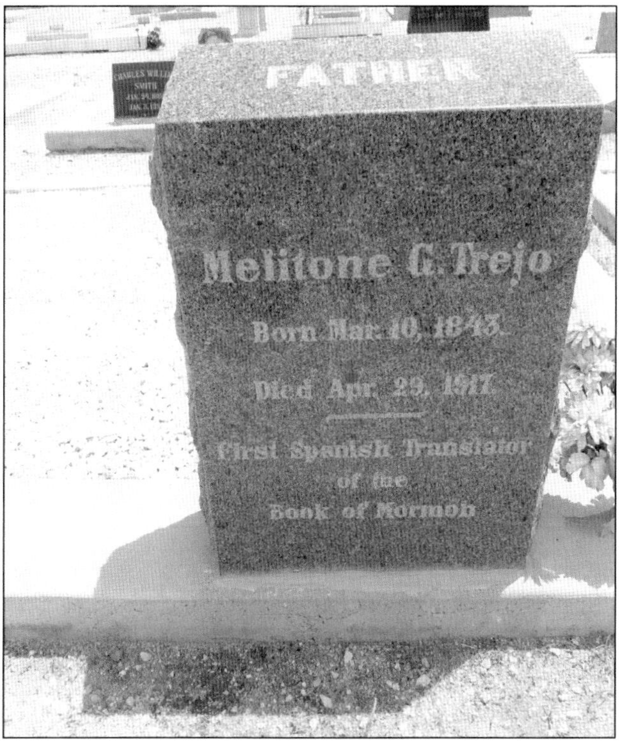

Meliton G. Trejo was born March 10, 1844, in Spain. His first name is spelled *Melitone* only on his gravestone; everywhere else, it is spelled *Meliton*. He died on April 29, 1917, in Willcox, Arizona, and is buried in the St. David Cemetery. Trejo married Emily Jones in 1884, and they had 10 children. He left the Spanish army after hearing about a group of "saints" being led by a prophet in the Rocky Mountains. He traveled to Salt Lake City, where he met Brigham Young, joined the Mormon church, and became the first Spanish translator of the Book of Mormon.

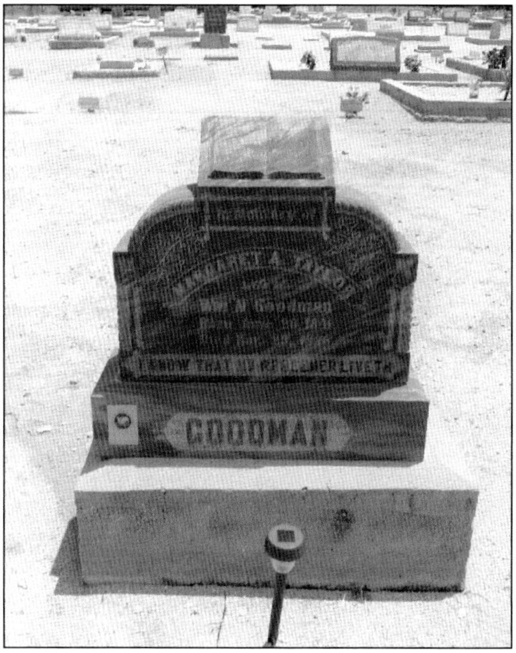

Margaret Ann Taylor was born June 20, 1841, in England. She married William Nicholas Goodman on February 27, 1864, and they settled in Minersville, Utah. William was in poor health, and they thought a warmer climate might help. In 1881, the family moved to Mesa, Arizona, before finally relocating to St. David. William died from a stroke on March 8, 1885, and Margaret sold their only cow to pay for funeral expenses. She bought bars of soap and small articles to sell out of her home and eventually founded Grandma Goodman's store; she worked in the mercantile business for 30 years. She also served as the postmaster in St. David for 20 years and boarded and roomed schoolteachers. Margaret died on March 29, 1926, from pneumonia. On top of her grave is an open book, and a solar collector in front of the tombstone lights up at night.

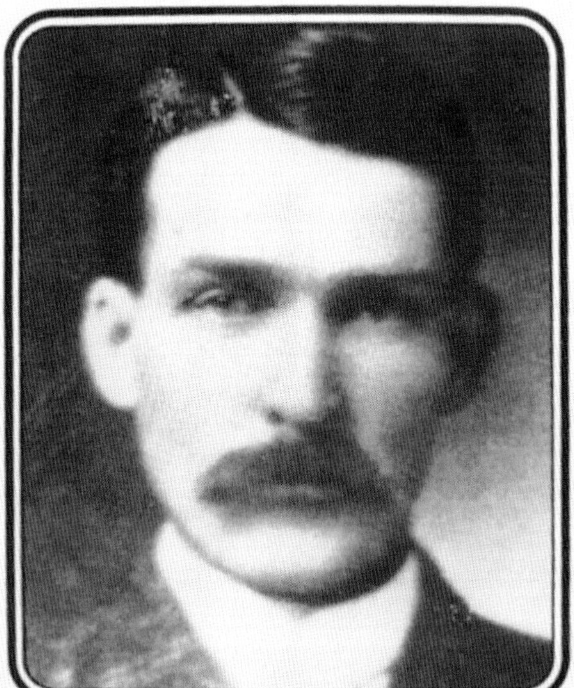

WARREN BAXTER EARP
Murdered 1900, in a Willcox, Arizona saloon.

Warren Baxter Earp, born March 9, 1855, in Pella, Iowa, died July 6, 1900, in Willcox, Arizona. The youngest of the Earp brothers, he came to Tombstone after Morgan Earp's death to help bring the body to California for burial. He joined his brother Wyatt in the vendetta ride to chase those whom they believed had murdered Morgan. Warren was killed by Johnny Boyett at the Headquarter Saloon in Willcox after Warren told Boyett that he knew that Boyett had been offered $100 or $150 by parties in town to kill him. Boyett denied this and told Earp he did not want any trouble, but added that if he had to fight him, he was not afraid.

On July 6, 1900, Warren Earp told Johnny Boyett to get his gun and said that he was fixed. Boyett walked over to the Willcox House, went behind the bar, and helped himself to a couple of guns. He returned to the saloon, and when Earp entered through the rear door, Boyett fired two shots at him. Earp went out a side door onto the sidewalk but re-entered a few minutes later. He advanced toward Boyett, opened his coat, and said, "You have the best of this, I have no gun." Boyett told him not to advance or he would shoot, but Earp kept coming. Boyett fired, and Earp dropped dead. Deputy Sheriff Page, George McKittrick, and Jim Hardin arrested Boyett and placed him in jail. A half-opened pocketknife was found in Earp's hand, but he was otherwise unarmed. (Courtesy of Richard Lapidus.)

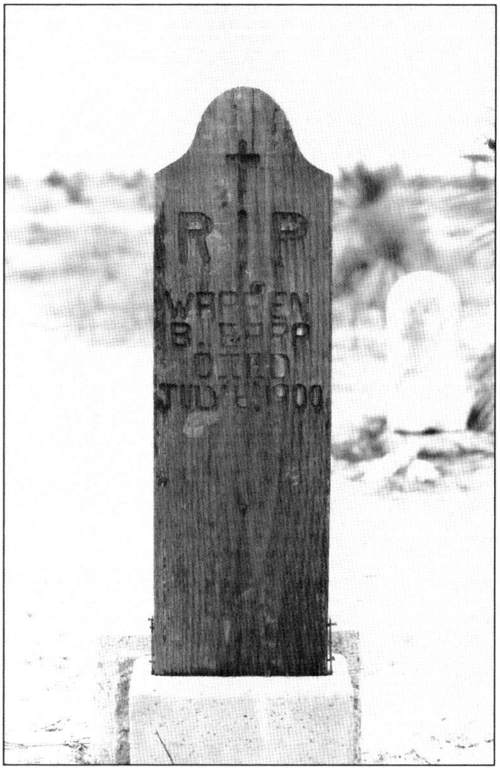

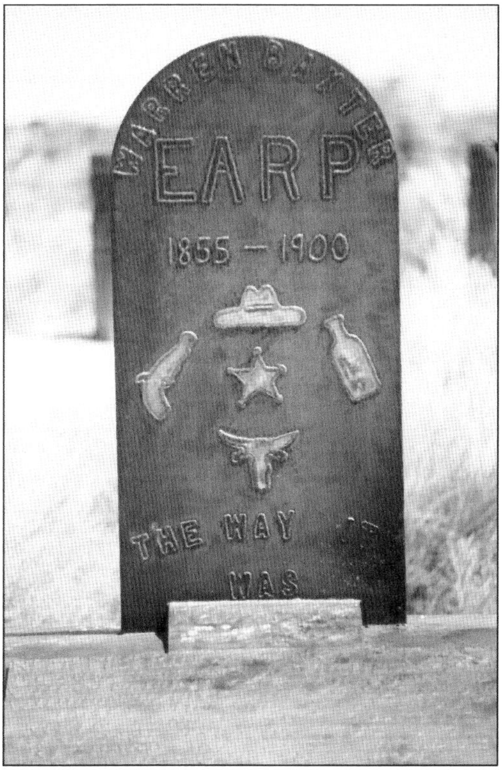

The next morning, Judge W.E. Nichols empaneled a coroner's jury, which rendered a verdict that Earp was killed by a bullet fired from Boyett's gun. Boyett had a preliminary hearing before Judge W.E. Nichols, and after evidence was heard, Boyett was discharged. Warren Earp has two tombstones in the old Willcox Pioneer Cemetery—the original one (pictured above) is from when he was actually buried, and the other (pictured at left) was erected a few years ago to commemorate the anniversary of his death. (Courtesy of Richard Lapidus.)

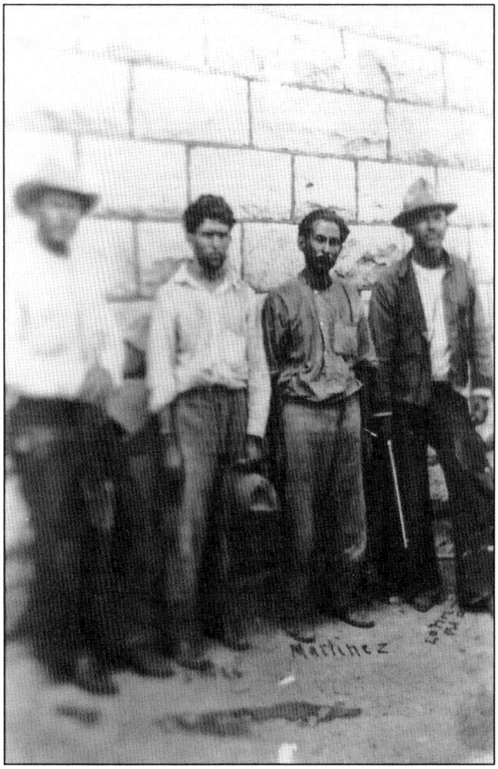

Santa Cruz County sheriff Harry Saxon and his deputy pose with two escapees who were involved in brutal murders at Ruby, Arizona. Saxon, the son of schoolteachers, was born July 24, 1882, in the mission town of San Gabriel, California. After his father's death, his mother moved the family to the ghost town of Calabasas in Santa Cruz County. Saxon's first job, besides herding his own cattle, was brand inspector. He died on August 11, 1964, in Willcox, and is buried next to his wife, Anna, in the Willcox Sunset Cemetery.

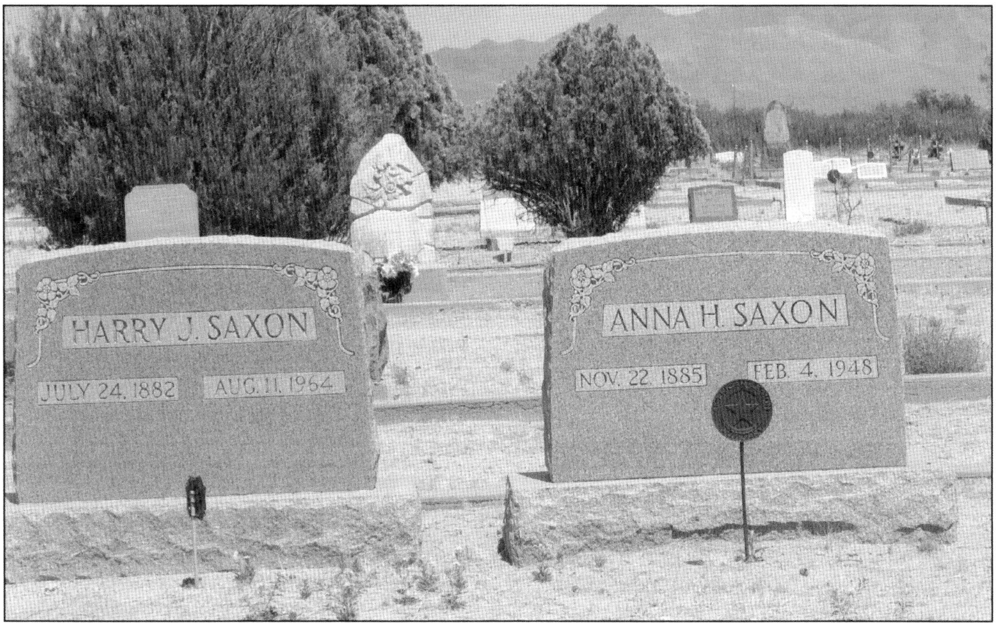

At the age of 22, Saxon was elected sheriff of Santa Cruz County. In addition to his roles as cattle inspector and sheriff, Saxon went on to serve as mayor of Willcox, organizer of the Three Links Cattle Company, chairman of the Santa Cruz Livestock Sanitary Board, president of the Sulphur Springs Valley Chamber of Commerce, and president of the Arizona Cattle Growers Association. Saxon also served in the House of Representatives of the First Arizona Legislature.

Four

Pima County Graves and Cemeteries

Almost all of the Pima County cemeteries are located within the Tucson metropolitan area. However, there are hundreds of small family cemeteries throughout the county. In cemeteries such as Evergreen and Holy Hope, areas are subdivided into smaller sections set aside for religious groups and fraternal organizations. All Faiths Cemetery is distinct in that the burials are in a natural desert setting, and it contains a cemetery for those of the Islamic faith. Binghamton Cemetery, established in 1899 by the Church of Jesus Christ of Latter-day Saints, was named after a small settlement that, at the time, was separate from Tucson. There are 12 varieties of evergreen trees planted throughout Evergreen Cemetery—the largest cemetery in Pima County—with more than 30,000 interments. Evergreen Cemetery, founded in 1907, is in a convenient location just outside of the Tucson city limits, and many remains from Tucson's earlier cemeteries were reinterred within Evergreen's manicured lawns. Holy Hope Cemetery was also founded in 1907 and was named by Bishop Henry Granjon. The first burials in Holy Hope were reburials of disinterred remains of family members who had originally been placed in what is now downtown Tucson.

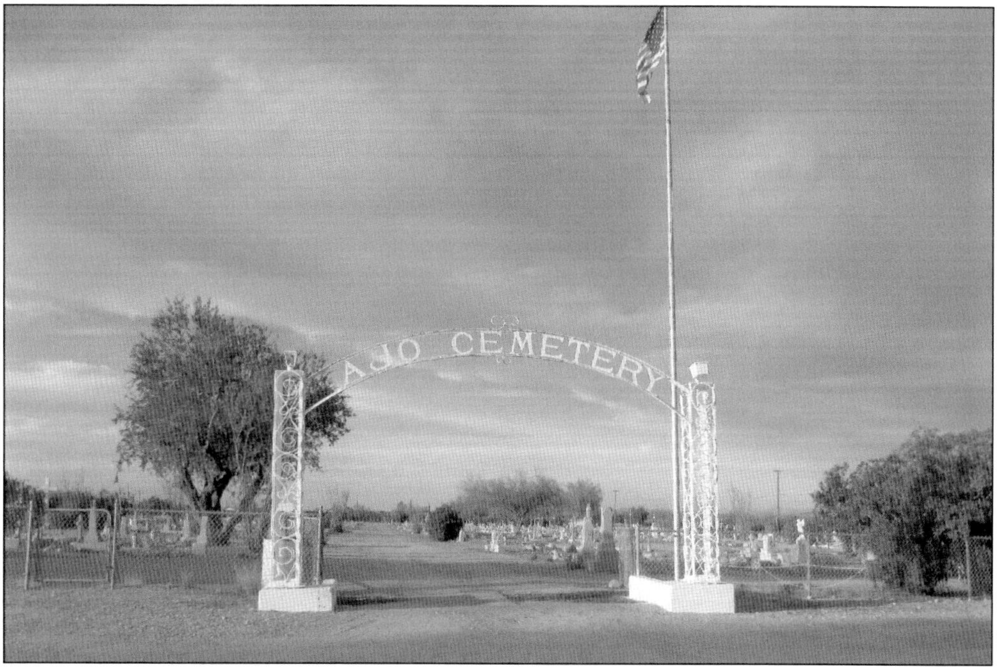

Many cemeteries have entrances flanked with an arched sign designating the name of the cemetery. The arch may be constructed of metal, wood, or brick, and it stands to remind visitors that they are entering a world of those who have left this life. In its heyday, Ajo, Arizona, was a primary producer of copper. Mexican miners are thought to have called the site "Ajo" after its abundant wild garlic, although they may have heard the O'odham word *au-auho*—meaning "red paint"—and named the area for the pigment in the ore-rich rocks. (Courtesy of Carolyn O'Bagy Davis.)

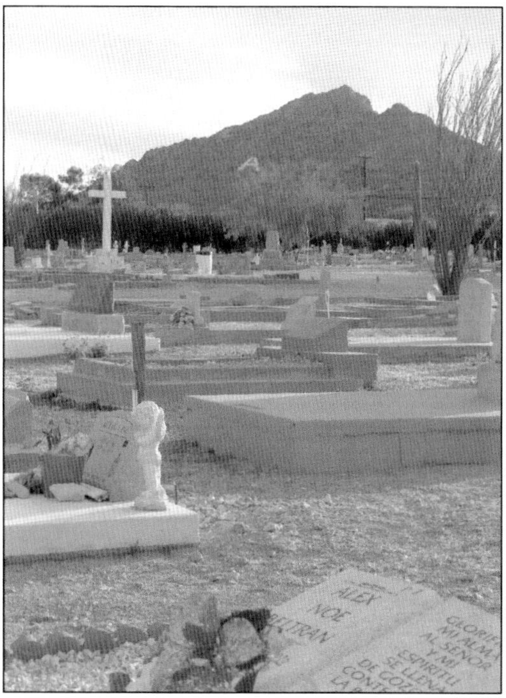

On their way to silver mines near Magdalena, Sonora, Tom Childs Sr. and his party discovered ore in the Ajo area in 1847. The Arizona Mining & Trading Company, formed by Childs's friend Peter M. Brady, worked the rich surface ores in the 1880s. However, the long supply lines and lack of water discouraged large mining companies. The first person to fully develop the Ajo area was John Campbell Greenway, a Rough Rider and star Yale athlete who became general manager of the Calumet & Arizona Mining Company. Greenway located the well that still provides water to Ajo. (Courtesy of Carolyn O'Bagy Davis.)

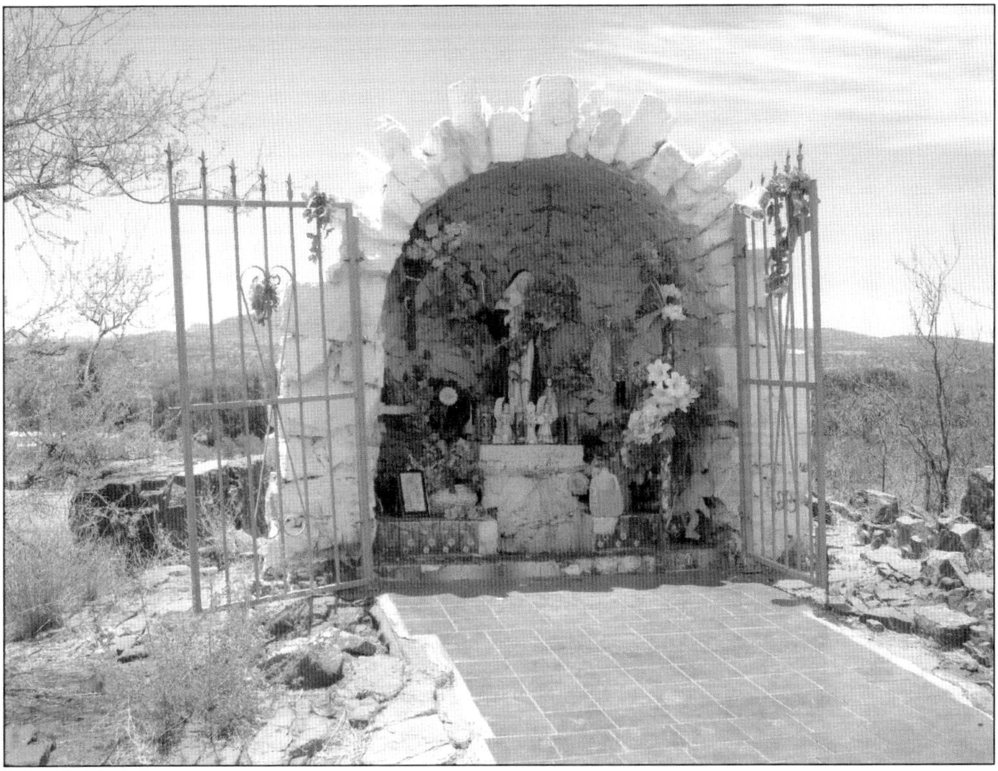

Throughout the Southwest and Mexico, roadside shrines mark individual deaths. People were once actually buried there, but the bodies have been removed to a cemetery, although a memorial shrine remains. Few are as beautiful and mysterious as the shrine of Santa Rita on the road to Arivaca. According to one legend, when Arthur Lee—owner of the nearby Sópori Ranch—was killed due to a fall from his horse, his wife had the grotto erected. Over the years, the shrine has been maintained by the Arivaca community and individuals who feel blessed by Santa Rita's presence. Santa Rita, the patron saint of desperate causes, has been credited with several miracles.

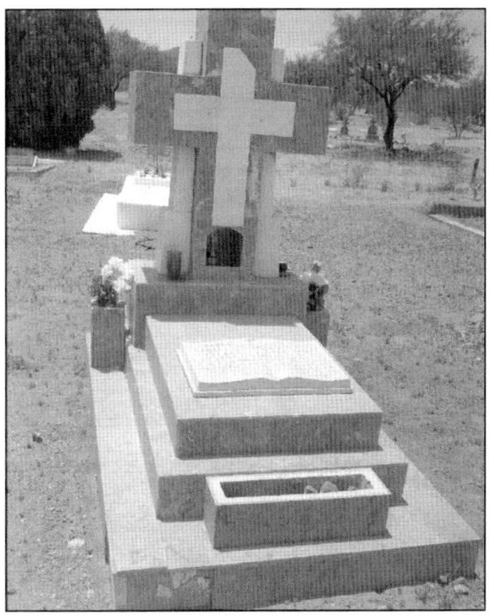

This is the grave of Pablo Celaya, who was born August 27, 1930, and died February 6, 1964. His grave's inscription is in Spanish on an open book. Bartolo Miquirray's tombstone—which is only partially visible behind Celaya's grave in this photograph—is the largest in the Arivaca Cemetery, and its inscriptions are in Spanish. Miquirray's birthday is unknown, but he died on July 26, 1914, in Santa Cruz County. His grave is somewhat mysterious, since almost nothing is known about this 18-year-old cowboy.

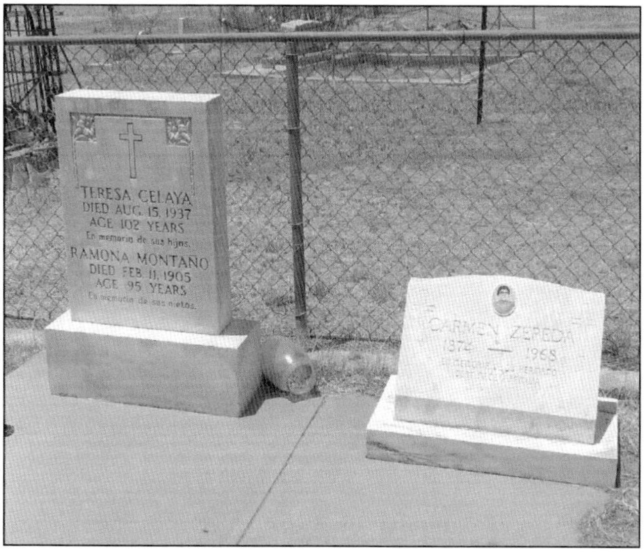

These three women lived a very long time and now rest together in the Arivaca Cemetery. Carmen Zepeda ran a store in Carmen, Arizona, for many years. She was born in 1874 and died in 1958. Teresa Celaya was born in 1835 and died on August 15, 1937, in Arivaca. Her brothers robbed the Vulture Mine, located near Wickenburg, of two gold bars and supposedly took refuge in Teresa's house, burying the gold bars in her backyard. Ramona Montano was born in 1810 and died on February 11, 1905, at age 95.

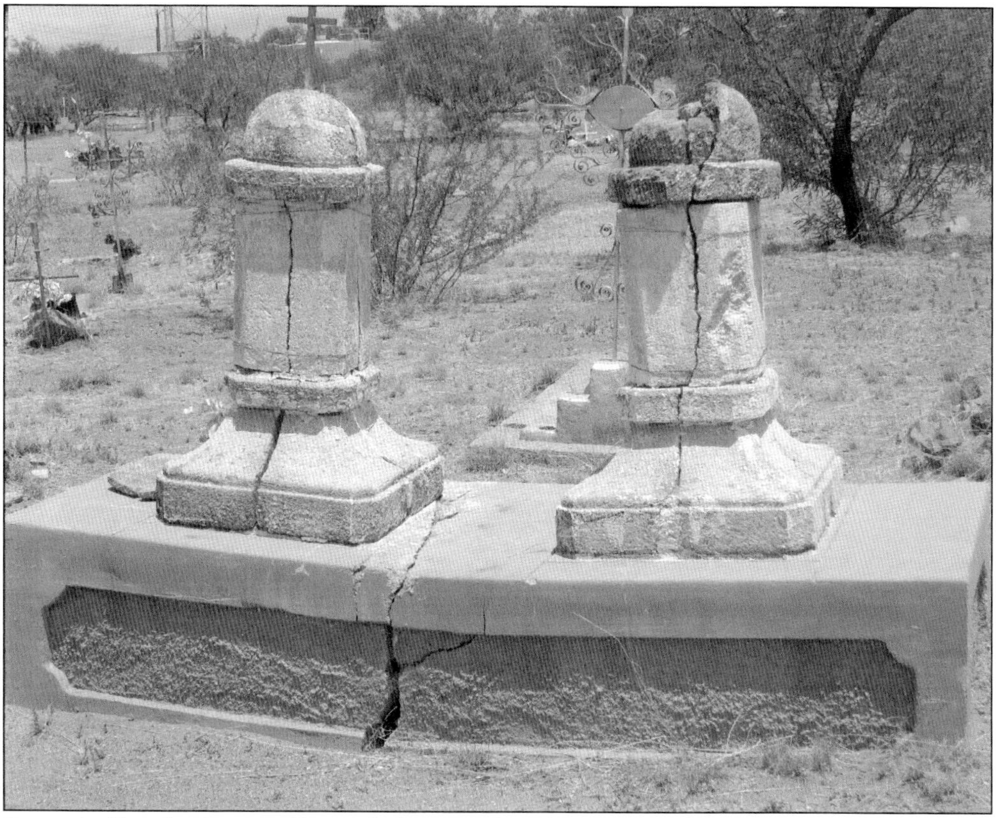

Bernardo Caviglia, born in Genoa, Italy, arrived in America in 1876. He spent time in Nevada, Colorado, and Tombstone, Arizona, before moving to Arivaca in 1887 and homesteading in Arivaca Canyon. Bernardo died in 1932. His son Angelo built Caviglia's Café and staged *tardeadas*, fiestas, and horse races. Bernardo and his wife, Pastora Vega, are buried in these crumbling graves in the Arivaca Cemetery. The Caviglia-Arivaca Branch Library is named for Diane Caviglia, daughter-in-law of Angelo and Luz.

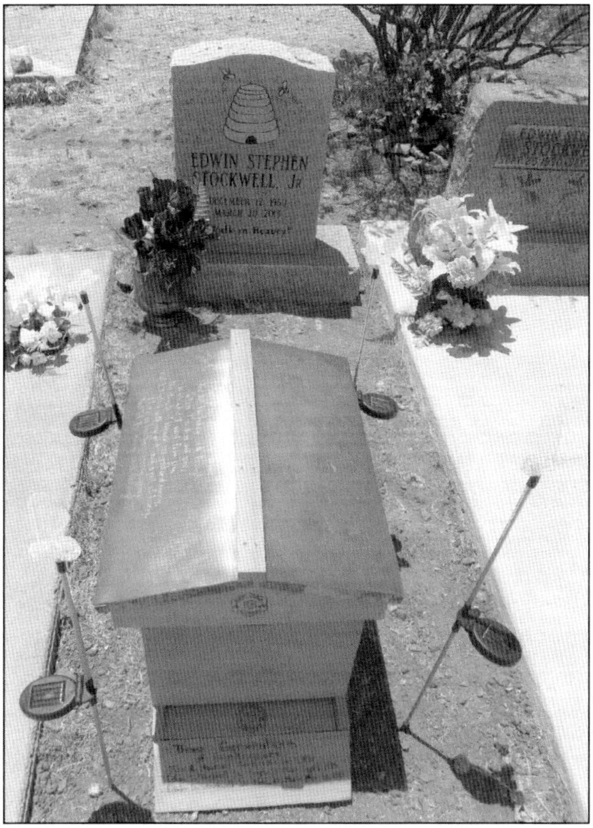

Edwin S. Stockwell Jr.'s grave marker celebrates three generations of Arivaca beekeepers. Stockwell was born on December 12, 1960, and died on March 20, 2013. The Stockwell Honey Company began in 1943. The inscription on the miniature beehive in the foreground says: "Place a beehive on my grave/And let the honey soak through/When I am dead and gone/ That's what I want from you/And I'll stick with my plot and a pot of honey/Place a beehive on my grave/ And let the honey soak through."

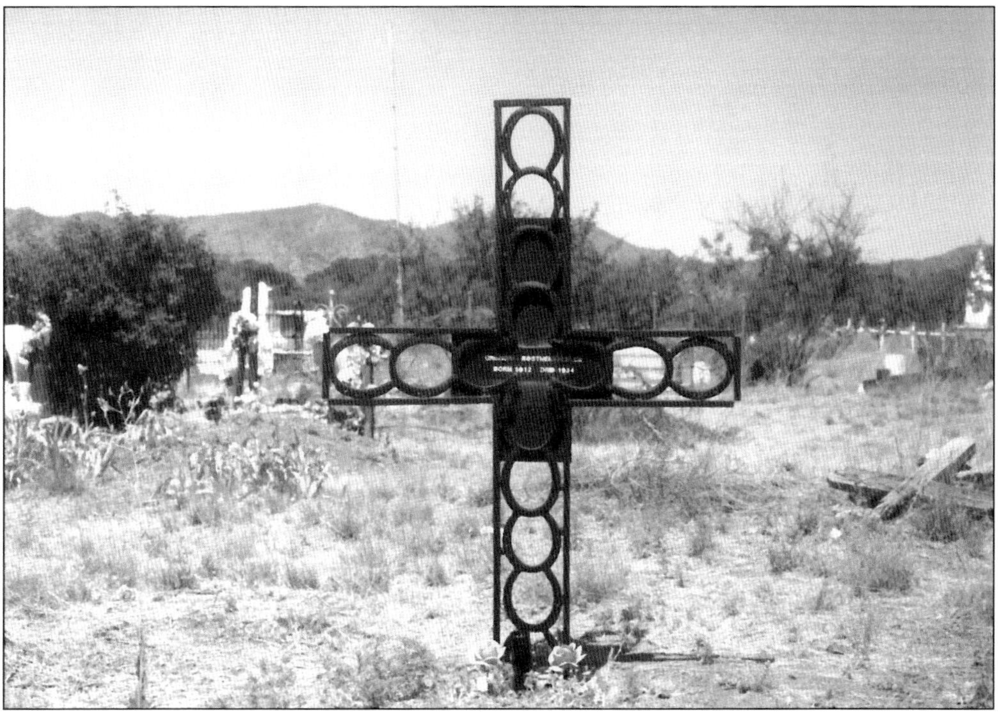

This young cowboy's tombstone, constructed with horseshoes, reflects his life.

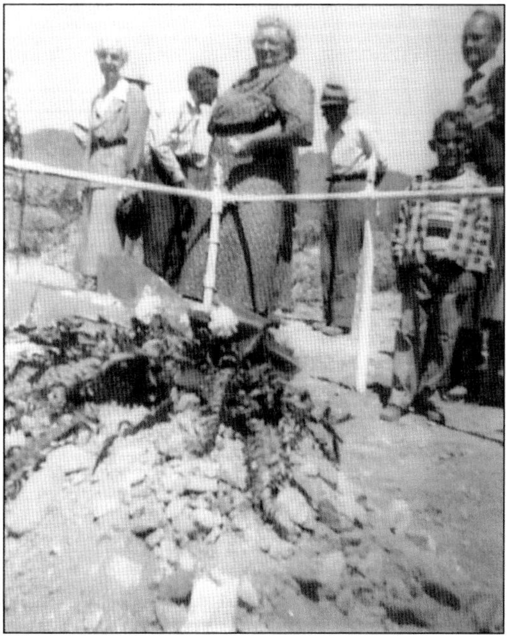

Goldie Preston (the large woman in the center of the image at left) was born in Kansas in 1896; at age 21, she married Marion Tracy and became his third wife. In 1927, the couple moved to Arizona. Goldie was 31, and Marion was 68 and in declining health. In 1932, they opened Tracy's Trading Post at San Simon on the Tohono O'odham Reservation. Goldie learned to speak the Tohono O'odham language and became one of the most respected white traders on the reservation. After Marion's death in 1936, Goldie continued to run the store and married Jim Richmond. She stitched quilts to sell in the trading post, and her exceptional designs won many blue ribbons and cash prizes. Her appliqué quilts depicting Tohono O'odham daily life are magnificent fabric portraits of the Sonoran Desert and its people. (Courtesy of Carolyn O'Bagy Davis.)

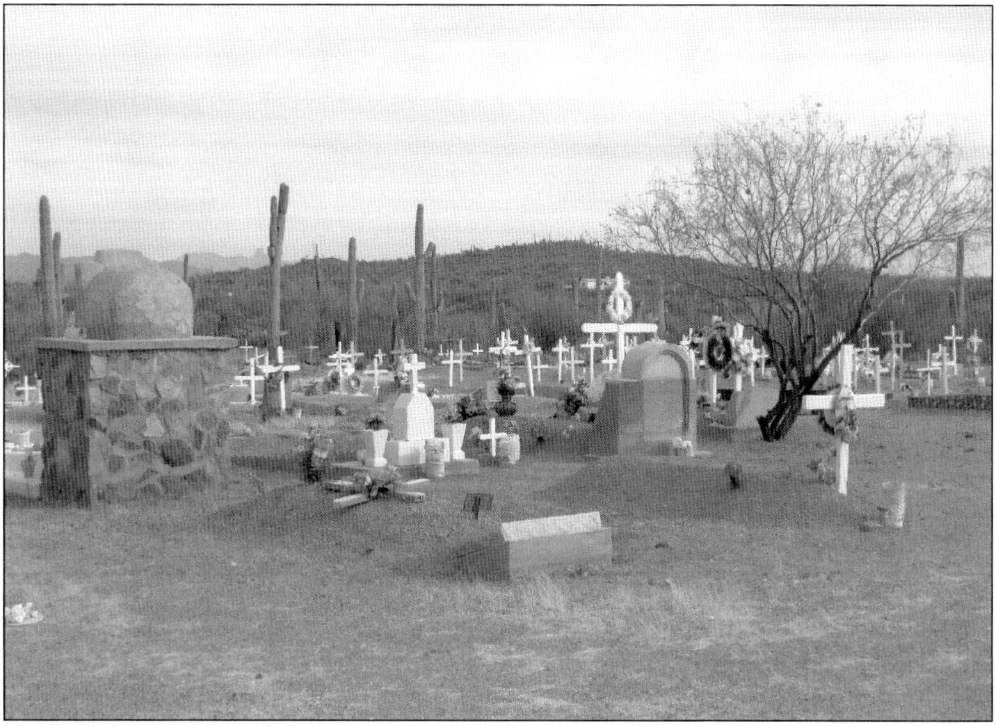

In the late 1960s, Goldie and Jim sold Tracy's Trading Post and retired to Mesa, Arizona, where she died in 1972. By the time word of her death reached the reservation, it was too late for people to make the long trip to attend her funeral. As a tribute to her life and friendship, O'odham friends held their own memorial service on the reservation, where she is still spoken of with respect and affection. Although Goldie is buried in Mesa, this grave in Quijotoa is typical of the small Indian community where she lived and worked. (Courtesy of Carolyn O'Bagy Davis.)

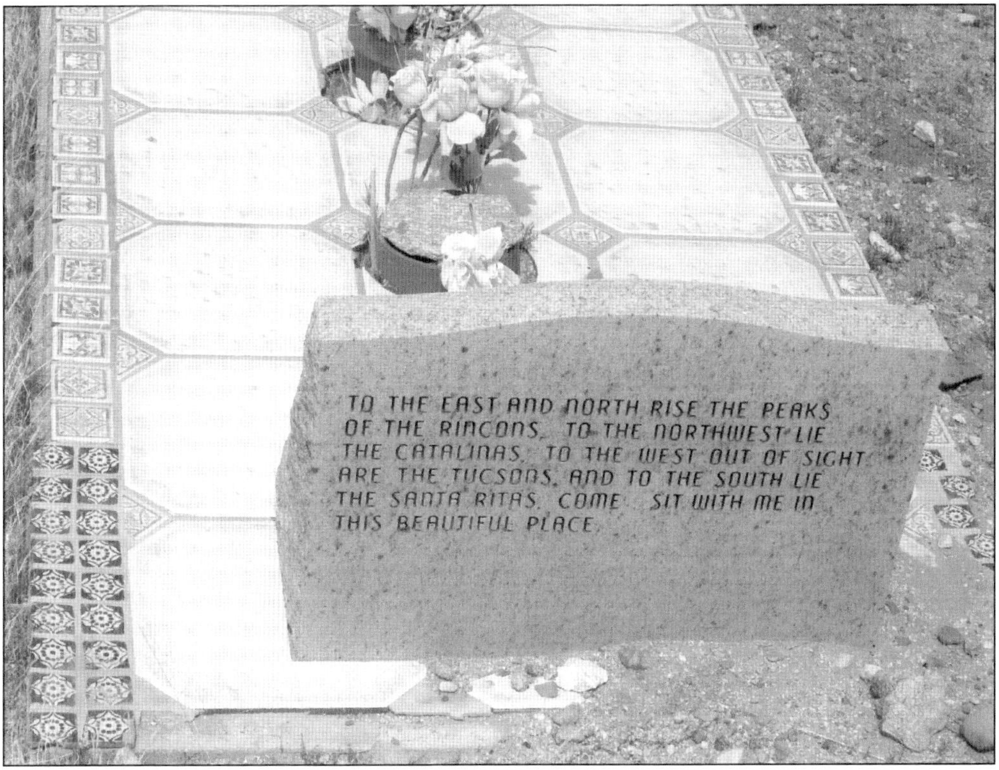

The Rincon Memorial Cemetery on Old Spanish Trail Road contains graves from the early 1900s and others as recent as 2009. It has a beautiful view from a hilltop, and the majority of graves look east to the Rincon Mountains. Many of the graves belong to those who were ranchers in the area. The inscription on this grave says it all.

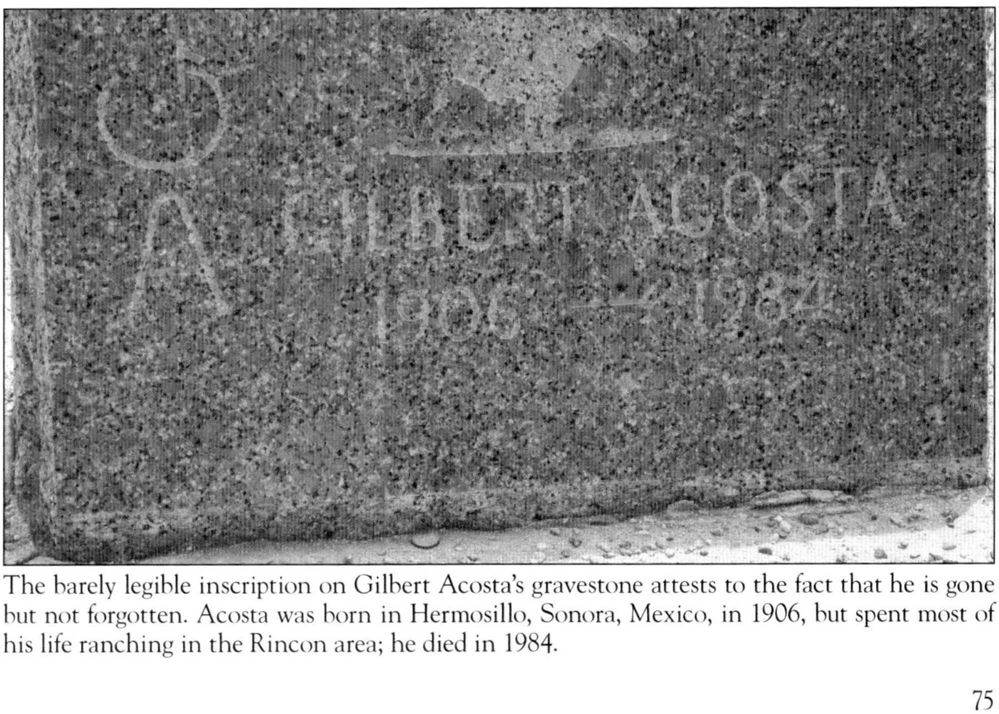

The barely legible inscription on Gilbert Acosta's gravestone attests to the fact that he is gone but not forgotten. Acosta was born in Hermosillo, Sonora, Mexico, in 1906, but spent most of his life ranching in the Rincon area; he died in 1984.

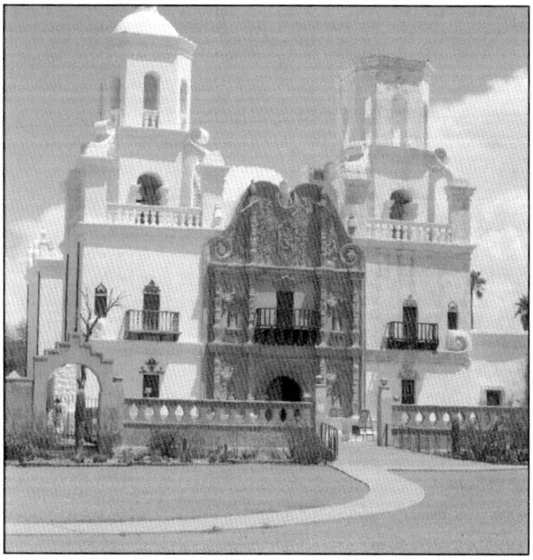

Mission San Xavier's interior is filled with beautiful statuary and murals. The church still ministers to the religious needs of its parishioners, who are predominantly members of the Tohono O'odham tribe. Some 200,000 visitors come each year to view what is widely considered to be the finest example of Spanish Colonial architecture in the United States. The current church dates from the late 1700s, when Franciscan missionary Fray Juan Bautista Velderrain hired architect Ignacio Gaona and a large workforce of O'odham to build it. With the Gadsden Purchase of 1854, the mission became part of the United States. In 1859, it became part of the Diocese of Santa Fe. In 1866, Tucson became a diocese, and regular services were held at the mission.

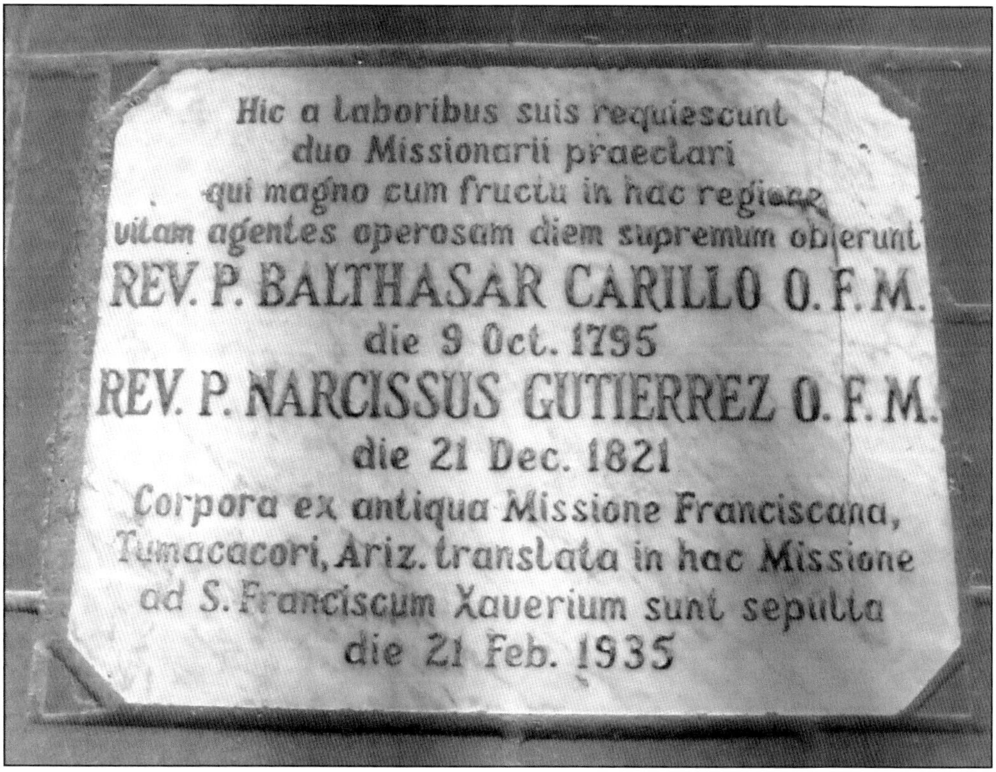

The San Xavier grounds contain a small mausoleum where two priests from Mission Tumacácori are buried. On the morning of February 21, 1935, Mass was said at Tumacácori by Rev. Francis Bree over the remains of two pioneer Franciscan priests. Then, the remains of Padre Baltazar Carillo and Padre Narciso Gutiérrez were escorted by three National Park Service employees from San José de Tumacácori to San Xavier del Bac. The padres had often made the long trip by foot or on horseback. Indians were stationed on the hill, and, upon seeing the procession, ran down the hill to tell others of the arrival. Hundreds of people welcomed the padres to the mission that had once been theirs. Two prelates of the church—Rev. Daniel J. Gercke, bishop of Tucson, and Rev. Edmund Gibbons, bishop of Albany, New York—joined in honoring the two pioneers.

"Because the love of a pet never dies," more people are providing their pets with funeral services, which can include cremation, blessings, chapel meditation, headstones, and caskets. At the Pet Cemetery of Tucson, owners are permitted to have their own cremains buried with their pet. Here, Milton the burro rests with cats, dogs, snakes, pot-bellied pigs, and humans in the afterlife.

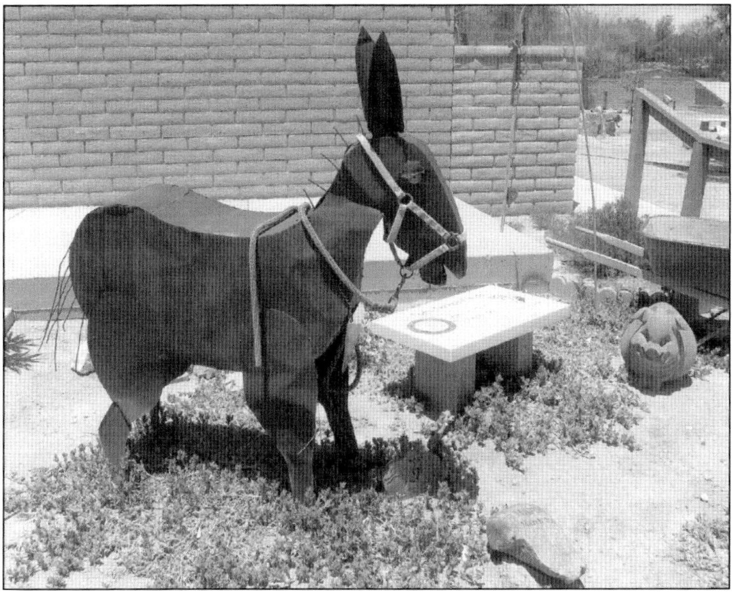

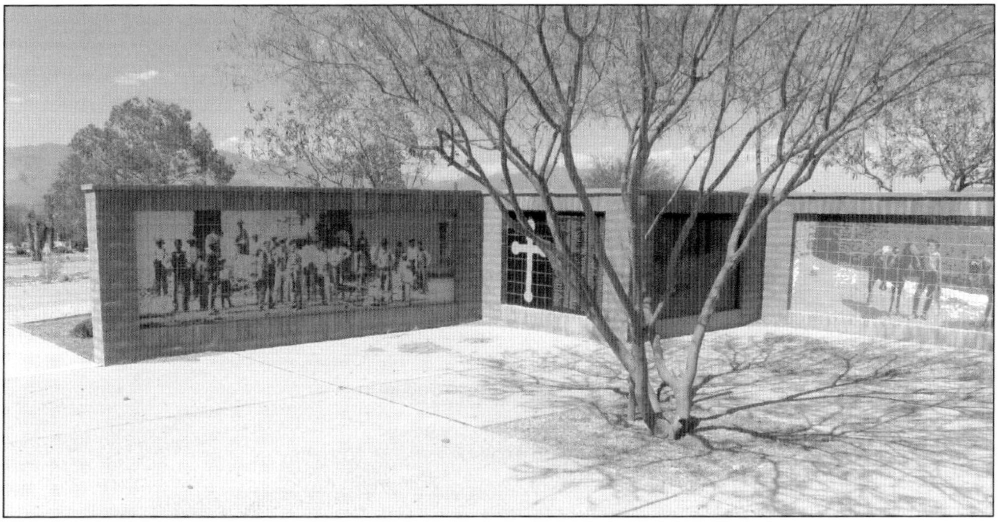

Between 1860 and 1875, Tucson's deceased were buried in a cemetery located at what is now the corner of Alameda and Stone Streets in downtown Tucson. Pima County exhumed more than 1,300 individuals between 2006 and 2008 in the course of construction in the area. About 1,200 were reburied at All Faiths Cemetery in February 2010, and the remaining 100 were buried at other sites. Individuals were placed in separate containers, and their names are etched on a wall. The dedication of the Memorial for Tucson's Historic Cemetery took place on June 26, 2010, and blessings were bestowed by Bishop Gerald Kicanas, Rabbi Thomas Louchheim, and Rev. John Lille. At the end of the service, doves were released.

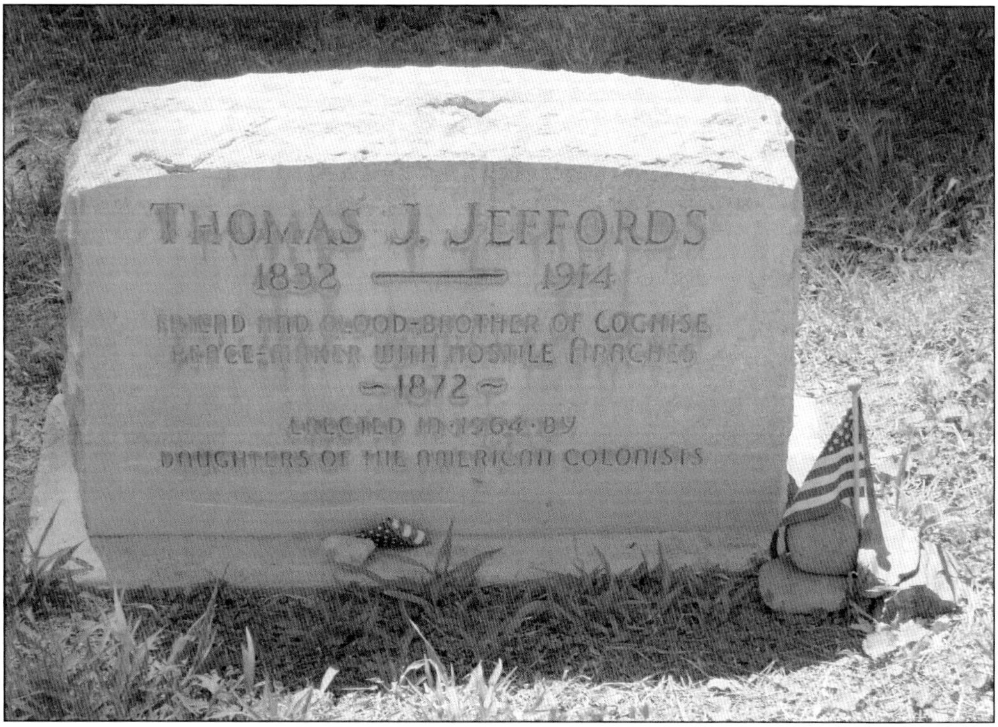

The graves closest to Oracle Road in Evergreen Cemetery are those of Arizona's most famous pioneers. Thomas Jonathan Jeffords was born on January 1, 1832, and died on February 19, 1914. In 1859 in the New Mexico Territory, he served as an Army scout and a teamster. He contacted the Apache chief Cochise in order to secure safe passage for his freight wagons through Apache territory. They became friends, and Jeffords provided the opportunity for Gen. Oliver O. Howard to meet with Cochise in 1871 and 1872 to negotiate an end to the war. Jeffords's and Cochise's friendship was depicted in the 1950 movie *Broken Arrow*.

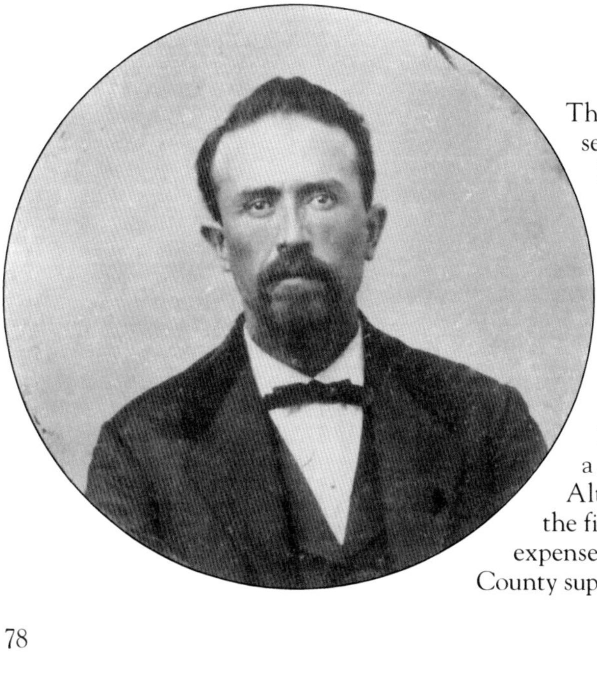

The Aguirre family, from Chihuahua, settled in New Mexico in the 1850s and later moved to Arizona to earn fortunes as freighters along the Santa Fe Trail. After the railroad ruined the wagon-freighting trade, they went on to become prominent Arizona ranchers, running more than 10,000 cattle per year on ranges near Tucson. Pedro Aguirre started the Buenos Aires Ranch, originally a stage stop, in 1864. In 1870, Aguirre made Arivaca a stop on his stage line from Tucson to Altar, Sonora, Mexico, and also built the first schoolhouse in Arivaca at his own expense. He later went on to become a Pima County supervisor.

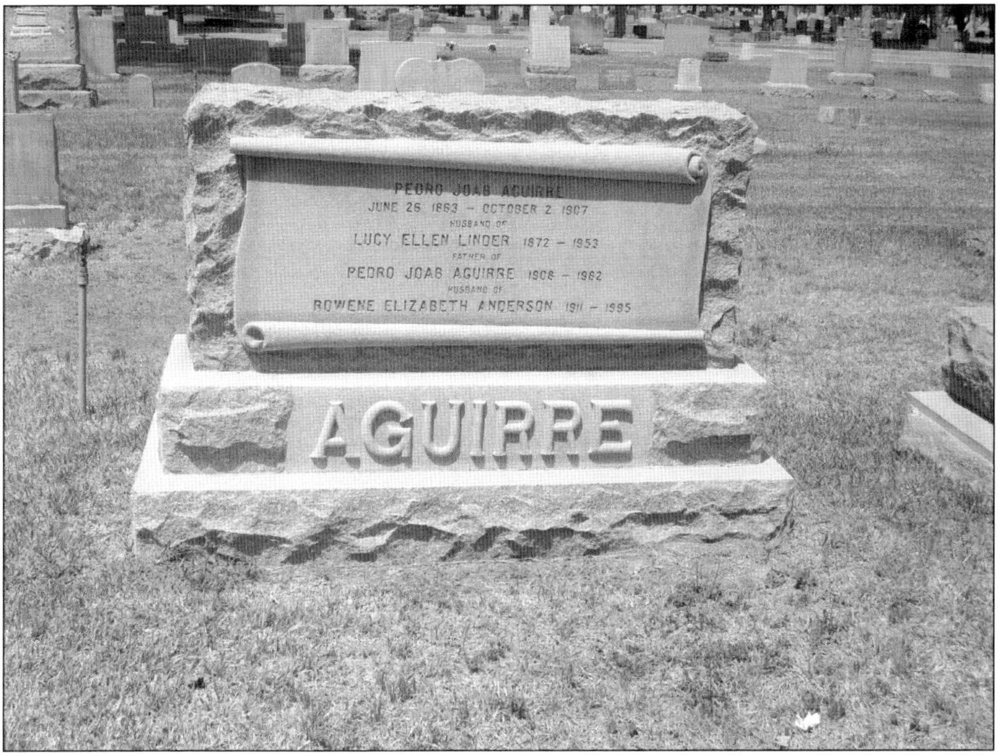

The Aguirre family gravestone features a large scroll naming those who are buried beneath it. Pedro married Ana Maria Redondo, daughter of a former governor of Sonora. Pedro's brother Epifanio, the husband of Mary "Mamie" Bernard, was killed by Indians on a freighting trip. Mamie's brother Noah (Nonie) W. Bernard had followed her to Arizona.

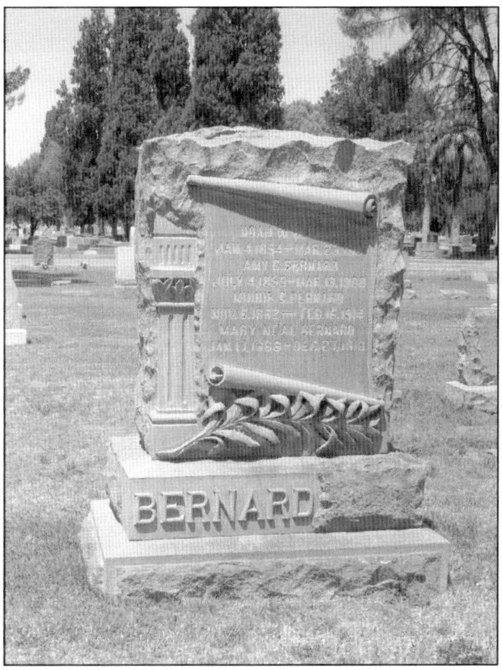

The massive Bernard tombstone features a scroll with the names of those making the final journey into eternity. It is adorned with a Greek column and acanthus leaves, which were used in funerary architecture as early as the fifth century BC. Noah "Nonie" W. Bernard was born in Baltimore, Maryland, on January 4, 1853. In Westport, Missouri, Epifanio Aguirre married Noah's older sister Mamie. When Epifanio was killed, Mamie taught school while Noah established himself in business. Noah joined Pedro Aguirre in Arivaca in 1877. His store, N.W. Bernard & Co., carried general merchandise. Noah and John Bogan went into partnership in the Arivaca Land & Cattle Company. Noah also served as a Pima County supervisor, representative to the Territorial Legislative Assembly in 1895, and a representative from Tucson to the 21st and 22nd Legislative Assembly in 1901 and 1903, respectively. He died in 1907 at age 54.

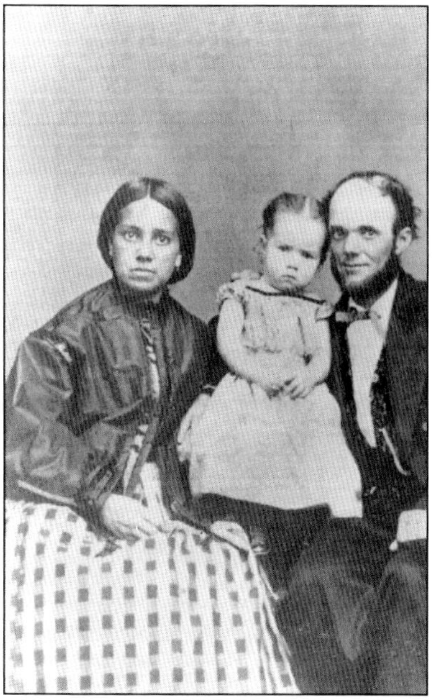

Samuel "Sam" Hughes was born in Wales in 1829, came to the United States in 1837, and died in Tucson in 1917. He had no formal schooling, and when both of his parents died, he helped raise and educate his siblings. Hughes became a successful merchant during the California Gold Rush, but he developed tuberculosis and got off a stagecoach outside of Tucson in 1858 expecting to die. He recovered, though, and when Confederate forces occupied Tucson, he moved to California. He left his financial interests to a friend until 1862, when he accompanied Union soldiers to Arizona and later fell in love with 13-year-old Atanacia Santa Cruz. They had 15 children, 5 of whom died in infancy. Hughes is the namesake of a school and a neighborhood, and he died in 1917. The image at left shows Atanacia and Sam with one of their children.

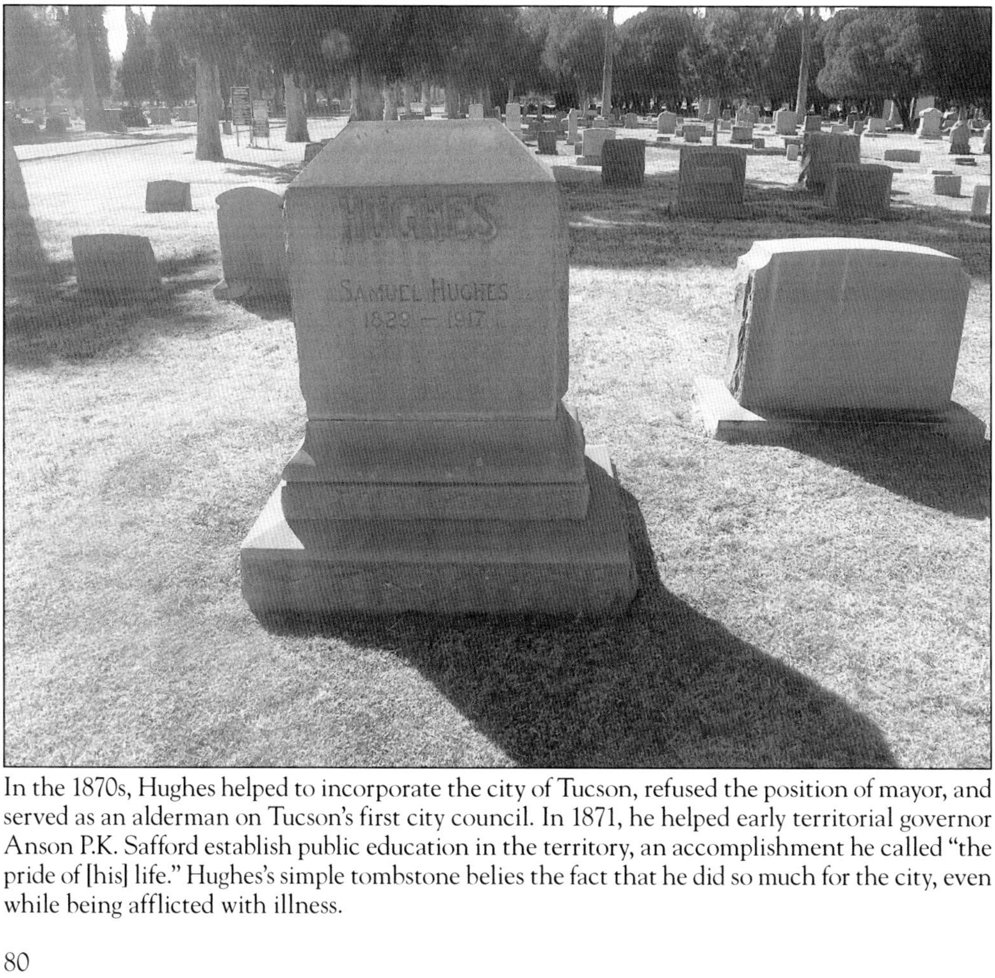

In the 1870s, Hughes helped to incorporate the city of Tucson, refused the position of mayor, and served as an alderman on Tucson's first city council. In 1871, he helped early territorial governor Anson P.K. Safford establish public education in the territory, an accomplishment he called "the pride of [his] life." Hughes's simple tombstone belies the fact that he did so much for the city, even while being afflicted with illness.

Louis Cameron Hughes—brother of Samuel Hughes—was born on May 15, 1842, in Philadelphia and died on November 24, 1915, in Tucson. He served as governor of Arizona Territory and, in 1877, started the *Daily Bulletin*, which eventually became the *Arizona Daily Star.* He grew up as an indentured servant to a Calvinist farmer. At age 16, his indenture ended, and he was given $15 and sent out into the world. He attended public schools in Meadville, Pennsylvania, before enlisting as a private during the Civil War. After the war, he earned a law degree. Like Sam, he had respiratory problems and moved to Arizona to help ease them. In 1871, he was admitted to practice law before the Arizona Territorial Supreme Court. He entered politics and was elected to the Tucson City Council in 1872 and served as Pima County attorney in 1873.

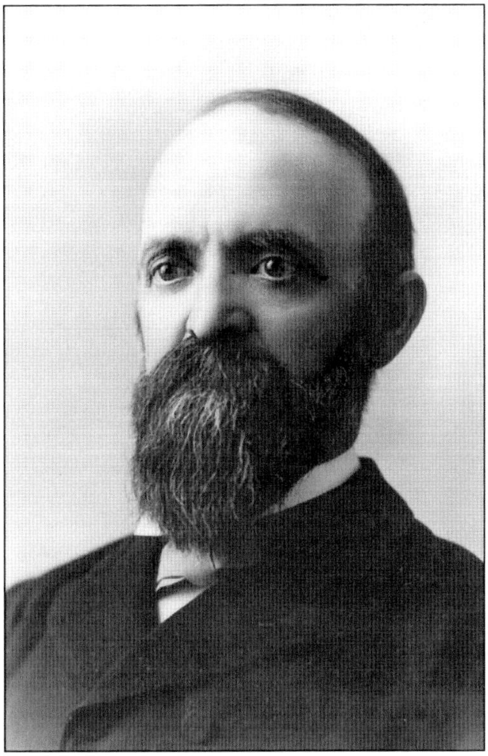

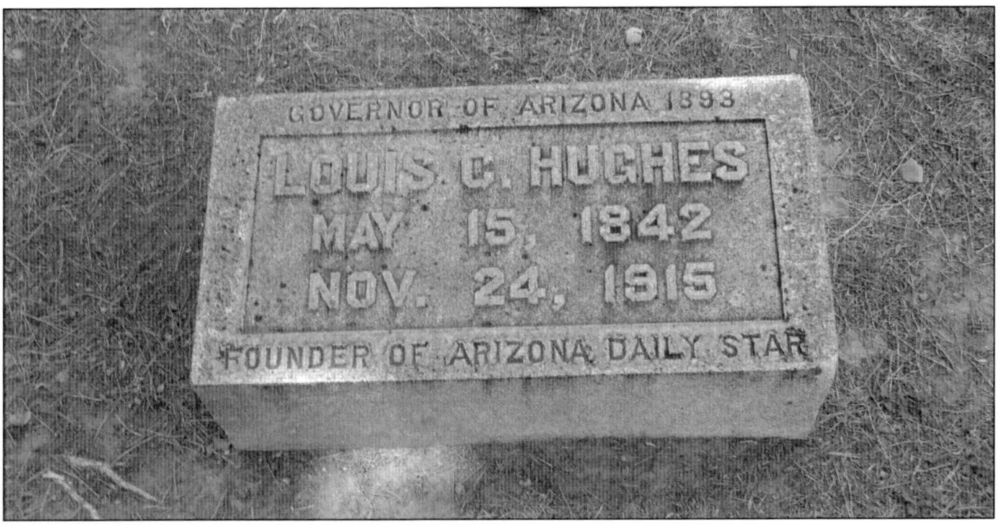

Louis Hughes was appointed territorial governor in 1893. He wanted to clean up the electoral process because voters were being bought with alcohol. He endorsed women's suffrage and the secret ballot and proposed a board of control for the territorial prison and the insane asylum. Hughes wanted to establish a board of immigration to encourage business to come to Arizona. In 1896, he reduced territorial debt and created a nonpartisan board of control before being removed from office in April of that year. He served on the University of Arizona Board of Regents in 1897 and returned to running his newspaper, the *Arizona Daily Star.* Pres. Theodore Roosevelt invited Hughes to the christening of the USS *Arizona*, but he refused because champagne was used in the ceremony. He is buried in Evergreen Cemetery near his wife, Josephine, and son Charles.

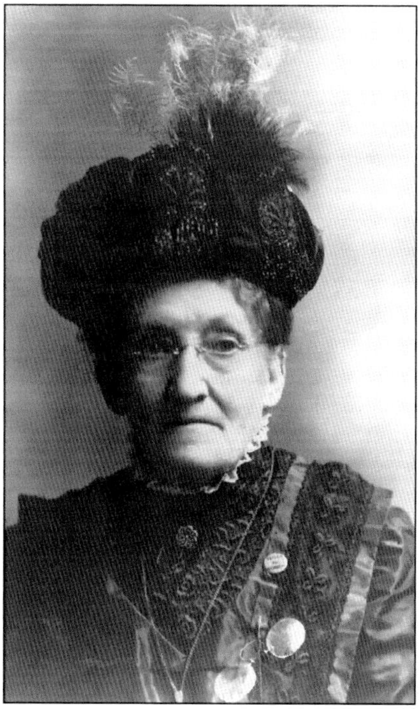

Josephine Brawley Hughes was born on December 22, 1839, in Meadville, Pennsylvania. She attended a rural school and then matriculated at Edinboro State Normal School. Upon graduation, Josephine taught for two years in public schools. While attending Edinboro, she met Louis C. Hughes, who was studying law at her father's law office and working at the local newspaper. They married in July 1869. Two years later, Louis sought the warmer climate of Tucson, where his brothers Samuel and Thomas had gone. He opened a law office in Tucson and, within a year, had saved enough money to bring Josephine and their child Gertrude there. Josephine had her parents send her candle molds, and candles soon illuminated her house and the homes around her. She installed a cistern, laid a carpet in her parlor, made paper fly brushes, and kept chickens.

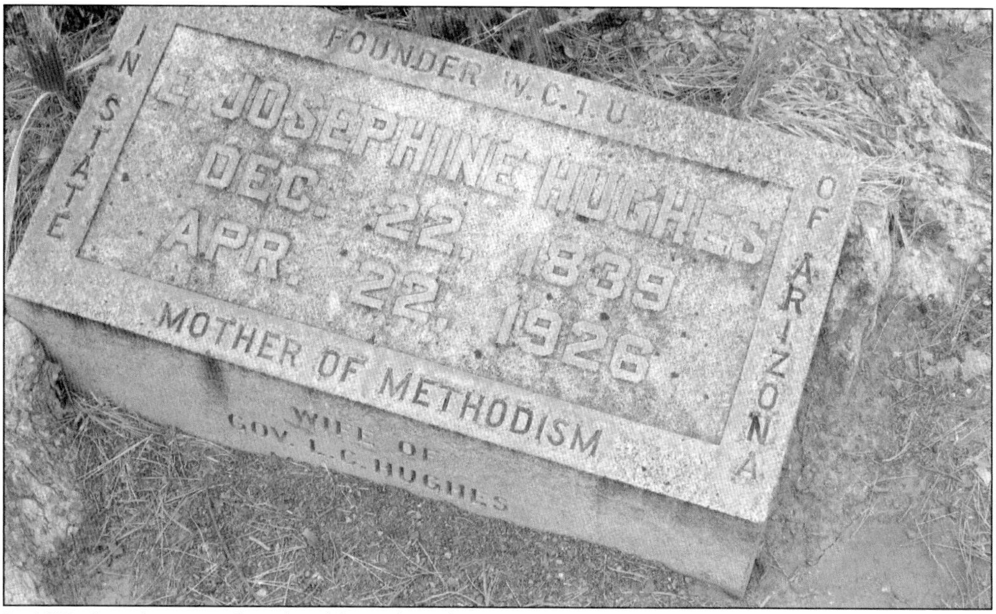

In 1872, Josephine taught school for girls and used a classroom in the Pioneer Brewery building. In 1875, she was appointed the Arizona commissioner to the Women's Department of the Centennial Exposition of 1876, which was held in Philadelphia. In 1876, Josephine helped organize the first Methodist church in Tucson. With her husband, Louis, serving as editor the *Arizona Daily Star* and Josephine serving as business manager, bookkeeper, and cashier, they advocated temperance, the complete removal of Apaches to Florida, and higher education. They opposed capital punishment and gambling. A couple of years after Louis's death, she moved to Hermosa Beach, California, to live with her daughter Gertrude. She died on April 22, 1926.

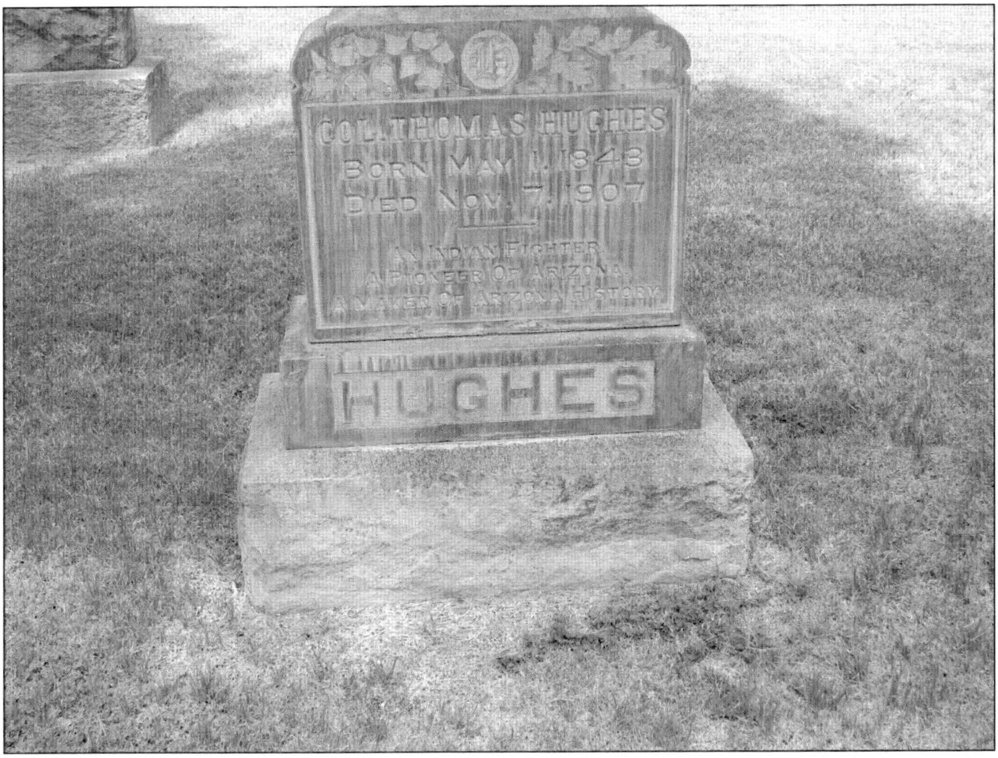

Thomas Hughes, brother of Sam and Louis Hughes, was born on May 1, 1843, and died on November 7, 1907. In 1796, Roque de Medina granted lands that included much of Tucson's present-day Barrio Anita. In 1828, Teodoro Ramírez bought the land for two muskets, sixteen pesos worth of tobacco, four serapes, a horse, and ten pesos. Hughes bought the land from the Arizona Territory on January 31, 1902. After his wife, Elena, died, his sister Annie helped him raise his children. Hughes named one of McKinley Park's streets—Annie Avenue—after his sister; it soon became Anita Avenue, and the area became known as Barrio Anita.

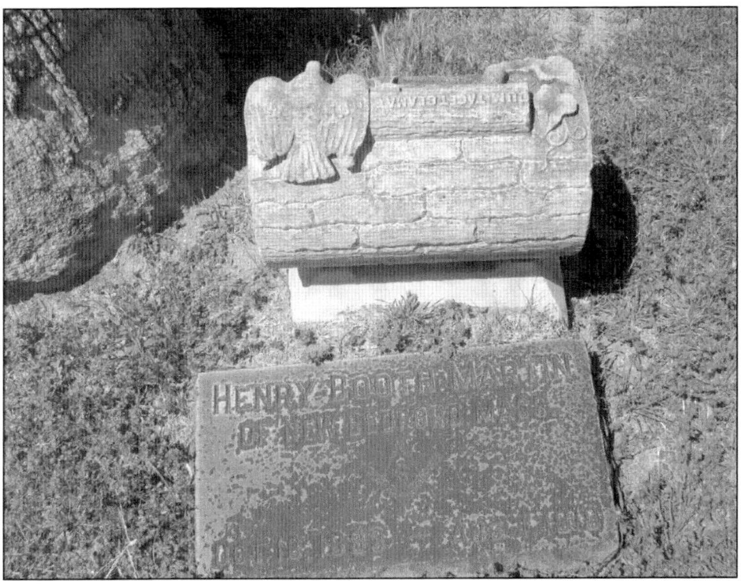

Little is known of Henry Booth Martin except that he was born on October 16, 1893, in Massachusetts, and he died a comparatively young man on August 1, 1919. If the treestone next to his marker belongs to him, it means that he was a member of Woodmen of the World.

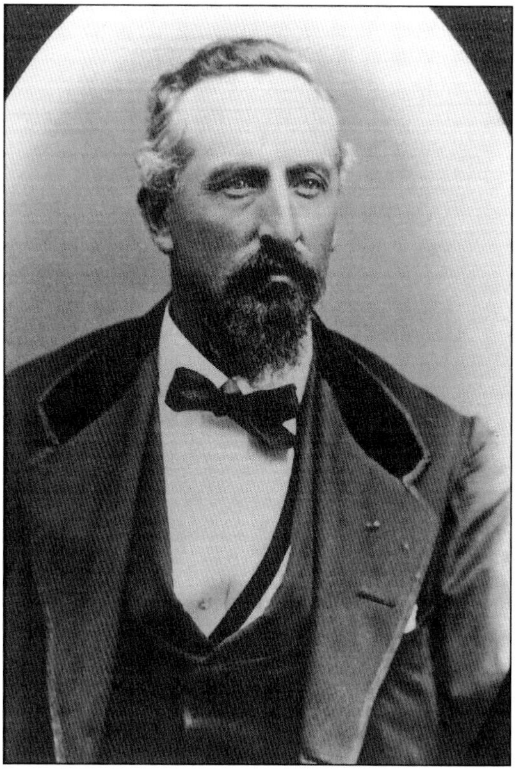

Sidney Randolph DeLong, born on December 28, 1828, in New York, died on November 24, 1914, in Tucson, Arizona. He served as a lieutenant in the Union army during the Civil War and came to Tucson with the military in 1861. Before Tucson incorporated as a town in 1871, the role of mayor had been an appointed position. When the town incorporated in 1871, DeLong became Tucson's first elected mayor. DeLong served as editor of the *Southern Arizonian*, which was established in 1859, from 1867 to 1869. He served in the territorial assembly and operated a trading post at Fort Bowie.

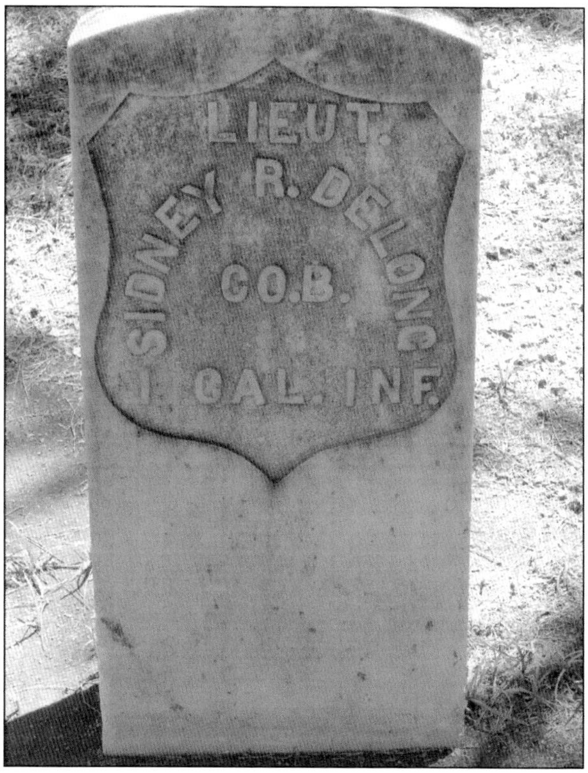

DeLong enlisted as a private at Amador, California, on August 18, 1861, and was mustered out February 19, 1863, to accept a commission as a second lieutenant. He then transferred to Company B. Lieutenant DeLong was mustered out in New Mexico Territory on July 11, 1866. He was a Republican, and at the time of his death, he was the oldest Mason in Arizona. His grave reflects his membership in the Grand Army of the Republic, an organization instrumental in establishing Memorial Day.

Daniel E. Garvey was born on June 19, 1886, in Vicksburg, Mississippi, and died in Tucson on February 5, 1974. He served as governor of Arizona from 1948 to 1951. He was a railroad accountant in Mississippi before he moved to Arizona in 1909 and became involved in politics. Garvey became Pima County treasurer in 1935 and Tucson city treasurer in 1938. In 1940, he was hired as an assistant to Secretary of State Harry M. Moore. Upon Moore's death in 1942, Gov. Sidney P. Osborn appointed Garvey to succeed Moore. Garvey assumed the governorship when Osborn died on May 25, 1948. That fall, he won a full term on the Democratic ticket.

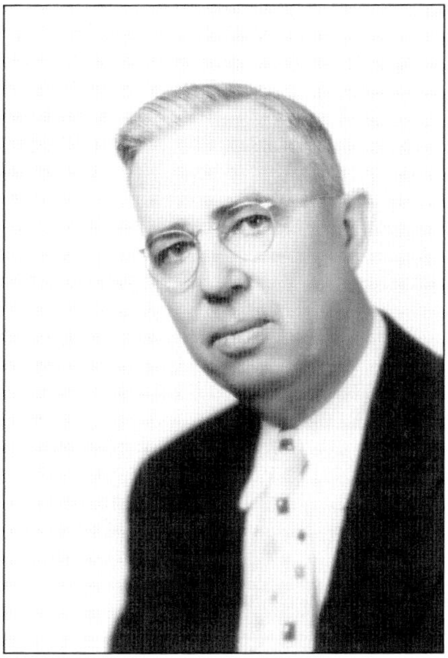

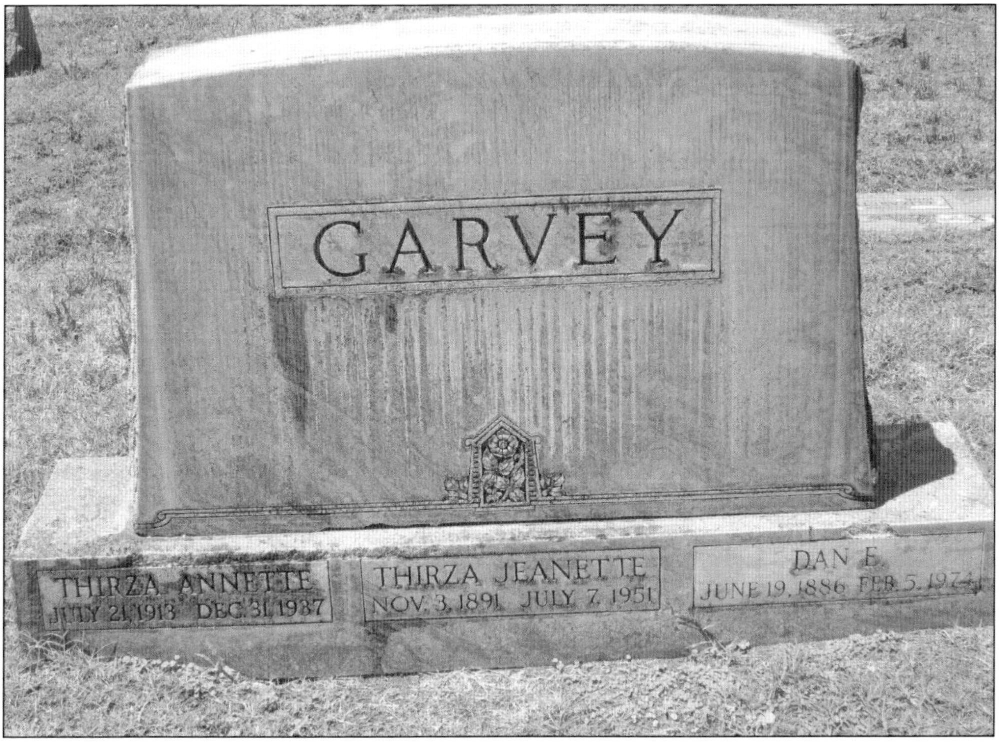

In 1950, Ana Frohmiller defeated Garvey in the Democratic primary. At the end of his elected term as governor, he was appointed Arizona administrator for the federal Reconstruction Finance Corporation. In 1955, Gov. Ernest W. McFarland appointed him state examiner, a post he held until his retirement in 1969. He returned to his business investments in Tucson upon leaving office in 1951. This modest tombstone marks the graves of Garvey and his wife and daughter, who were both named Thirza.

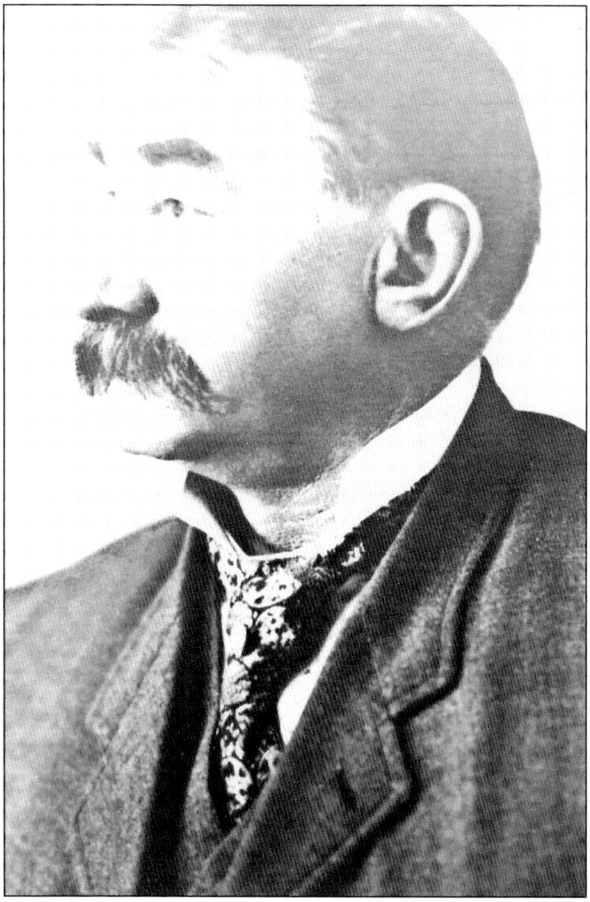

Benjamin Franklin Daniels was born in Illinois on November 4, 1852, and died in Tucson on April 20, 1923. Daniels lost his mother, two brothers, and four sisters to cholera, and at age 11, he moved with his father and stepmother to Kansas. By age 16, he was working as a cowboy in Texas. He returned to Kansas as a buffalo hunter. Daniels later earned a living as a gambler and, in the 1880s, as an assistant city marshal in Dodge City. He was a policeman and gambler in Cripple Creek, Colorado. After serving with the Rough Riders, Daniels settled in Nogales, Arizona, and invested in mining properties. In 1901, Pres. Theodore Roosevelt appointed Daniels as a US marshal in Arizona. When it was discovered that Daniels, at age 18, had served time in a Wyoming prison for horse theft, he was forced to resign. In 1904, Arizona governor Alexander Brodie appointed Daniels superintendent of the territorial prison.

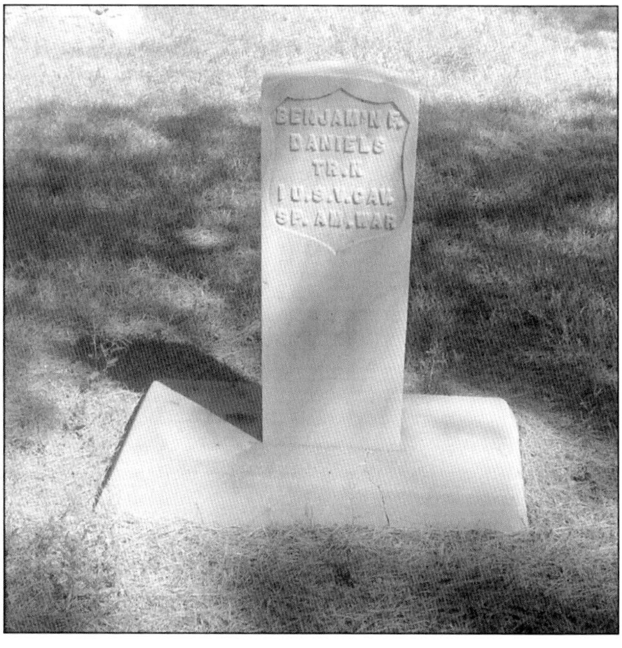

In 1906, Roosevelt determined that Daniels had atoned for his youthful lawlessness and once again appointed him a US marshal. The appointment was supported by Sen. Frederick Dodge (a former Wells Fargo agent and Rough Rider) and William "Bat" Masterson. Daniels served as a marshal until the end of Roosevelt's term. On July 15, 1908, he married Annie Stakebake. His military tombstone commemorates his service during the Spanish-American War.

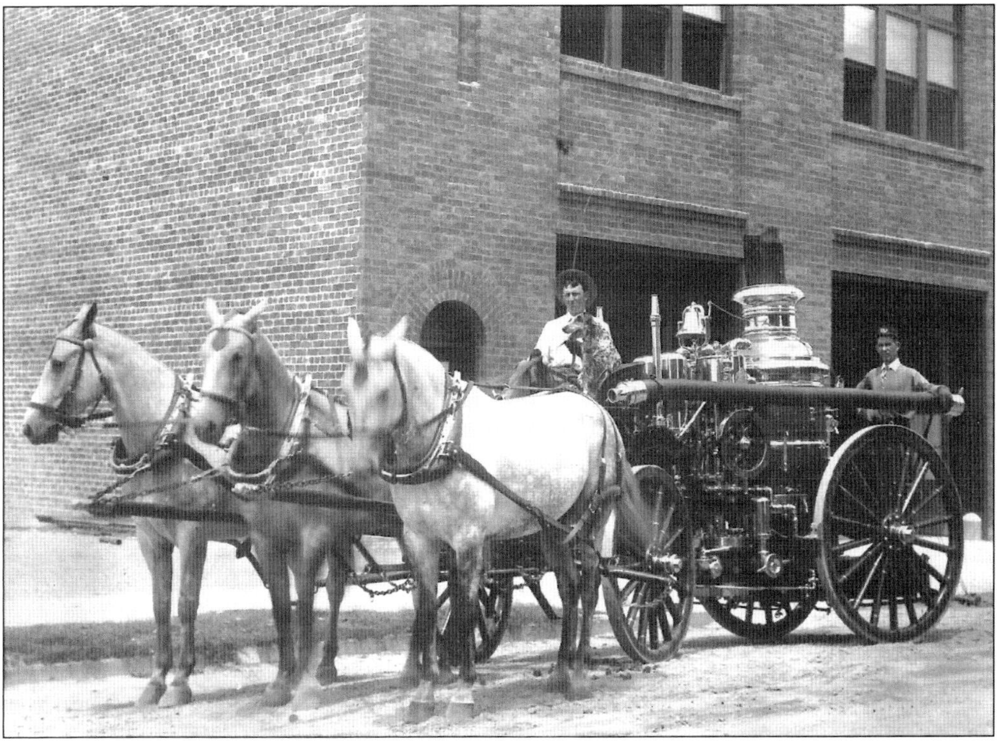

This beautiful old fire engine is now on display at the headquarters of the Tucson Fire Department. David John "Jack" Boleyn, born in 1842, died in Tucson on November 20, 1910, as a result of injuries sustained while fighting a structure fire at the Goldering Furniture Stores. Water was trapped on top of a metal roof and heated by a fire underneath; when the roof failed, Boleyn was scalded by the boiling water and struck across the stomach by a falling timber. He had been foreman of Tucson's Pioneer Hose Company in 1881, fire chief of the Tucson Volunteer Fire Association in 1882, and fire chief of the Tucson Fire Department until his death.

Upon his death, it was learned that Boleyn had a wife in Canada as well as one in Tucson. An ugly lawsuit ensued over his estate, which was worth approximately \$22,000—a substantial sum in those days. His tombstone was set on September 11, 2008, with etchings of firefighting tools.

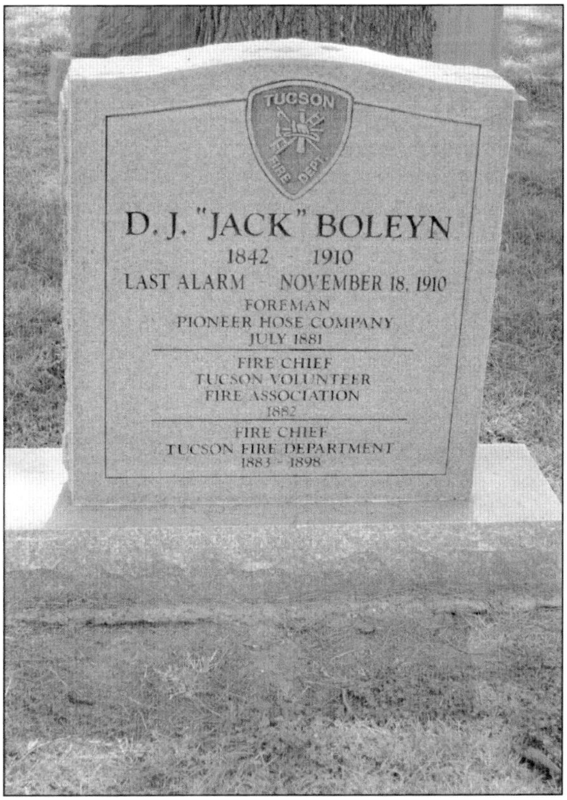

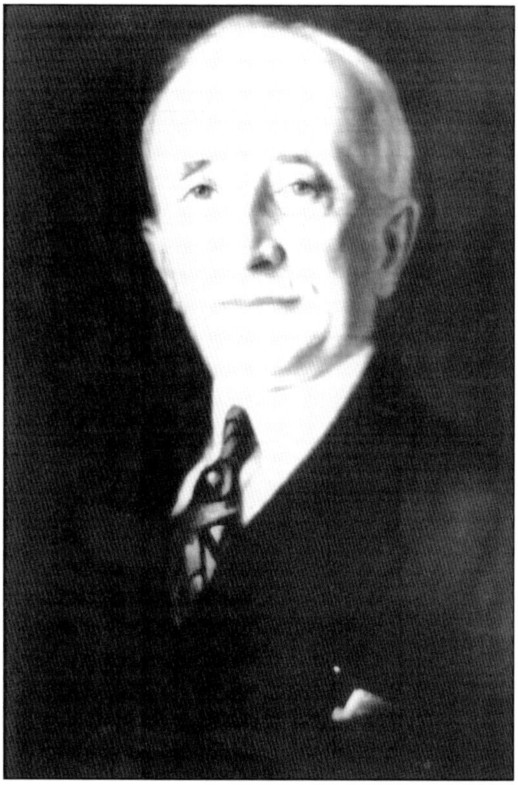

Albert Steinfeld, born in Germany on December 23, 1854, died in Tucson in 1935. It was said that his first impression of Tucson moved him to tears. In 1872, he built one of the finest department stores in Tucson, and he also served as president of the Consolidated National Bank of Tucson. Steinfeld was educated in New York City public schools. Beginning in 1869, he worked in a dry goods house for about two years before coming west. In Tucson, he became connected to Zeckendorf & Co., which was controlled by his uncles Adolph and Louis Zeckendorf. After several years, he was admitted to the firm as resident partner and manager.

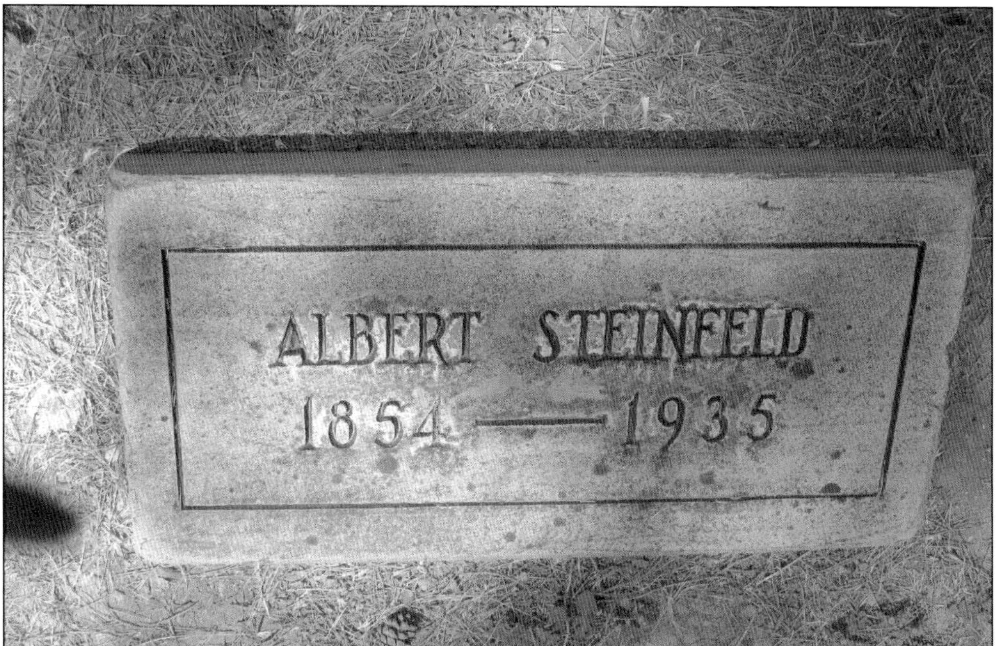

Steinfeld was elected president of the Tucson Chamber of Commerce, and, later, vice president of the Board of Trade (when it replaced the chamber of commerce). He was prominent in Masonic affairs and was married to Bettina V. Donau on February 15, 1883, in Denver.

Mary Page Handy was born in 1860 and died in 1893. Her father, John Page, was killed by Apache Indians, and her mother, Larcena Pennington, survived capture by the Apaches. Mary was 16 when she married Dr. John Handy, a prominent Tucson physician and surgeon for the US army at Camp Thomas. Doctor Handy moved to Tucson in 1871 and was selected as the first chancellor of the University of Arizona in November 1886. He abused Mary, chaining her to a bed in their home and administering morphine to her until she became addicted. Two years later, he filed for divorce, accusing Mary of being "a morphine fiend and a common slut." Handy publicly stated that any lawyer who defended her would be sorry. In 1889, after Handy won the divorce trial and custody of their five children, he sent them to live with his mother.

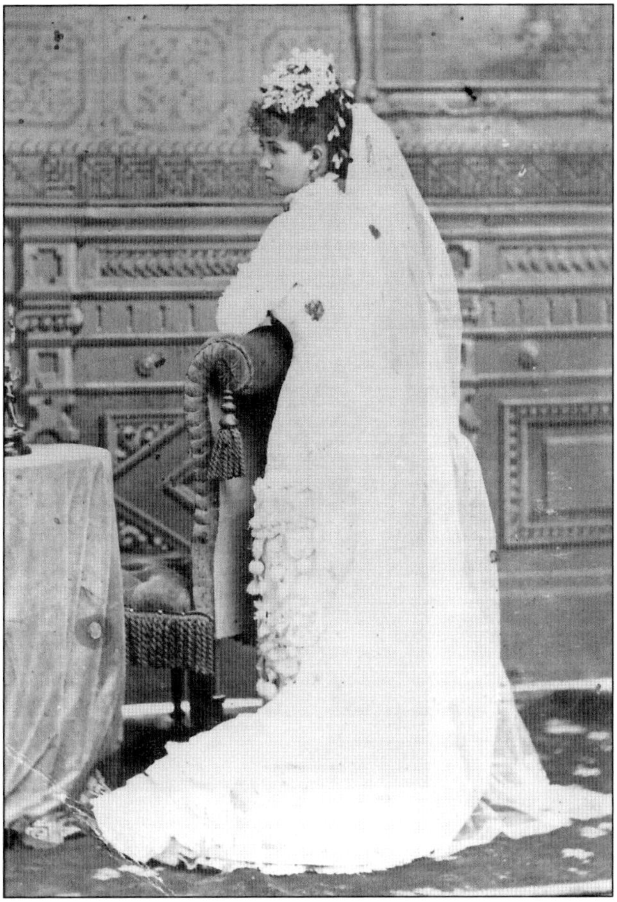

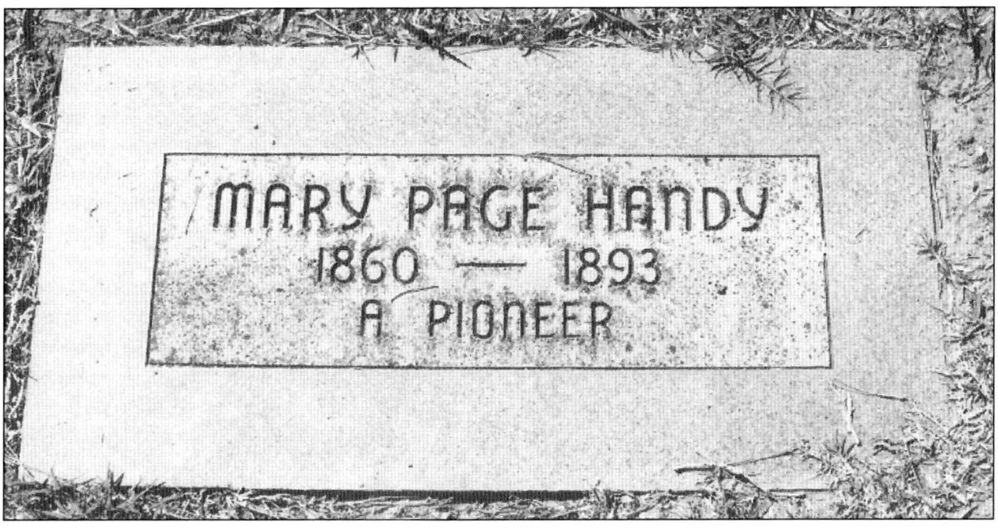

Handy tried to evict Mary from the home that the court had awarded her, and he protested the $30/month alimony. On September 24, 1891, he attacked her attorney on the streets of Tucson, and the attorney shot him in what was ruled an act of self-defense. When Mary died of cancer in 1893, she had not seen her children for two years. She has a simple, flat marker in Evergreen.

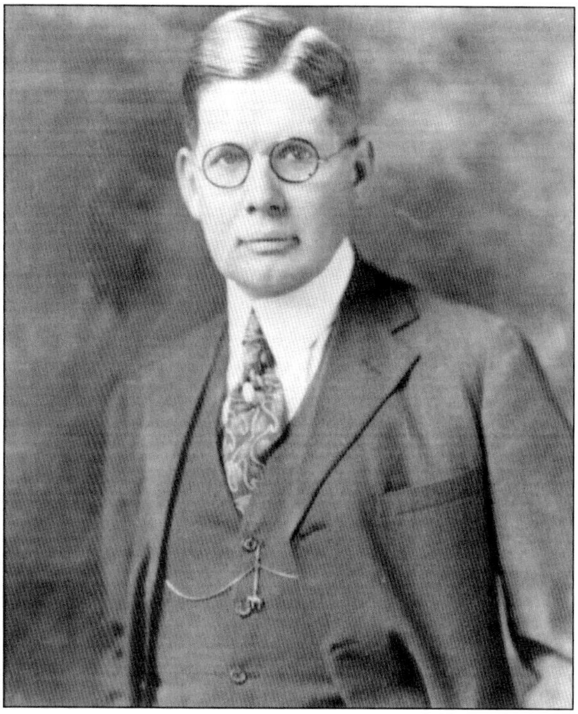

Allan Brown Jaynes, born on December 4, 1879, in Ohio, died in Tucson on November 7, 1920. He became the editor and publisher of the *Tucson Daily Citizen* in 1910, when he and fellow Republicans James T. Williams Jr. and John B. Wright bought the *Citizen* and returned it to its Republican roots and editorial policy. The previous owners invested heavily in the paper, and Jaynes took advantage of those improvements. On February 4, 1912, fire struck the *Citizen*. The paper, which had been campaigning for Arizona's statehood, hoped to be the first newspaper in the state to herald the state joining the Union. The *Arizona Daily Star* allowed the *Citizen* to use its printing press until it could install a new one. Jaynes's name is also associated with Jaynes Station Road.

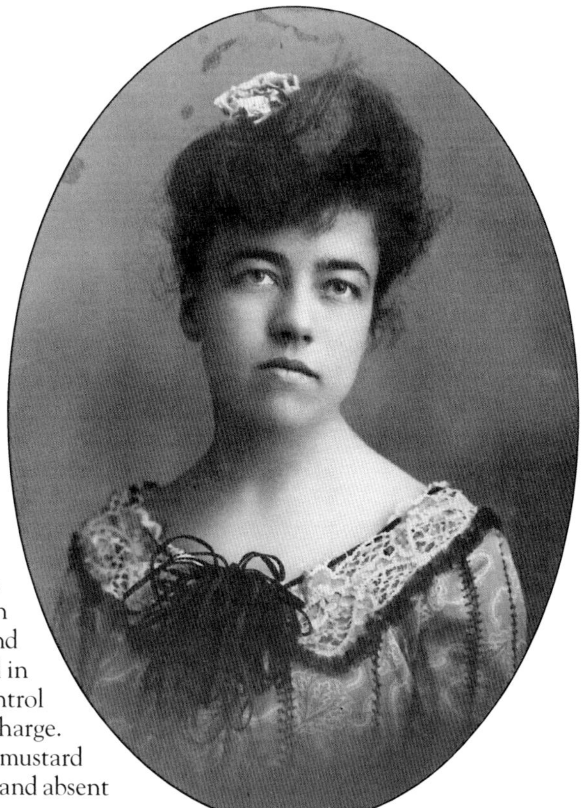

On February 14, 1912, the *Tucson Daily Citizen* announced Arizona's statehood. In 1914, the paper moved to a building at the corner of Stone Street and Jackson Avenue—its eighth relocation in 30 years. It remained there for 26 years. Allan Brown Jaynes's wife, Kathryn Feighan Jaynes, was born in 1880 in Kentucky and died in Tucson in 1951. After Jaynes died in November 1920, Kathryn took over control of the paper and put her son Oliver in charge. Oliver, however, had been poisoned by mustard gas in World War I and was frequently ill and absent from work.

Allan and Kathryn Jaynes and their son, Willis, are buried in Evergreen Cemetery.

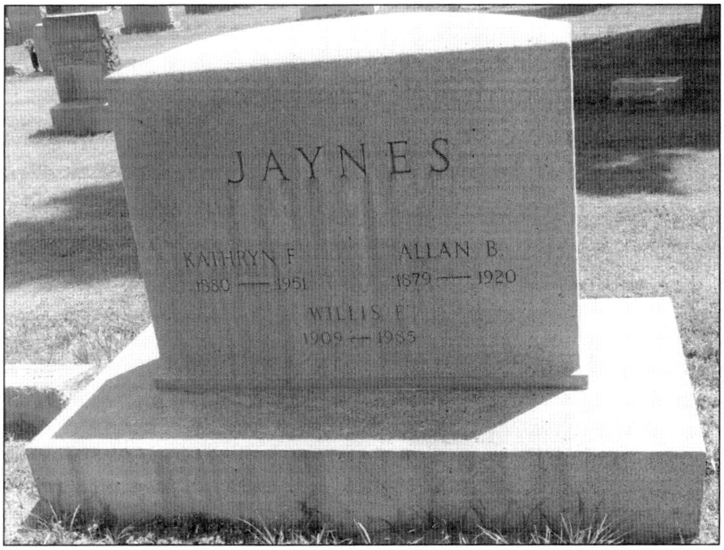

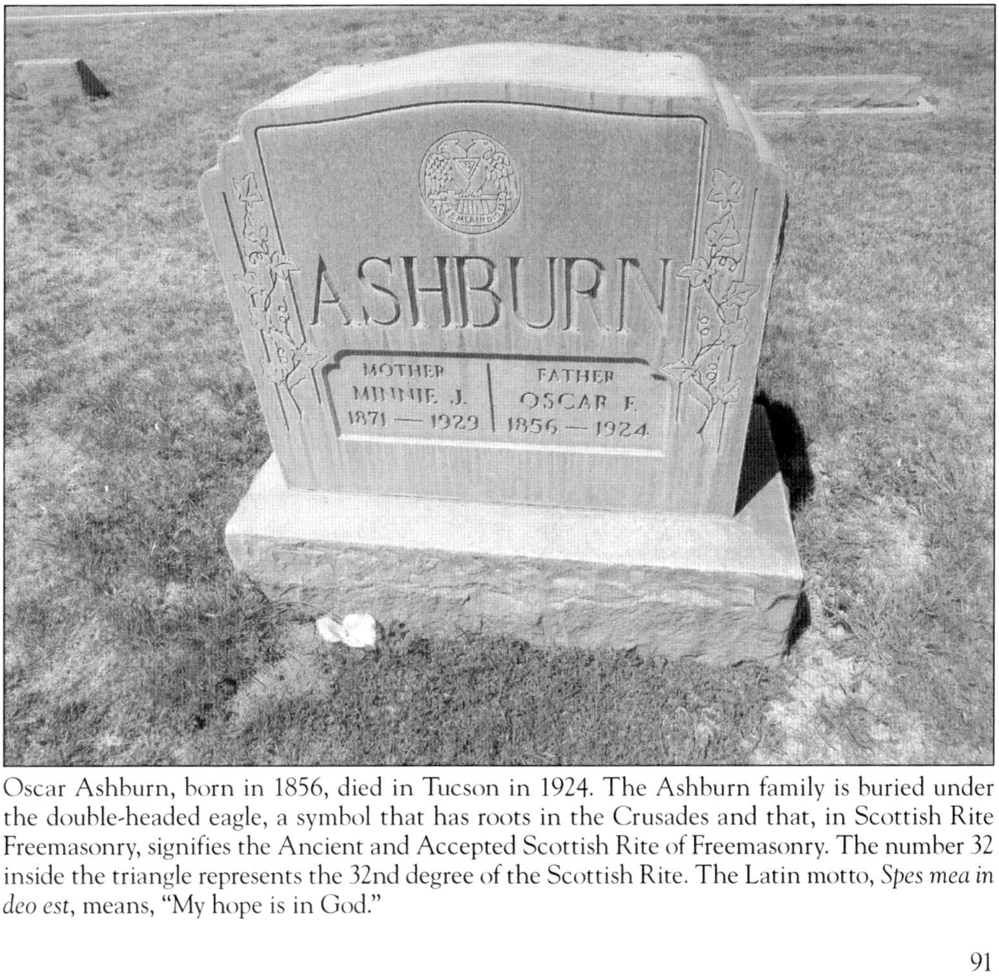

Oscar Ashburn, born in 1856, died in Tucson in 1924. The Ashburn family is buried under the double-headed eagle, a symbol that has roots in the Crusades and that, in Scottish Rite Freemasonry, signifies the Ancient and Accepted Scottish Rite of Freemasonry. The number 32 inside the triangle represents the 32nd degree of the Scottish Rite. The Latin motto, *Spes mea in deo est*, means, "My hope is in God."

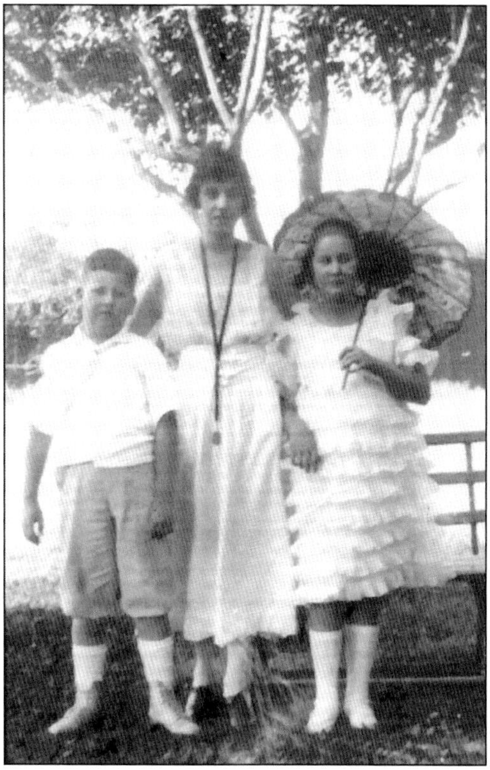

Frank O. Sutherland's wife, Sofia, and their two children are pictured at left. Sutherland, born December 29, 1883, in Florence, Arizona, died June 20, 1917, in Tucson. He married Sofia Elias, who was born in Arizona on September 28, 1882, and died in Tucson on April 29, 1959. On January 13, 1899, William H. Sutherland was appointed guardian for Ray and Frank Sutherland, who were minors. Their estate consisted of 350 head of horned cattle. On November 17, 1916, the *Tucson Citizen* carried an advertisement announcing that Frank O. Sutherland was running for Pima County sheriff. Frank was a property owner and taxpayer who was interested in everything related to the welfare and prosperity of the state. Fully aware that laws were being openly violated—especially those forbidding gambling and liquor distribution—he pledged that, if elected, he would devote his efforts to the eradication of these disgraceful behaviors. Frank lost the election by a small margin. He served as undersheriff to John Nelson, who was his ranching partner. (Courtesy of Catherine Sutherland Hartline.)

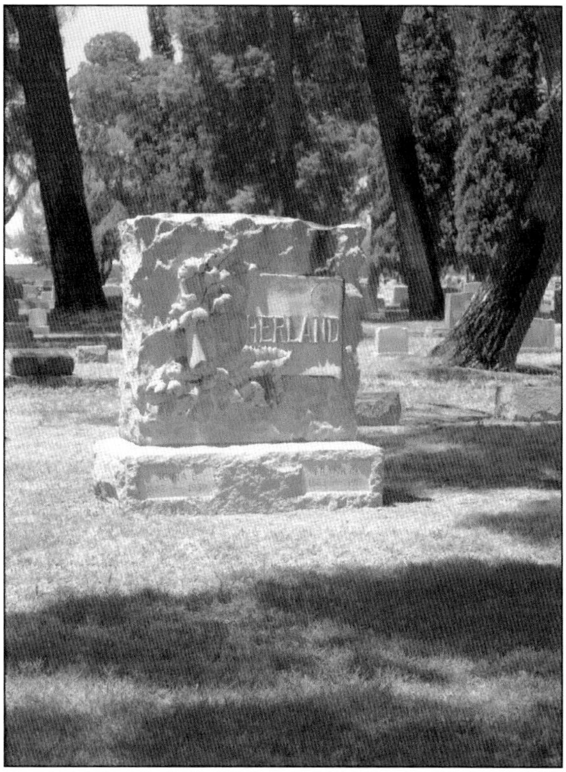

In 1917, Frank became ill and went to California to see physicians; however, he returned very disheartened with his illness still undiagnosed. Tucson physicians decided that he had appendicitis. The day before his surgery in St. Mary's Hospital, he made his will. He died the following day, after his operation, at the age of 34. Sutherland was a member of the Elks, and the funeral was held under the auspices of the organization with a large number of Elks attending. Frank and Sofia's ranch is now part of the Miraval Spa. Their tombstone in Evergreen Cemetery is a massive display of swirling shells and features the logo of the Benevolent and Protective Order of Elks (BPOE).

John Nelson was born in Sweden on November 11, 1868, and died on December 24, 1947, in Tucson, where he had served as a Pima County sheriff and was a rancher. He was a territorial sheriff for two terms and had the distinction of becoming the first state Pima County sheriff when Arizona was granted statehood in 1912. On January 21, 1913, during Nelson's tenure as Pima County sheriff, deputy Joe W. Meeks was shot and killed by Calistro Villareal. Villareal fled to Mexico, and Nelson and a posse chased him but came back empty-handed.

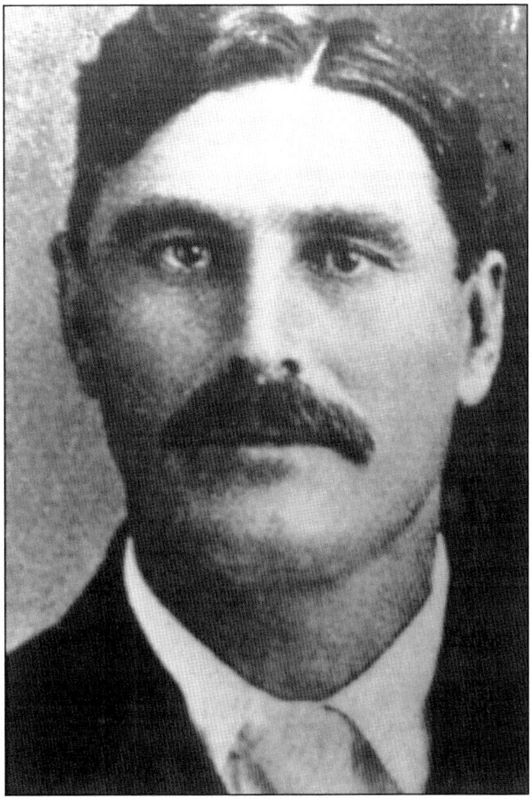

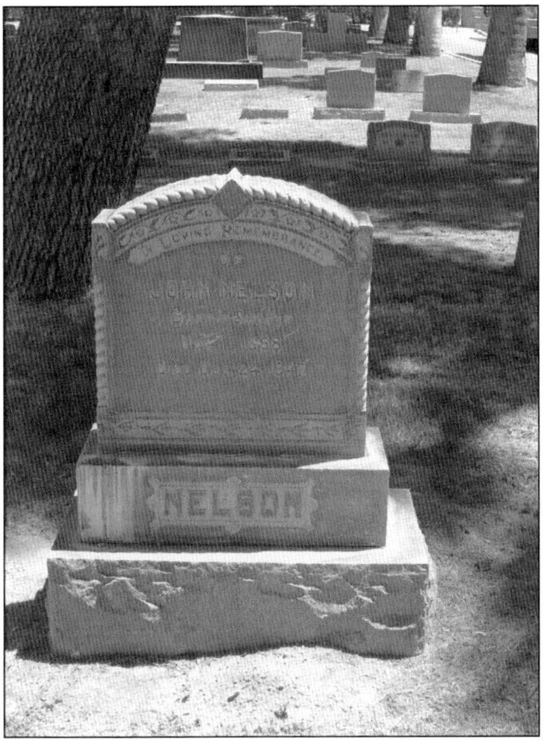

Nelson jailed stockbroker Frank O'Brien for swindling W.V. Elliot out of $2,000, which was supposed to have been used to purchase stock in the Ray Consolidated Mining Company. O'Brien had a passion for poker and wanted to break into Tucson's exclusive circles.

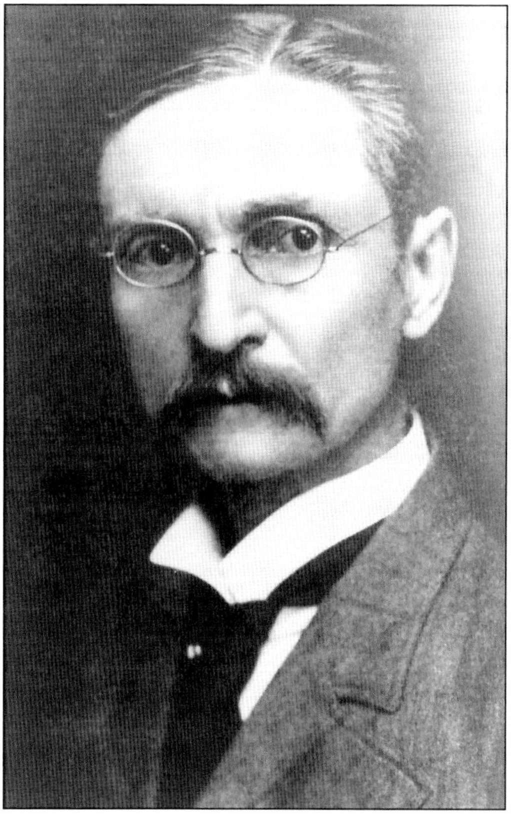

Henry Buehman, born on May 15, 1851, in Germany, died in Tucson on December 19, 1912. He and his family dominated professional photography in Tucson for three generations. He opened a portrait studio in 1874, and his son Albert took it over in 1913. Henry's grandson Remick began running the business in 1946. Buehman served as mayor of Tucson, and in 1897, he complained that the Tucson streets were filthy and needed a general cleanup. The Arizona Historical Society's photograph collection contains over 250,000 negatives taken by the Buehman family between 1874 and 1960.

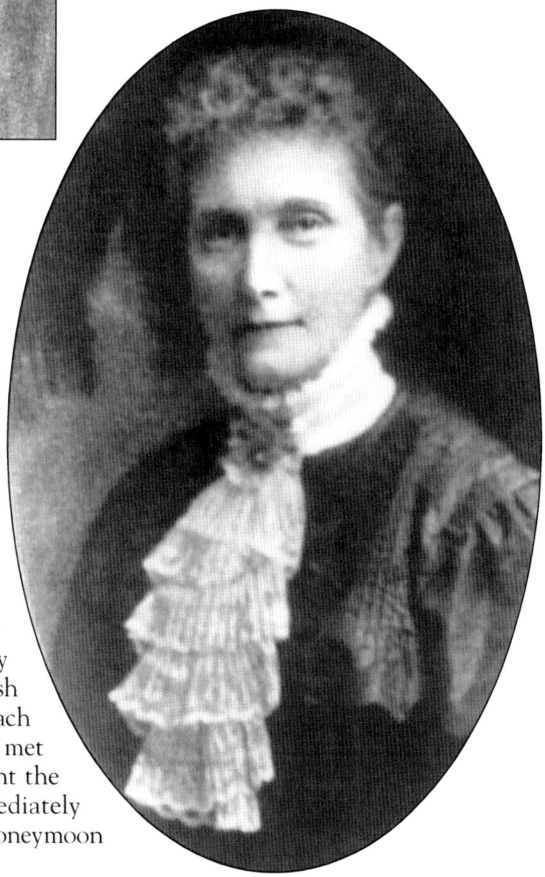

In 1882, Henry Buehman married Estelle Morehouse, a schoolteacher and the founder of Tucson's first kindergarten. Estelle was born in Portland, Michigan, on September 28, 1846, and was of New York Dutch ancestry on her mother's side and Scotch and English on her father's side. She travelled west to teach school and ended up in Tucson, where she met Henry. She returned to Michigan and spent the summer preparing for her wedding. Immediately after the wedding, the Buehmans left for a honeymoon in Canada. Estelle died in 1916.

In November, the Buehmans returned to Tucson and settled down in a home on Convent Street. Estelle took charge of the portrait studio when her husband, Henry, was out of town. She worked with him in the reception room of their studio, which was located above the Tucson post office on Congress Street.

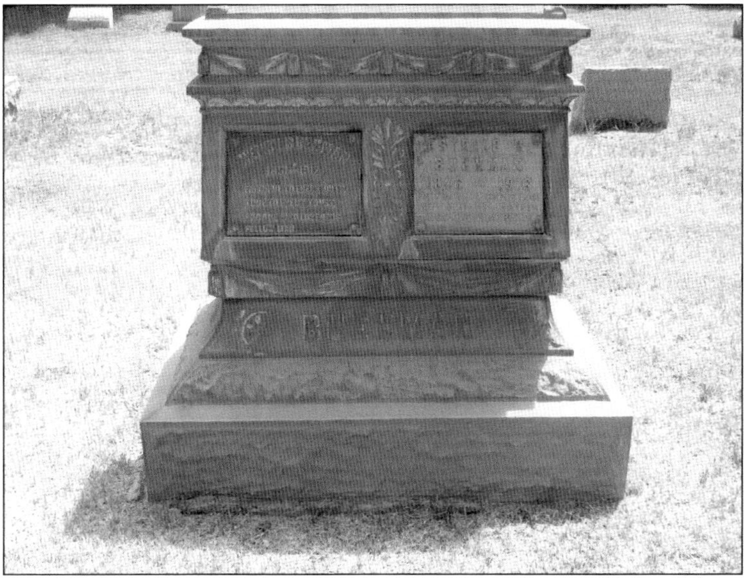

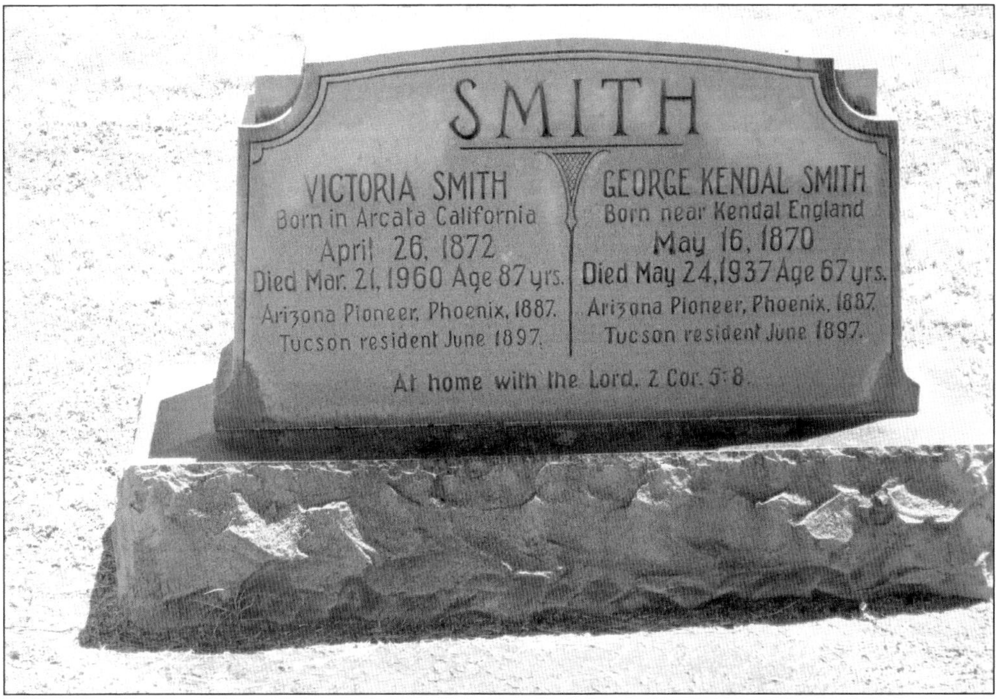

George Kendal Smith was born May 16, 1870, in Carlisle, England, and died May 24, 1937, in Tucson, Arizona. His wife, Victoria Shaw, was born in California. George learned the dyer trade before immigrating to Los Angeles with an uncle. He subsequently opened his own business in Phoenix and finally settled in Tucson, where he operated the American Cleaning Company. Besides serving as mayor of Tucson during the Great Depression, Smith was a member of the volunteer fire department, the Elks, the Rotary Club of Tucson, the Tucson Merchants' Association, and the Tucson Sunshine Club. In 1931, he was elected mayor of Tucson and oversaw the rewriting of the city charter. When he took office, the city budget was $15,000 in arrears, but at end of his term, the city was in the black.

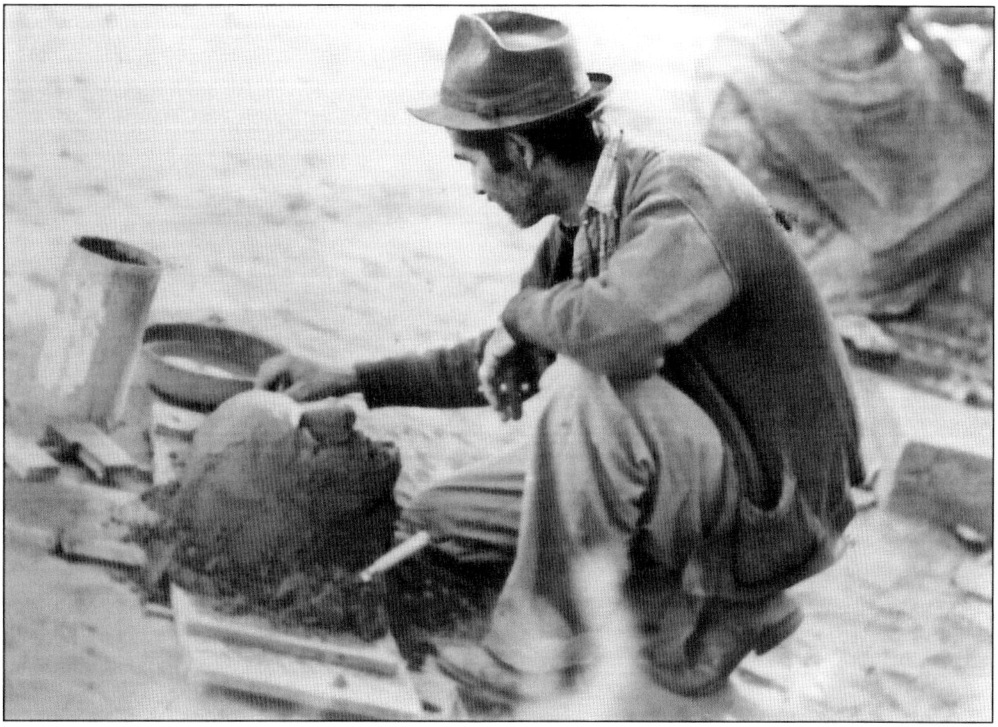

Felix Lucero, born in Colorado on May 9, 1895, died on January 23, 1951. A homeless artist, he arrived in Tucson in 1938. He found odd jobs and lived in a shack beneath the Congress Street Bridge. While fighting in France during World War I, Lucero was critically injured and promised God that, if he lived, he would commit his life to sculpting statues of Christ. In 1945, he began sculpting the promised statues from sand, concrete, and debris along the bank of the Santa Cruz River. Floods would wash his work away, and he would start all over again. His creations were admired by most locals, many of whom threw him coins from the bridge, but some ridiculed him for his efforts. If the elements did not claim his work, vandals did (and still do).

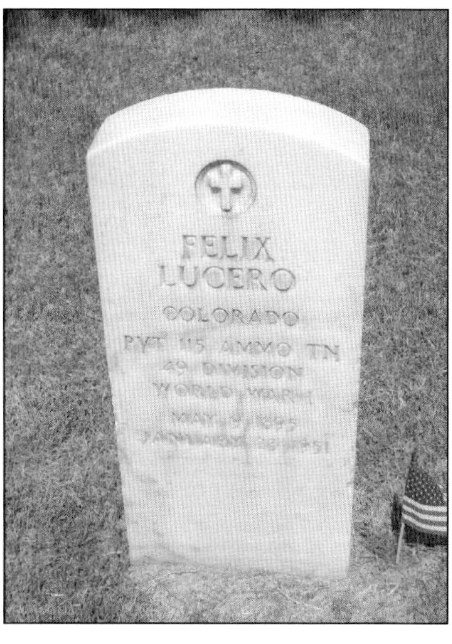

Lucero's Garden of Gethsemane—a tiny park under the Congress Street Bridge in downtown Tucson—features life-size statues of the Last Supper, Mary and Joseph, Jesus on the Cross, and the body of Christ in the tomb. Lucero's shack caught fire in 1951, and he suffered terrible burns from which he never recovered. As a veteran, Lucero received a military funeral and tombstone.

Cy Young (left) and Louis "Lou" Criger are pictured at right. Criger was born February 3, 1872, in Elkhart, Indiana, died in Tucson on May 14, 1934. He played major-league baseball for the Cleveland Spiders, St. Louis Cardinals, Boston Americans/Red Sox, St. Louis Browns, and New York Highlanders. Criger was the catcher for most of Cy Young's 511 victories and many of his 316 losses. He caught every inning for eight games with Boston in the first-ever World Series in 1903, helping his team win the championship. In 1908, Boston traded him to the St. Louis Browns. (Courtesy of the National Baseball Hall of Fame.)

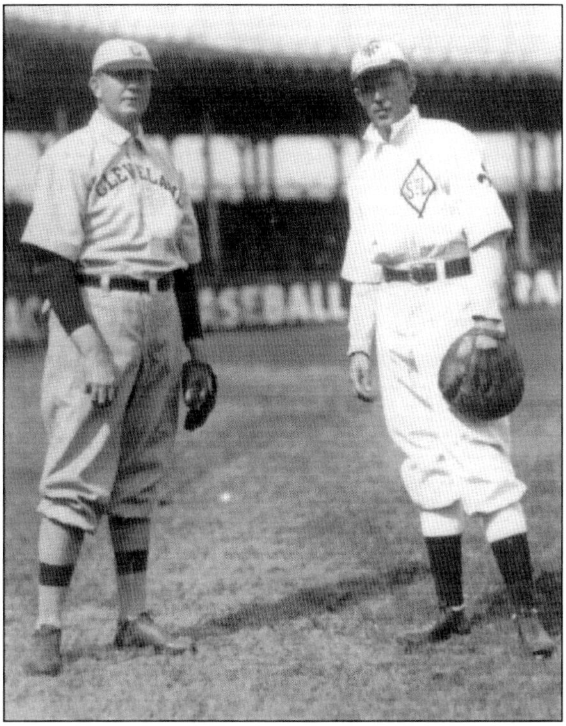

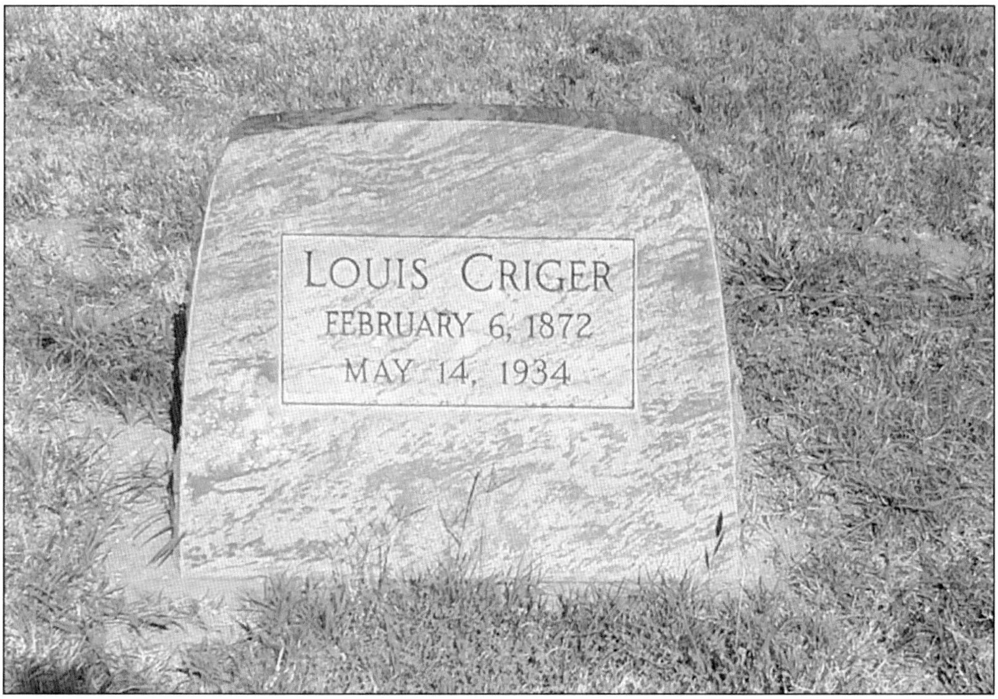

Criger and his wife, Belle, and their six children lived in Elkhart until 1909, when the family moved to a farm at Bair Lake, Michigan. In 1914, Criger developed tuberculosis in his left knee, and the following year, his leg had to be amputated. He moved to Nevada and relocated again in 1924 to the dry climate of Arizona, spending winters in Tucson and summers in Flagstaff.

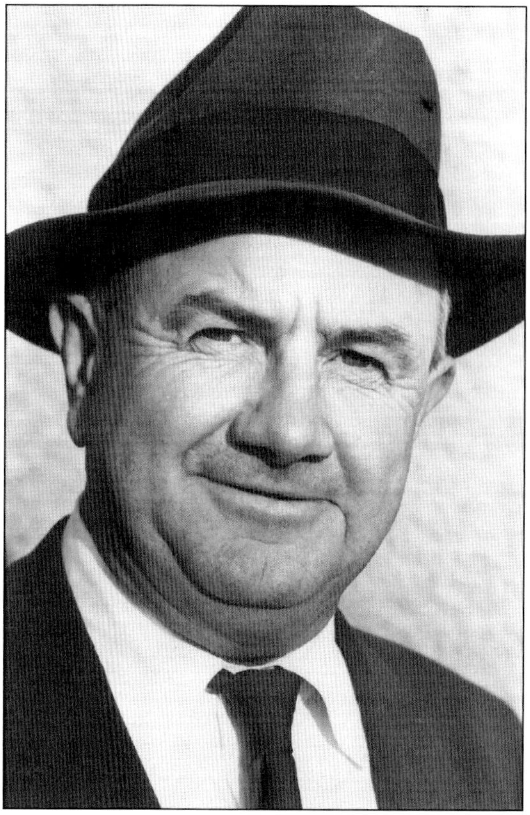

Hiram "Hi" Corbett was born in Tucson on September 13, 1886, and died there on July 5, 1967. Corbett helped found the Cactus League for major-league spring training in Tucson. Hi Corbett Field was built in 1927. The initial home teams included the Tucson Waddies, the Tucson Cowboys, the Tucson Missions, and the Tucson Lizards. In 1946, the Cleveland Indians moved their spring-training operations to Tucson. Corbett was enthusiastic about golf—which was introduced in Tucson in 1915—and he helped establish the area's first golf course. He served six terms in the state senate, and for 13 years he was a member of the selective service board. His other affiliations included the Knights Templar, the Shriners, the Masons, and the Republican National Committee.

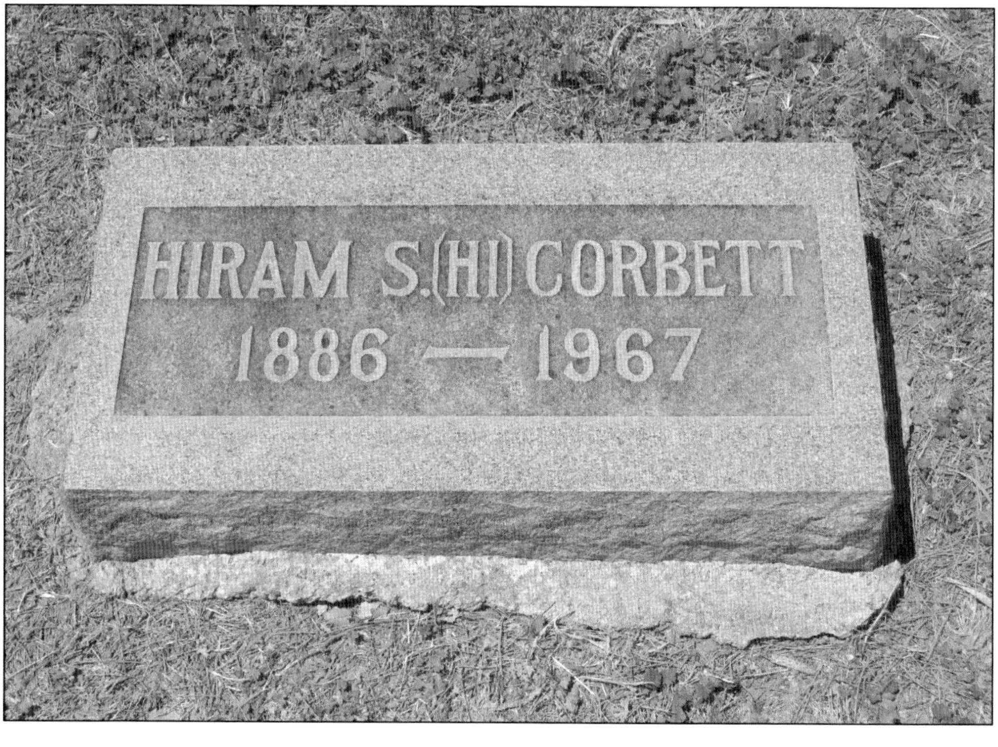

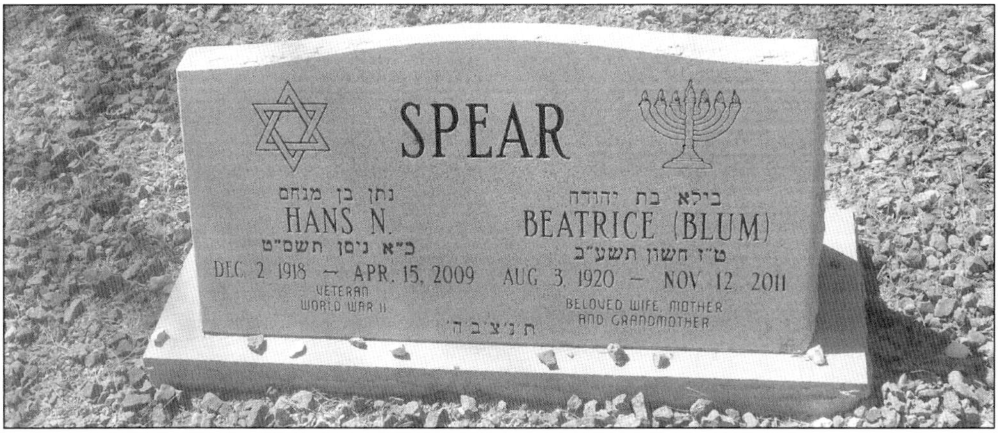

Hans Norbert Spear died on April 15, 2009. Born in Germany on December 2, 1918, he came to America in 1938. Hans married his childhood sweetheart, Beatrice, in New York in 1939. He served in the US army during World War II and trained at Camp Ritchie, Maryland, which was featured in the documentary *The Ritchie Boys*. He received four Battle Stars and was awarded the Bronze Star Medal in 2008, 63 years after having originally been denied the honor because he was Jewish. His tombstone features the Star of David and the menorah, along with inscriptions in English and Hebrew. He is buried in the B'nai B'rith section of Evergreen Cemetery.

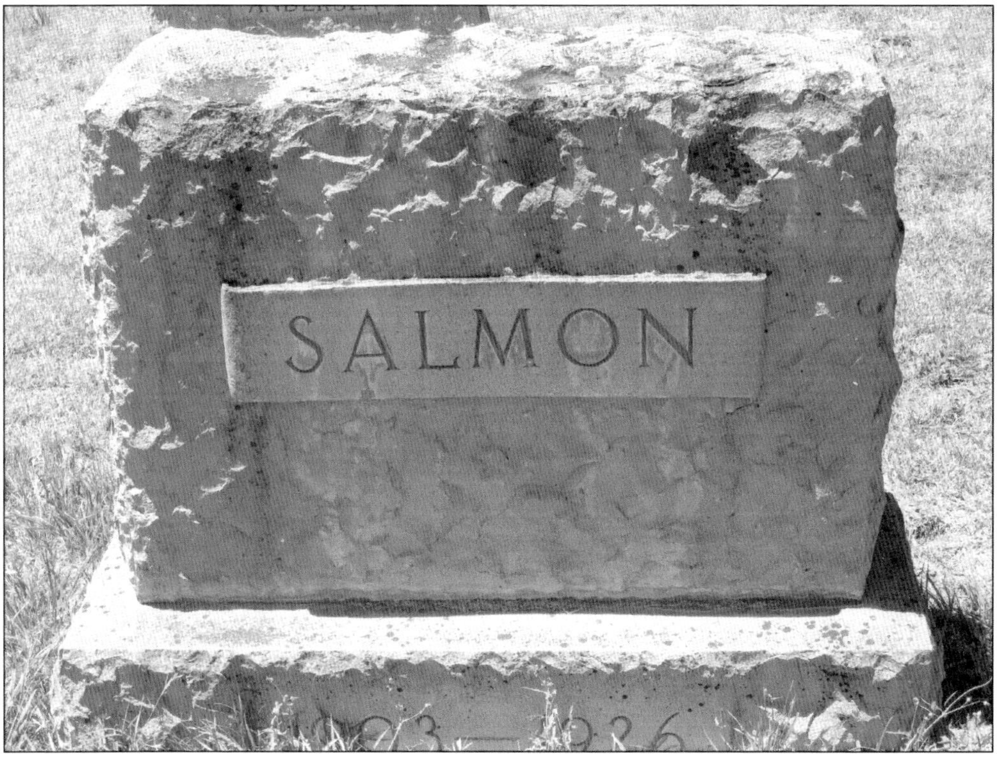

John "Button" Salmon, born October 22, 1903, died October 18, 1926, as a result of injuries from a car crash. Despite his small size, he played football at the University of Arizona. His supposed deathbed words—"Bear Down"—became the rallying cry for the University of Arizona. Students were allowed to paint the slogan on the roof of the new gymnasium, and band director Jack Lee composed the "Bear Down Arizona" song.

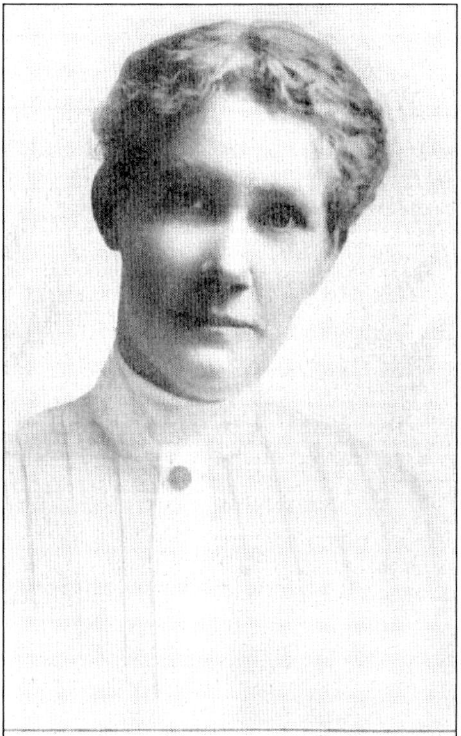

SARAH HERRING SORIN

Sarah Herring Sorin, born January 15, 1861, in New York, died of bronchial pneumonia and influenza on April 30, 1914, in Globe, Arizona. After the death of her brother Howard Ford Herring, she gave up a career as a teacher to help her father run his law firm, which eventually became Herring & Herring. Sarah read law and passed the bar exam.

In 1893, Herring became the first woman to practice before the Arizona Supreme Court, and in 1913, she became the first woman to argue a case before the US Supreme Court unassisted by male counsel. She soon became the attorney of choice for Arizona mining firms. Herring's husband, Thomas Sorin, was a miner, rancher, and publisher (with John Clum) of the *Tombstone Epitaph*. Sarah and Thomas were married on July 22, 1898.

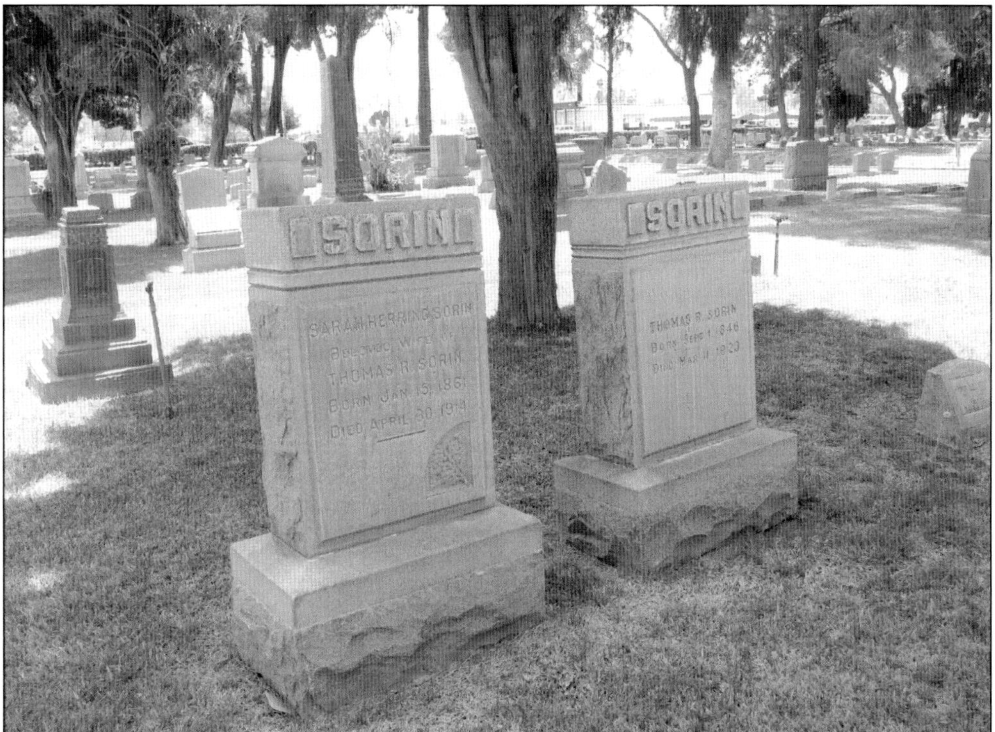

Mose Drachman, born November 16, 1870, in San Francisco, died on October 2, 1935, in Tucson. He worked as a delivery boy and a messenger for the *Tucson Citizen*, at Zeckendorf's store, at his uncle's cigar store, and at the Tucson Steam Laundry. Drachman bought land near the University of Arizona and invested in cattle and mining businesses. He served on the Board of Equalization, on the Tucson City Council, in the Arizona State Senate, and as a regent at the University of Arizona. He was elected to the Tucson District 1 School Board in 1920 and was reelected each year until his death in 1935.

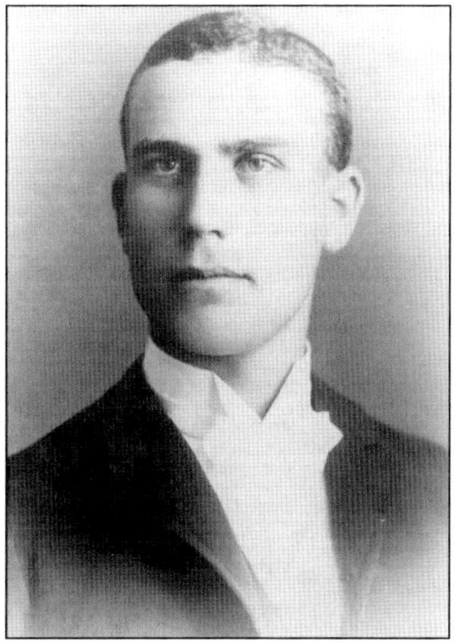

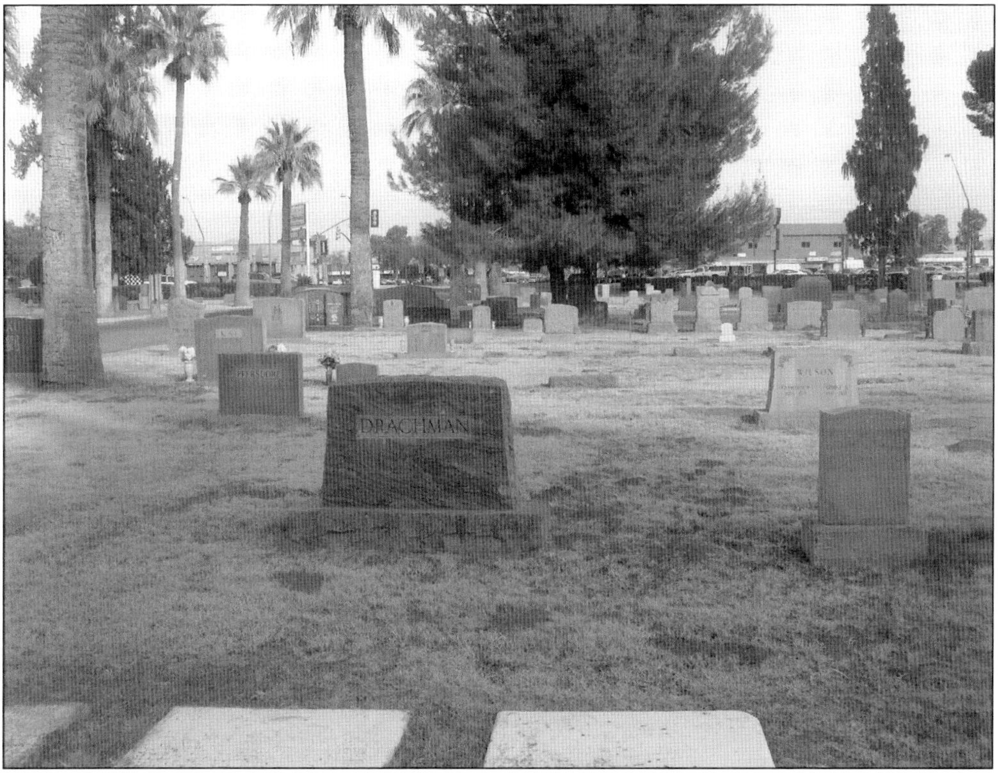

Emanuel "Manny" Drachman was born in Tucson on August 1, 1872, and died there on December 28, 1933. His first job was taking care of the horses and buggies used in his father's transportation business. He worked in the blacksmith shop of the Southern Pacific Railroad before enlisting in the Spanish-American War in 1898. He purchased the first motion picture–projection machine for Tucson. He also brought, via railroad, the first "aeroplane," which was first flown on February 20, 1910. Millie Royers, a singer from Los Angeles, came to Tucson to give a concert, and she and Manny were married on November 3, 1905. This grave marker is simple, but it speaks to centuries of Tucson history.

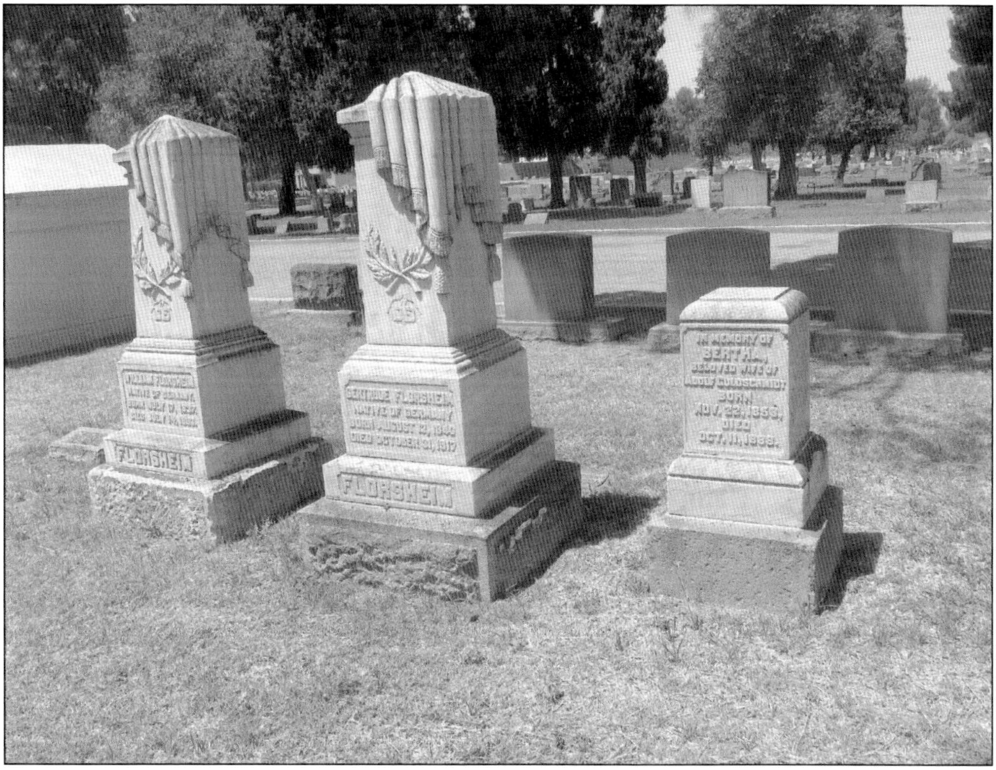

Gertrude and William Florsheim's tombstones are among the most beautiful in Tucson's Evergreen Cemetery. The Florsheims were natives of Germany. Gertrude—the sister of Leo Goldschmidt—was born August 12, 1840, and died on October 31, 1917; William was born on July 17, 1837, and died on July 14, 1889. In the Jewish faith, the drapery (or veil) covered the Ark of the Covenant to protect mortals from its radiance. The Hebrew symbols—commonly found on Jewish graves—say *po nikbar*, meaning "here lies."

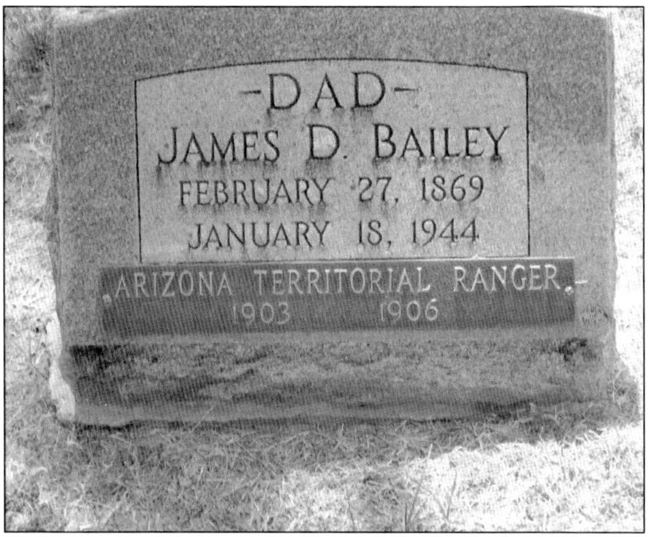

The Arizona Rangers agency was created by the Arizona Territorial Legislature in 1901, disbanded in 1909, and re-created as a volunteer group in 1957. The rangers were an elite, well-trained group mounted on quality horses and equipped with modern weapons; they dealt with outlaws along the Mexican border. James D. Bailey enlisted at age 33 and served from 1903 to 1905. He was born on February 27, 1869, in Webster County, Kentucky, and died in Tucson on January 18, 1944.

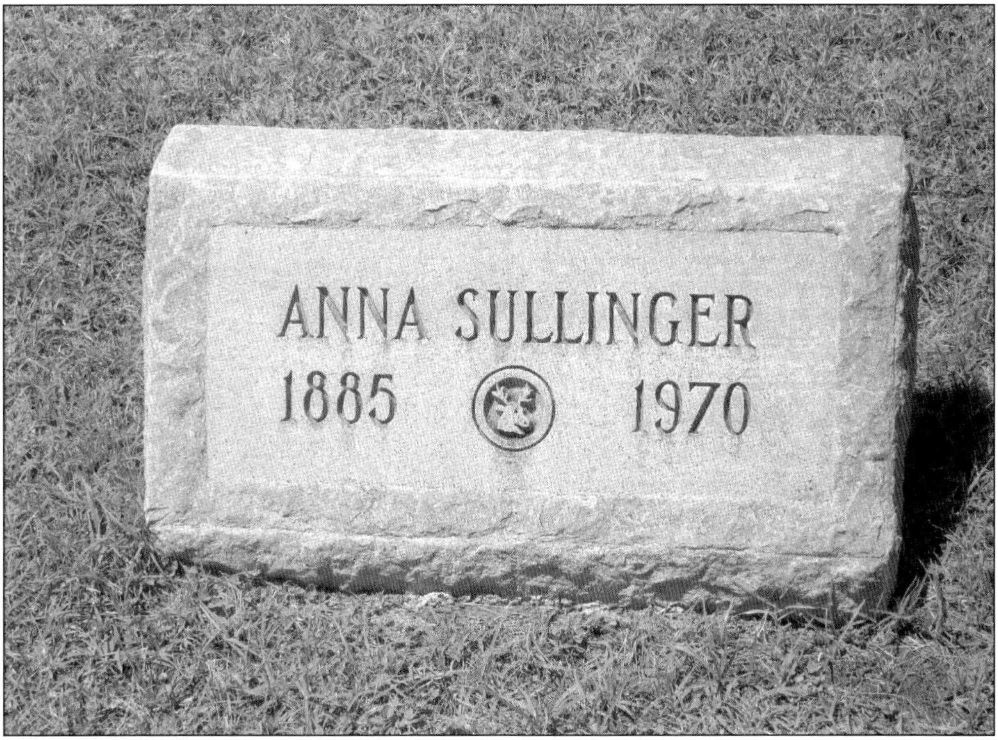

Anna Sullinger served as the Pima County recorder for 18 consecutive terms and died in 1970, just two weeks after announcing her retirement. She was 84 years old and living in a home that her mother built in 1908. Anna's husband, Wilford Sullinger, held several political posts and was secretary at the Elks Lodge. Anna has the Elks symbol on her tombstone.

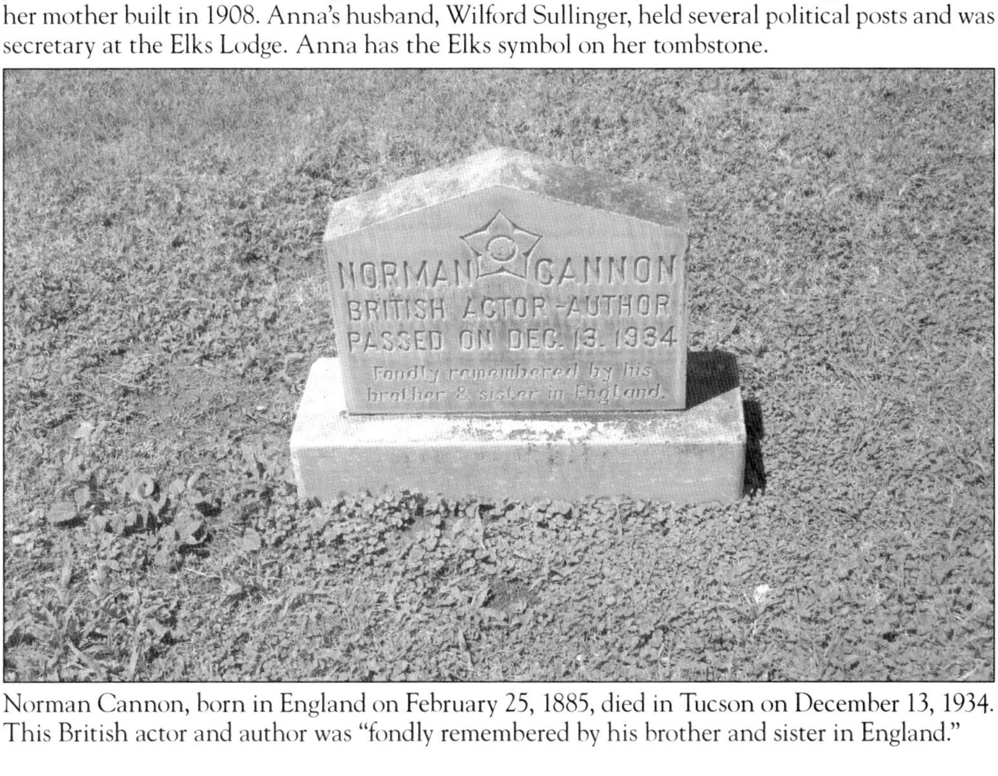

Norman Cannon, born in England on February 25, 1885, died in Tucson on December 13, 1934. This British actor and author was "fondly remembered by his brother and sister in England."

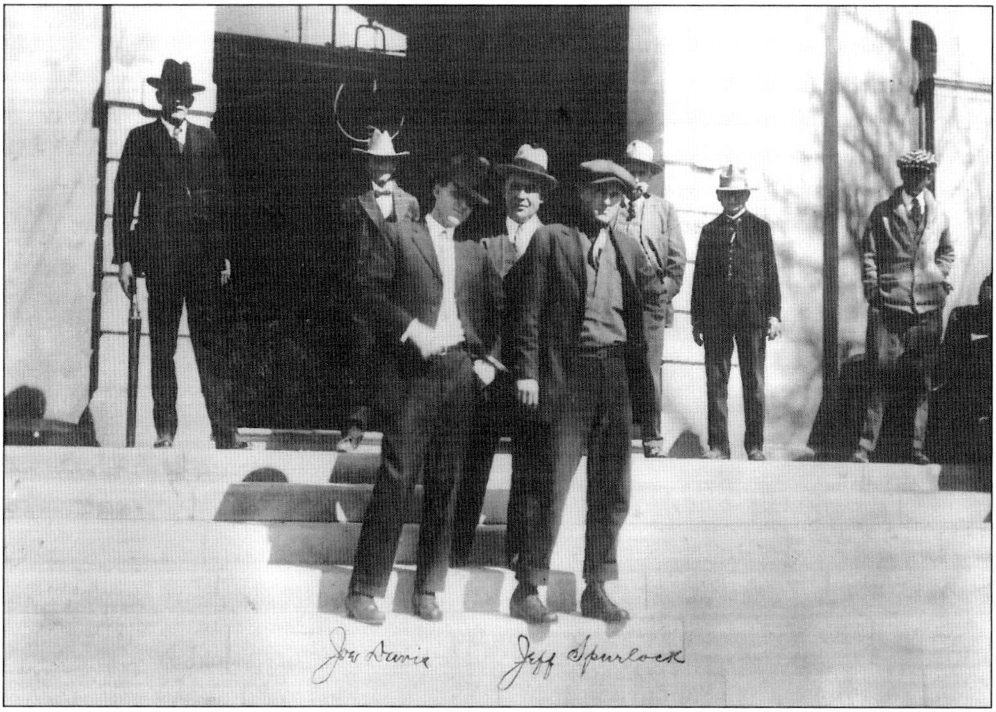

Louis Ezekiels stands at far right on the top step. He is guarding handcuffed prisoners John Davis and Jeff Spurlock. Davis and Spurlock were tried in federal court in 1917 for the Golden State Robbery near Rodeo, New Mexico, and each was given a 25-year term in prison.

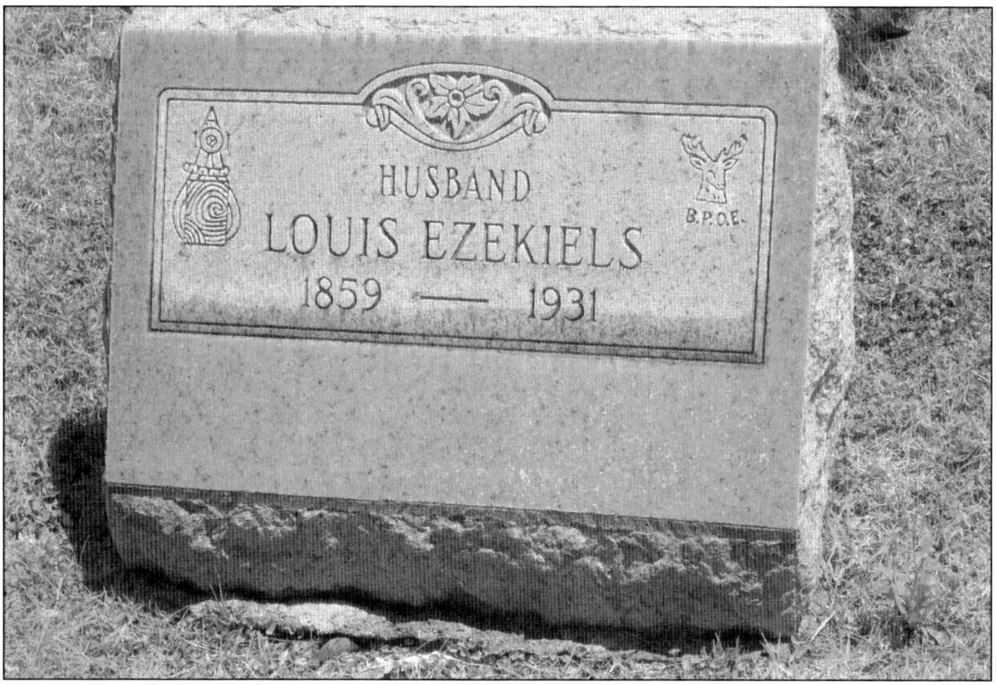

Ezekiels spent many years in law enforcement in Tucson. His grave is decorated with the Elks logo and a lamp signifying eternal light.

Homer LeRoy Shantz (1876–1958) was born in Michigan. He received his doctoral degree in botany from the University of Nebraska in 1905. Shantz traveled widely and documented vegetation in his photographs. He served as president of the University of Arizona from 1928 to 1936, when he was forced to resign after disagreements with the state legislature and the University of Arizona Board of Regents. He served as chief of the Division of Wildlife Management of the US Forest Service from 1936 until his retirement in 1944.

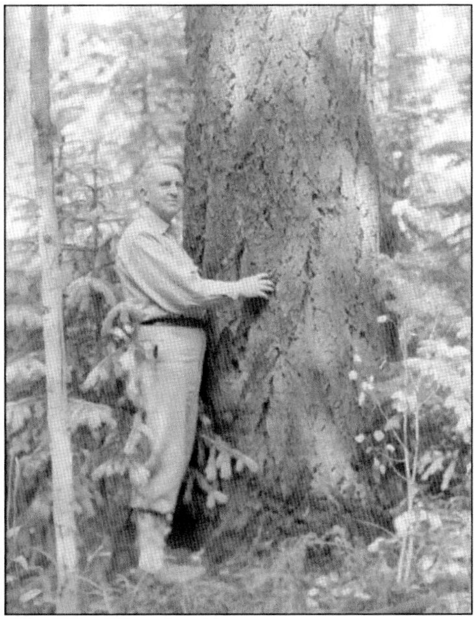

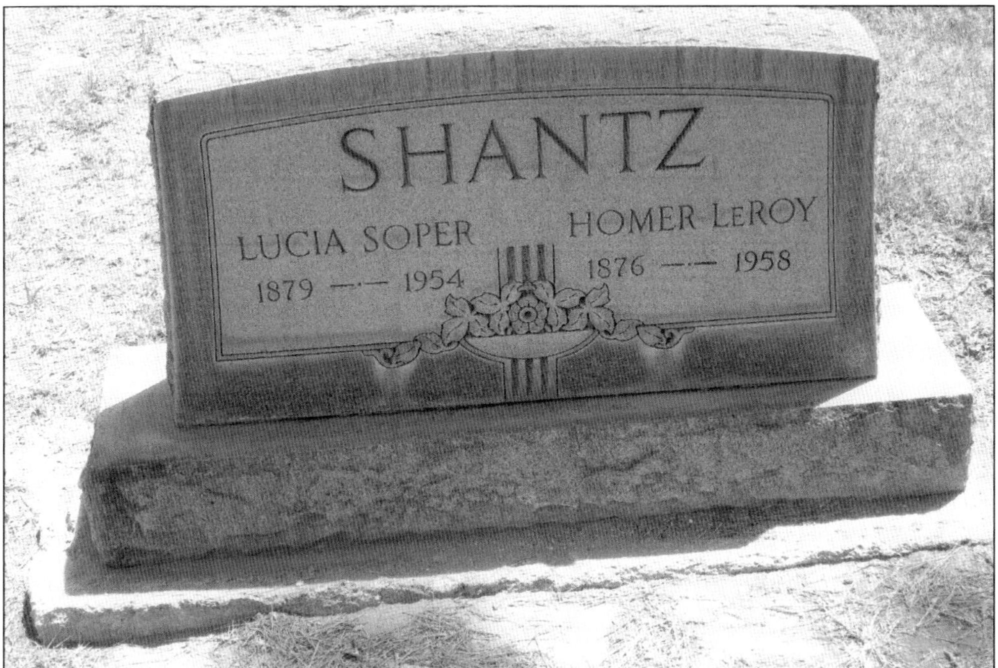

In 1920, the first attempt to set aside land to protect the saguaro cactus failed for lack of funds. When Shantz became president of the University of Arizona, he contacted the National Park Service. The NPS was not interested, so Shantz committed university funds and commissioned a person to buy 480 acres of saguaro land. At the end of his term as president on March 1, 1933, Herbert Hoover signed the executive order proclaiming the Saguaro National Monument. University funds were dwindling in the face of the Great Depression, and Shantz was fired for his reckless improvidence. It was a long road for Saguaro National Monument to attain national park status, but Shantz started it.

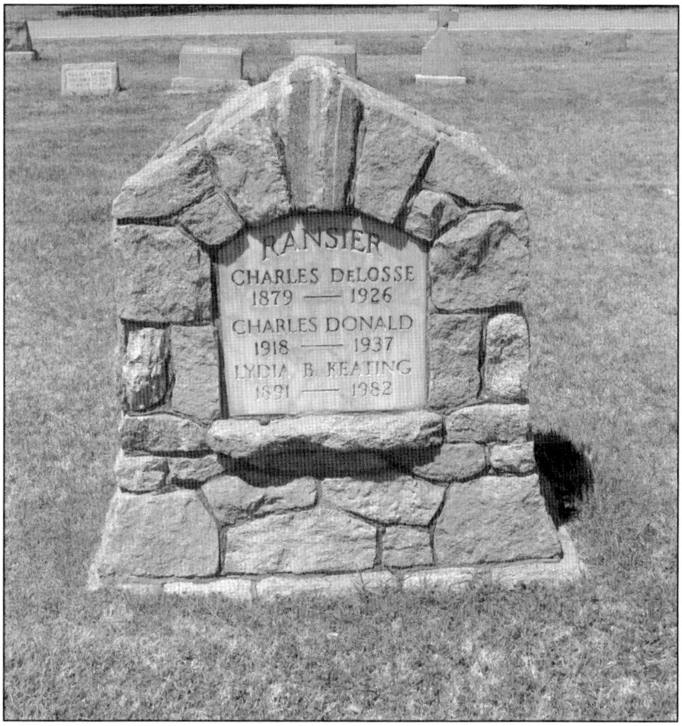

Charles D. Ransier, born in 1879, came to Tucson from Wisconsin in 1914. He accepted a manual-training position at the Tucson Indian School. After three years, he took the same position at Tucson's Safford School. Ransier was also an adjutant of the Ben Daniels camp of Spanish-American War veterans and a member of the local Masonic lodge and Alton Kol Grotto, an auxiliary body restricted exclusively to Master Masons. His gravestone in Evergreen Cemetery consists of rough rocks in the shape of a house. Ransier died of pneumonia on January 25, 1926.

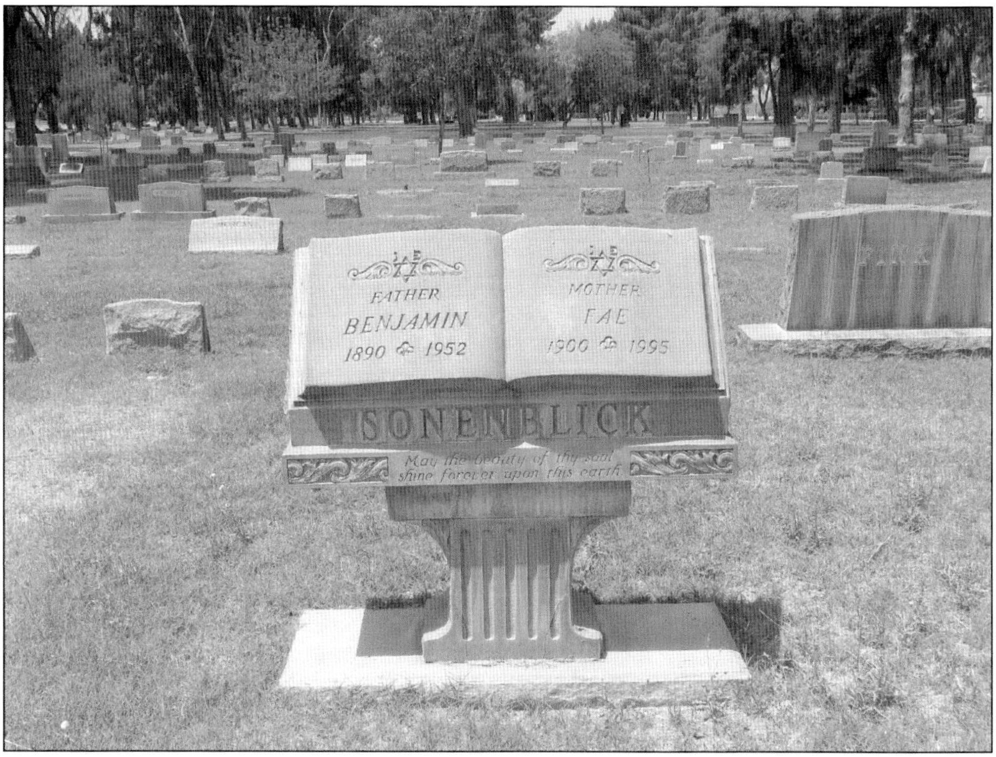

Benjamin and Fae Sonenblick chose a beautiful, massive, open book on a pedestal for their tombstone. Above each name are a Star of David and the Hebrew symbols for "here lies."

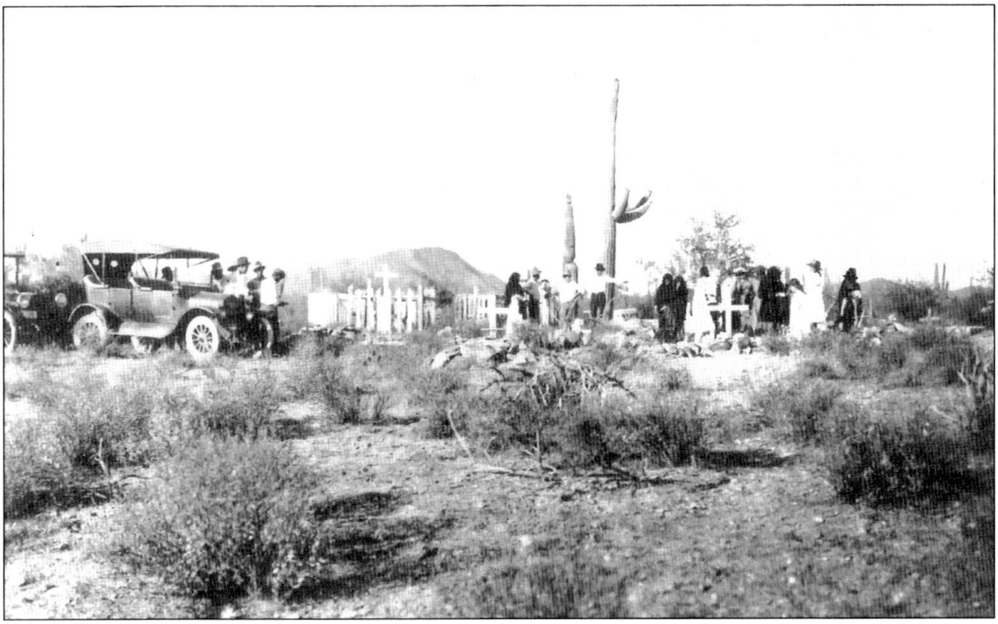

This old image—possibly from the 1920s, judging by the cars—shows a Catholic funeral at Holy Hope Cemetery, located just north of Evergreen Cemetery in Tucson. In 1907, Bishop Granjon acquired the 200 acres for the cemetery, which is located off of present-day Oracle Road.

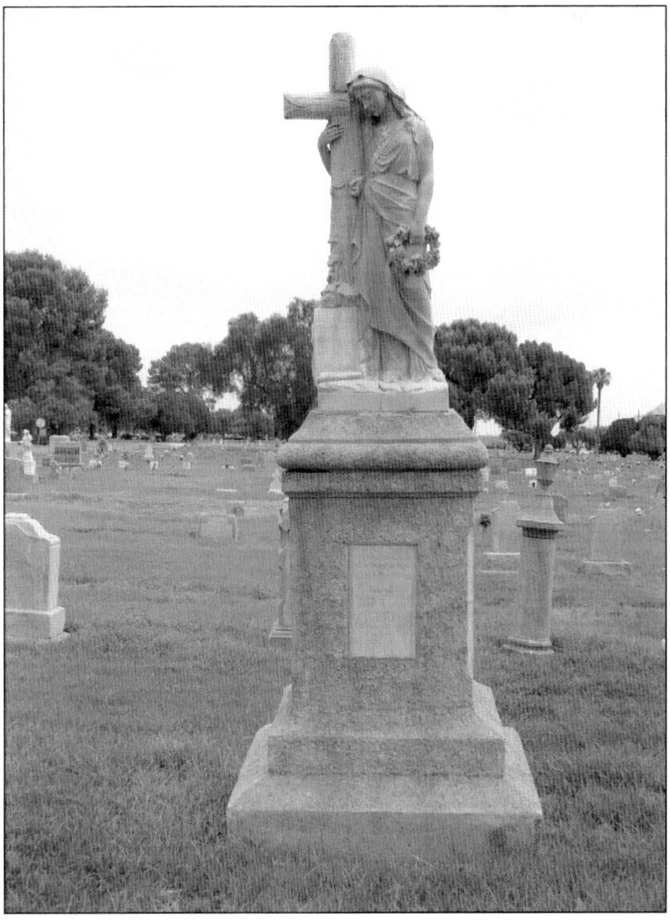

Eloisa Durazo was born in Tucson in March 1866 and died there of heart trouble on January 20, 1911. The statue on her grave appears to depict Mary grieving at the cross and clutching what seems to be a crown of thorns.

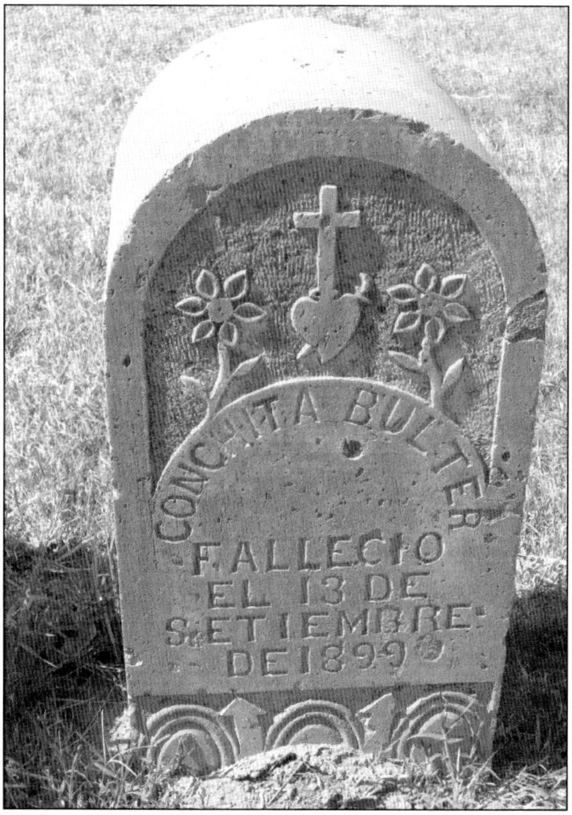

This graceful, arched tombstone covers the remains of Conchita Bulter. Her date of birth is unknown, but she died in Tucson on September 13, 1899. Bulter's marker is adorned with six-petaled primroses and a cross stabbing a heart, indicating deep grief.

This is possibly the strangest tombstone in Holy Hope Cemetery. There are many others with clasping hands, but none with the handshake spanning the top of the tomb. The hands appear to be those of a male and a female, so this may mark the grave of a husband and wife.

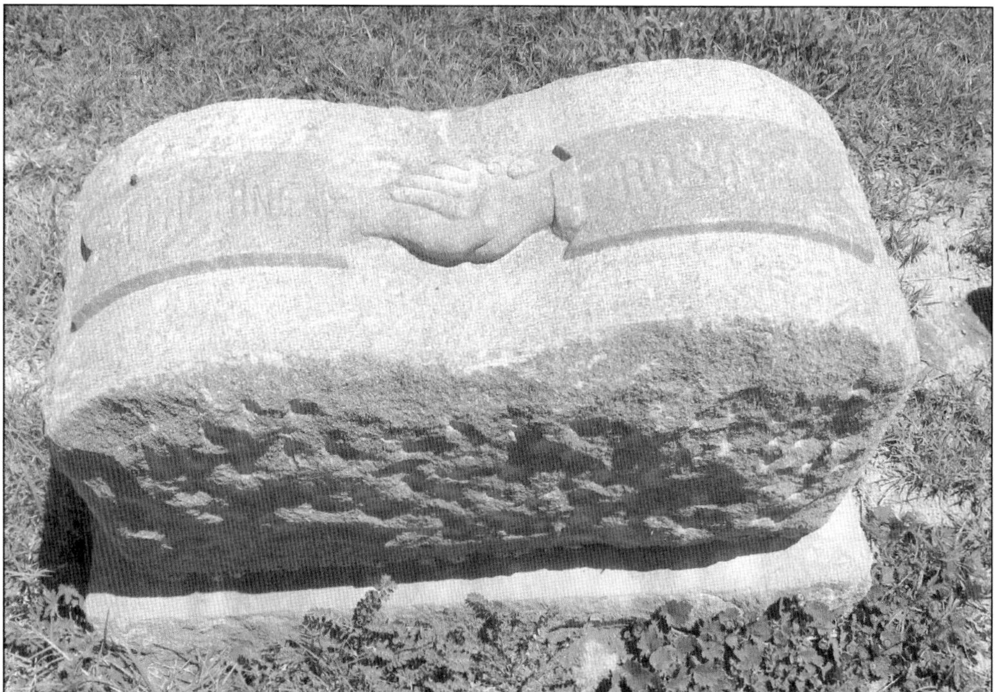

Solomon Warner was born in Warnerville, New York, on February 8, 1811. At age 26, he went to work on riverboats plying the Mississippi River. In 1849, he joined the California Gold Rush. When he did not find gold, he travelled to the Isthmus of Panama and worked in Nicaragua. In 1853, Warner moved to San Francisco, where he worked as a mason for the Quartermaster Corps; this took him to Fort Yuma, Arizona, where he met William F. Hooper and Francis Hinton, who hired him to lead a 13-mule train loaded with merchandise for Tucson. He arrived in Tucson on February 29, 1856, just 11 days before Mexican troops withdrew from the area in accordance with the Gadsden Purchase. He purchased land and partnered with Mark Aldrich in opening a general store.

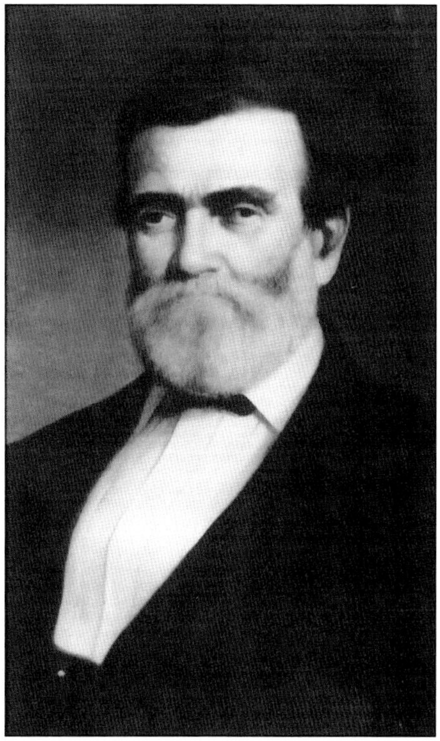

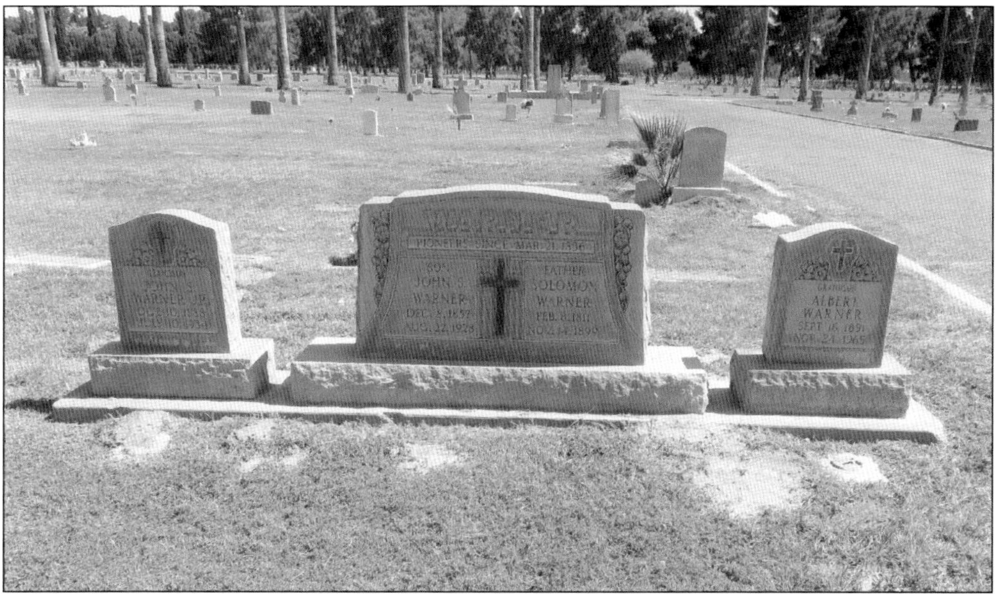

When Confederate troops arrived in Tucson in February 1862, Warner refused to take their loyalty oath. As a result, his property was seized, and Warner was forced to leave town. He spent the duration of the war in Sonora, where he married a wealthy widow. After the war, on January 29, 1870, Warner was wounded by Apaches while returning to Tucson and was permanently crippled. Between 1874 and 1875, he built a flour mill and a small dam along the Santa Cruz River. He spent his final years obsessed with building a perpetual-motion machine. Warner died from cancer on November 14, 1899, in Tucson.

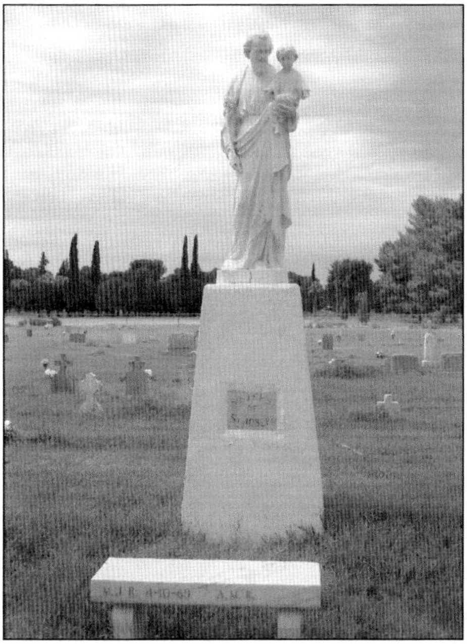

The burial sites for the Sisters of St. Joseph of Carondelet are marked with lawn plaques, which surround this statue of St. Joseph. All except Sr. Monica Corrigan and Sr. Martha Peters died in Tucson. Sr. Emerentia Bonnefoy, born in 1823, died on August 1, 1874; Sr. Euphrasia Suchet, born in 1838, died on April 10, 1904; Sr. Maxime Croissat, born in 1840, died on February 14, 1882; Sr. Ambrosia Armichaud, born in 1834, died on May 13, 1888; and Sr. Hyacinth Blanc, born in 1835, died on July 13, 1904.

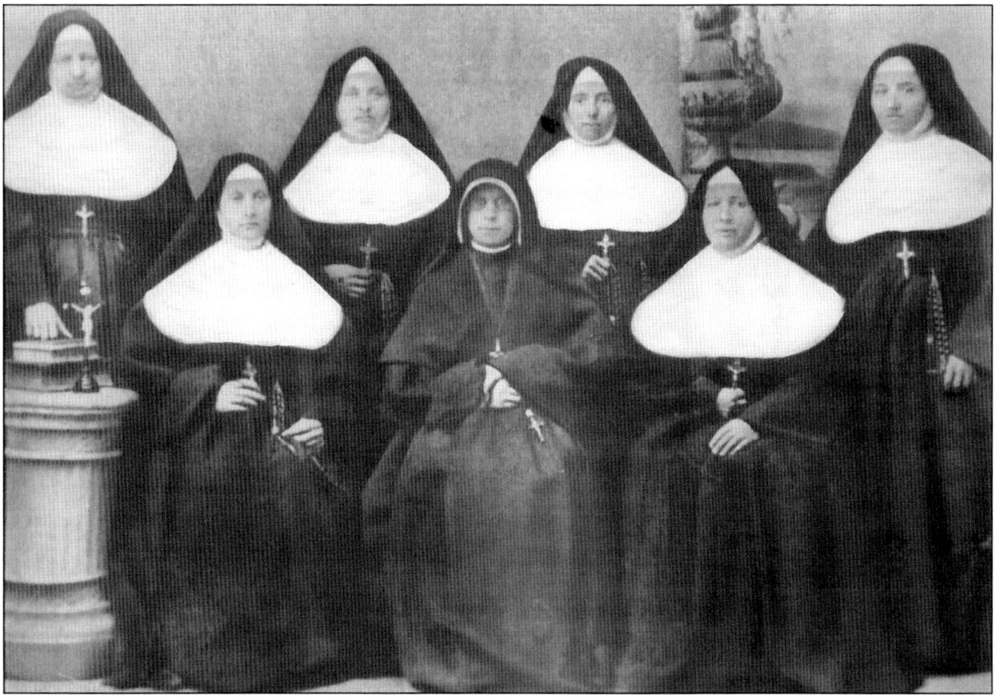

Pictured here are, from left to right, (first row) Sr. Maxima Croissat, Sr. Martha Peters, and Sr. Euphrasia Suchet; (second row) Sr. Ambrosia Armichaud, Sr. Hyacinth Blanc, Sr. Monica Corrigan, and Sr. Emerentia Bonnefoy. Tucson's seven Sisters of St. Joseph of Carondelet arrived in Tucson in 1870. In 1880, Bishop Salpointe asked the sisters to serve the sick in the 12-bed St. Mary's Hospital. They borrowed large sums of money and mortgaged their properties to build a sanitarium for the hospital and to enlarge St. Joseph's Female Academy, the school they founded in 1885. (Courtesy of Albert Carmack.)

Holy Hope is the final resting place for many clergy who have served the Catholic community of Tucson. Included are Archbishop Jean Baptiste Salpointe (1825–1898), Archbishop Peter Bourgade (1845–1908), Bishop Henry Granjon (1863–1922), Archbishop Daniel James Gercke (1874–1964), the Most Reverend Francis J. Green (1906–1995), and the Most Reverend Manuel D. Moreno (1930–2006). Their graves have lawn plaques in Holy Hope's Garden of the Apostles.

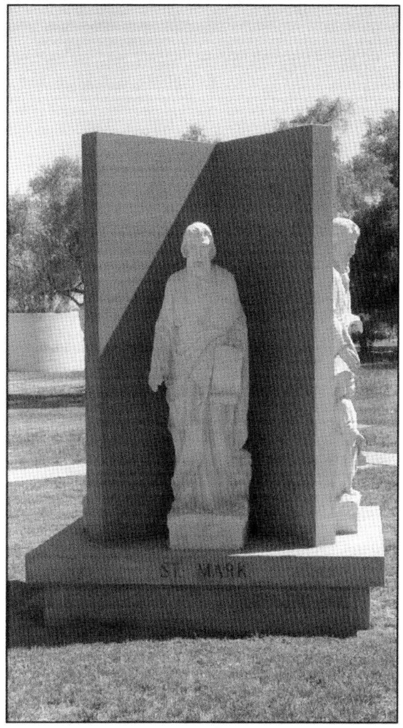

Bishop Daniel James Gercke (center) is flanked by Herbert Drachman (left) and author Harold Bell Wright. Gercke was born October 9, 1874, and died March 19, 1964. Born in Philadelphia, he attended St. Joseph's College, where he obtained a bachelor of arts degree in 1891. He studied at St. Charles Borromeo Seminary in Overbrook and was ordained on June 1, 1901. Gercke went to the city of Vigan in the Philippines in 1903. Upon returning to Philadelphia in 1919, he served as rector of the Cathedral of SS. Peter and Paul. On June 21, 1923, Gercke was appointed the third bishop of Tucson by Pope Pius XI, a position he held until 1960. He was the first American-born head of the Tucson diocese.

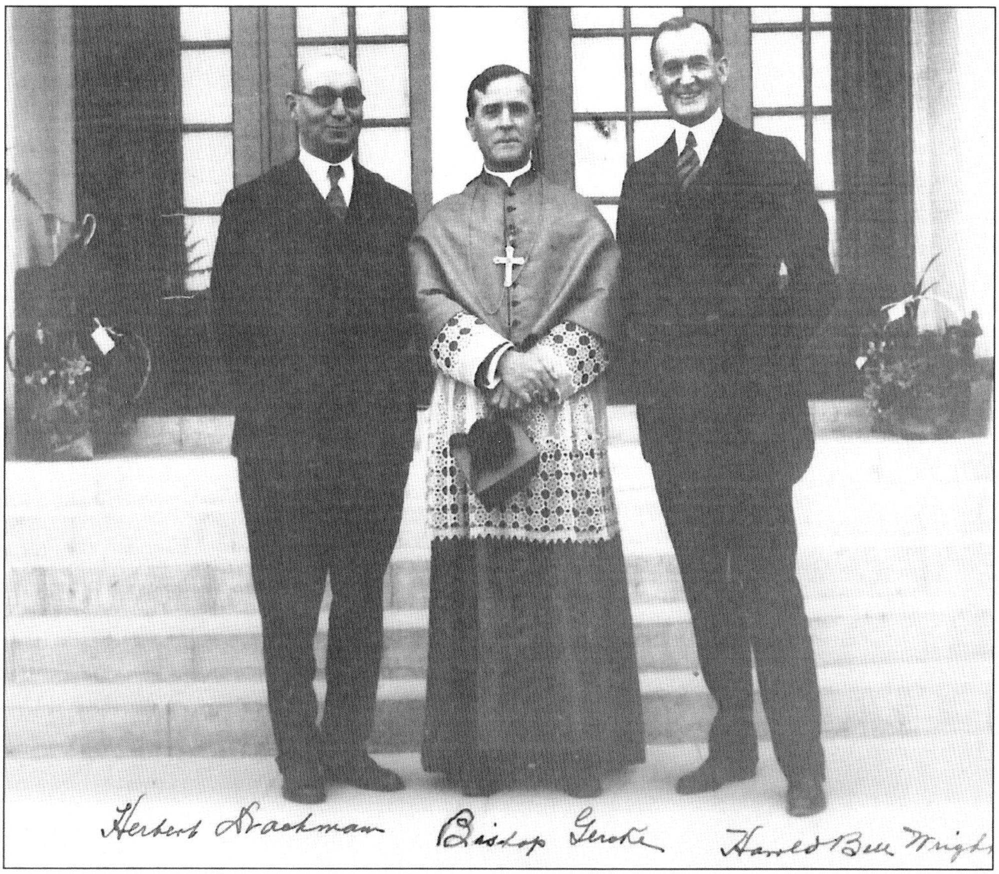

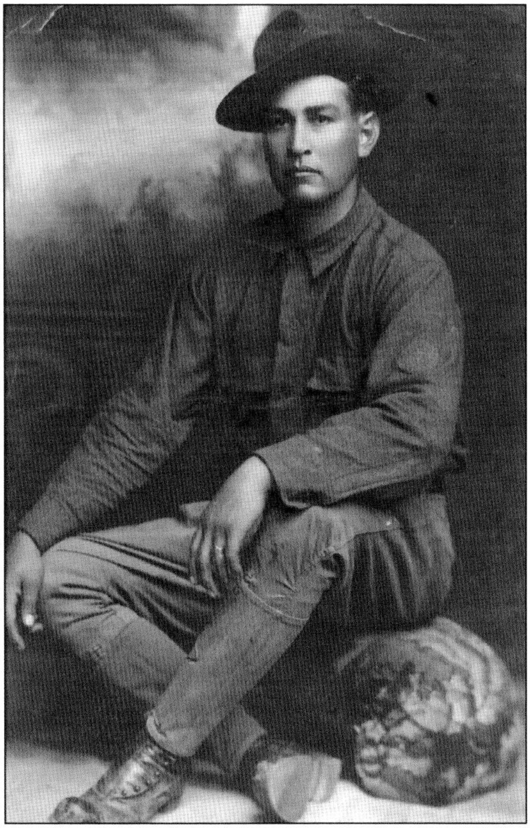

Jesus Camacho was born on April 22, 1883, in a house near St. Mary's Road and Grande Avenue, and he died in Tucson on February 20, 1949. Camacho was known in Tucson as the "mayor of Meyer Street." During a 26-year career that began in 1910, he held every position on the police force, from rookie to acting chief. (Courtesy of Art Solano.)

Jesus Camacho captured one big-time criminal and killed two men in the line of duty. He walked the beat on Meyer Street before becoming a mounted patrolman. He and his horse, Babe, were well known in Tucson. In 1926, he had a misunderstanding with chief of police Jack Dyer and opened up his own detective agency. They eventually straightened out matters, and Camacho rejoined the force. When he died in 1949 at age 66, a Mass was held for him at St. Augustine Cathedral. Jesus and his wife, Ramona Camacho, are buried in Holy Hope Cemetery.

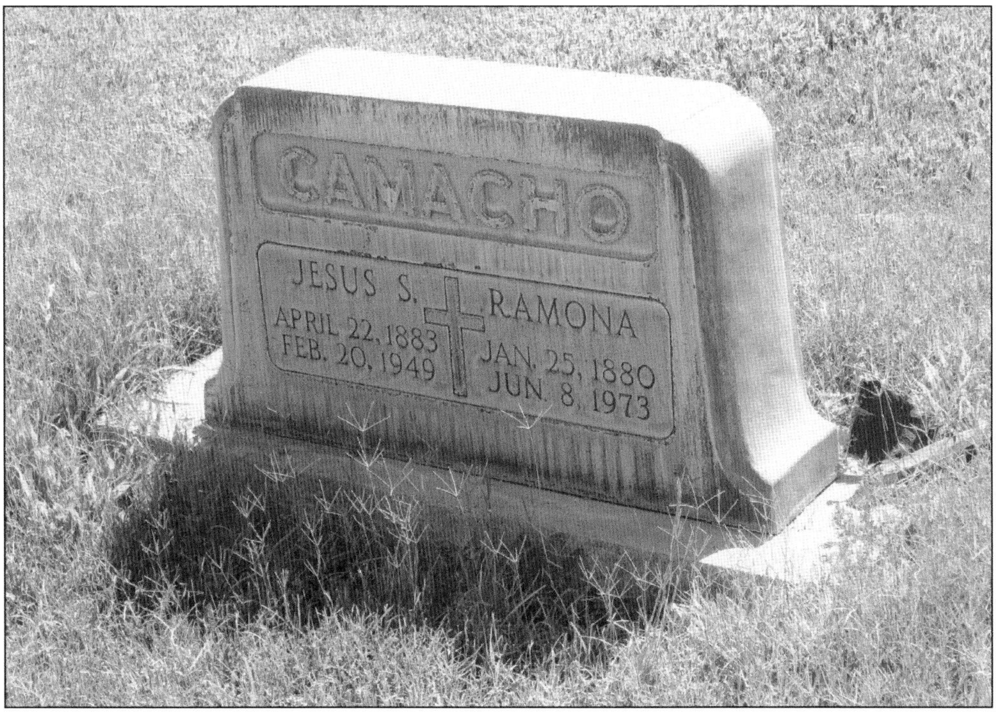

Pictured here are Atanacia Santa Cruz Hughes (left), Guadalupe Santa Cruz de Martinez (center), and Petra Santa Cruz Stevens. Guadalupe was the aunt of the two orphaned sisters. Atanacia, born in Tucson on August 14, 1850, when it was part of Mexico, died on November 12, 1934. She and her sister Petra were raised by their aunt—Guadalupe—after their parents died. Atanacia married Samuel Hughes on May 27, 1863, at Mission San Xavier del Bac.

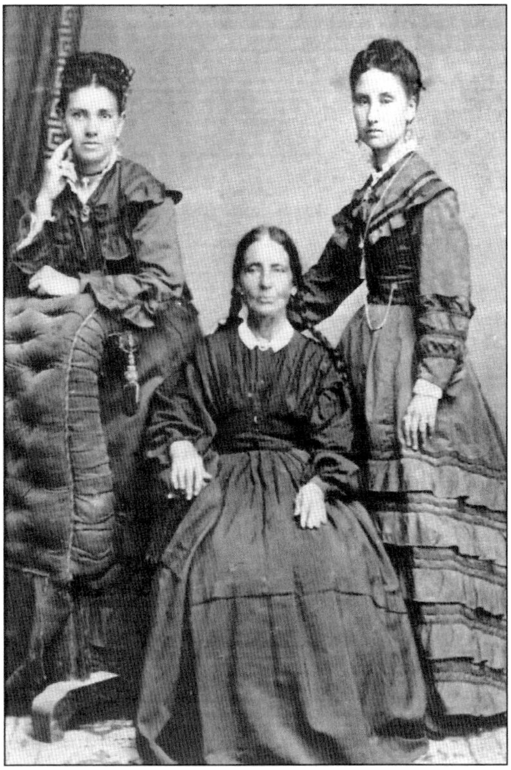

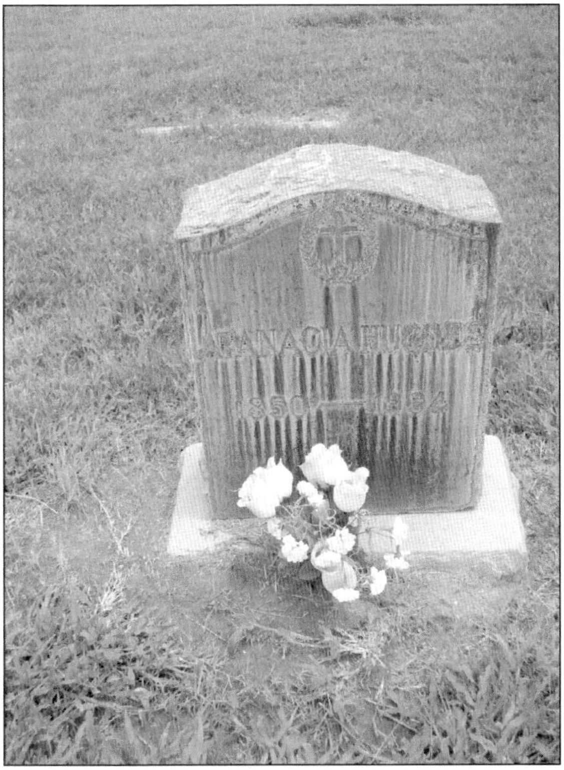

Atanacia died at St. Mary's Hospital in 1934 from an intestinal obstruction. Her sister Petra Santa Cruz Stevens was born on October 19, 1848, and died on July 30, 1916; she is buried at Holy Hope. In 1893, depressed over business setbacks, Petra's husband, Hiram Stevens, shot Petra and then killed himself. She survived the shooting and stipulated that, when she did die, she was not to be buried near her husband; he is buried at Evergreen Cemetery.

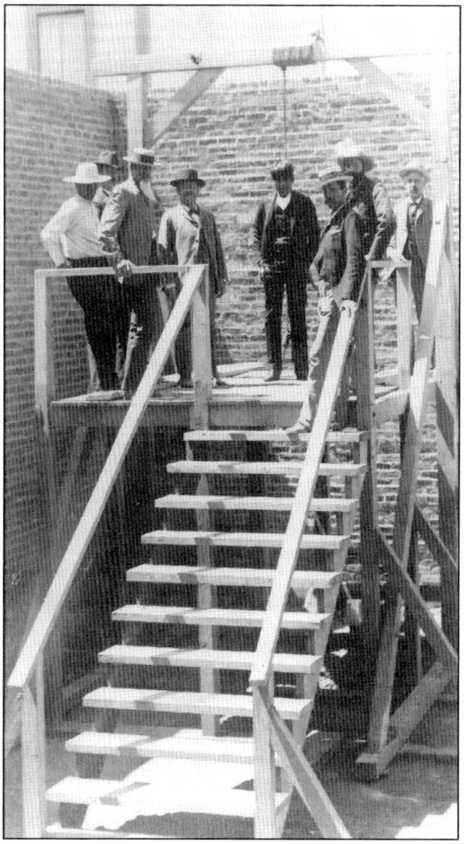

In the image at left, Pima County sheriff Nabor Pacheco is standing on the top step leading up to the gallows. He was born November 11, 1861, in Tucson and died there on February 14, 1920. He died from acute uremia at his home at 337 South Sixth Avenue.

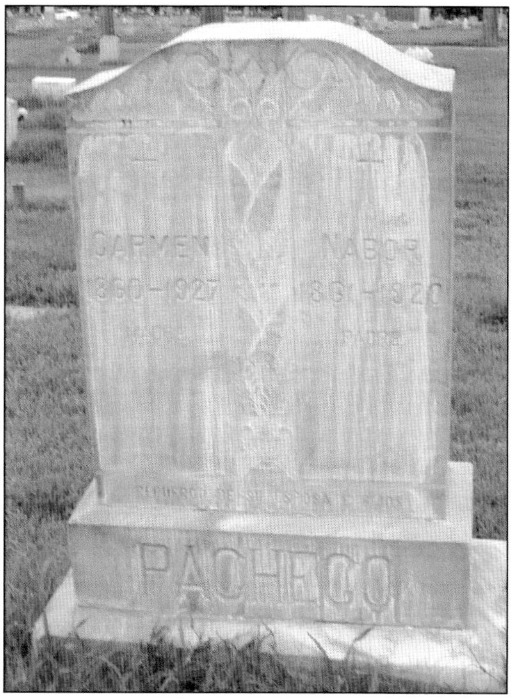

Nabor Pacheco was the first native Tucsonan to be elected Pima County sheriff. He served as a Tucson police officer and a constable before serving two terms as sheriff. His engraved Colt .45 revolver is on display at the Arizona Historical Society. In 1908, he performed two hangings within a month, and he was largely responsible for having legal executions moved to the state prison in Florence. After leaving office in 1909, he served for eight years as Tucson's chief of police.

This is a photograph of a young Louisa Done (1868–1965). Tucson's Binghampton Cemetery is a Mormon cemetery, and Louisa Matilda (Haag) Abegg Done was a Binghampton pioneer. In Germany, the Haag family was financially comfortable, with a lovely home and servants. Louisa believed in the truthfulness of the Mormon gospel, and at age 13, she sought baptism. Because of Mormon persecution, the baptism took place in the middle of the night through broken ice on the Neckar River. (Courtesy of Jeanette Done.)

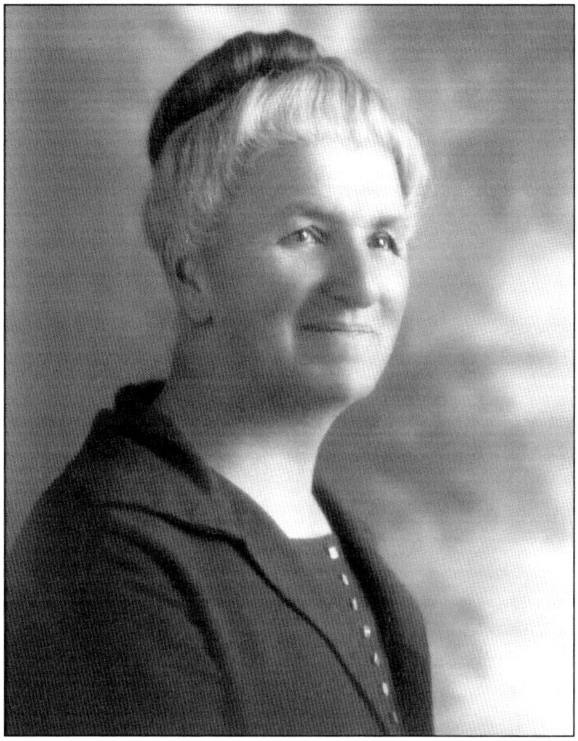

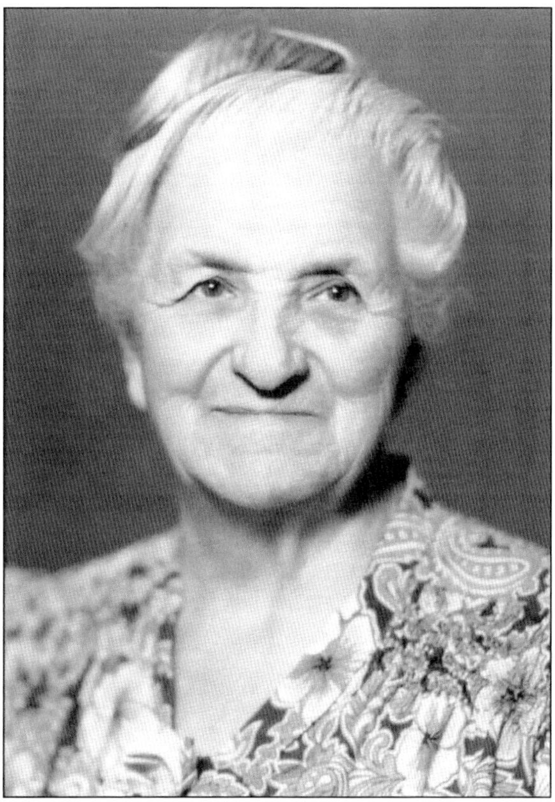

This is Louisa Done in later years. Louisa came to America with her mother and several of her brothers and first lived in Payson, Utah. Their father never joined the family. Louisa married Arnold Abegg in the Logan Utah Temple at age 15. She had four children—two daughters and two sons, one of whom was Eli Abegg, who became the first caretaker of the Binghampton Cemetery. Widowed at age 27, Louisa became the sole provider for her four children. She moved to Mexico and became one of the wives of Abraham Done in Colonia Dublan (at the time, polygamy was still practiced in the Mormon colonies). She had five more children, one of whom was Richard Haag Done, father of M. Boyd Done, who served as bishop of the Binghampton Ward. After leaving Mexico during its revolution, Louisa came to Binghampton, near Tucson. Her husband lived in Mesa with his first family, leaving her the sole breadwinner for her nine children. (Courtesy of Jeanette Done.)

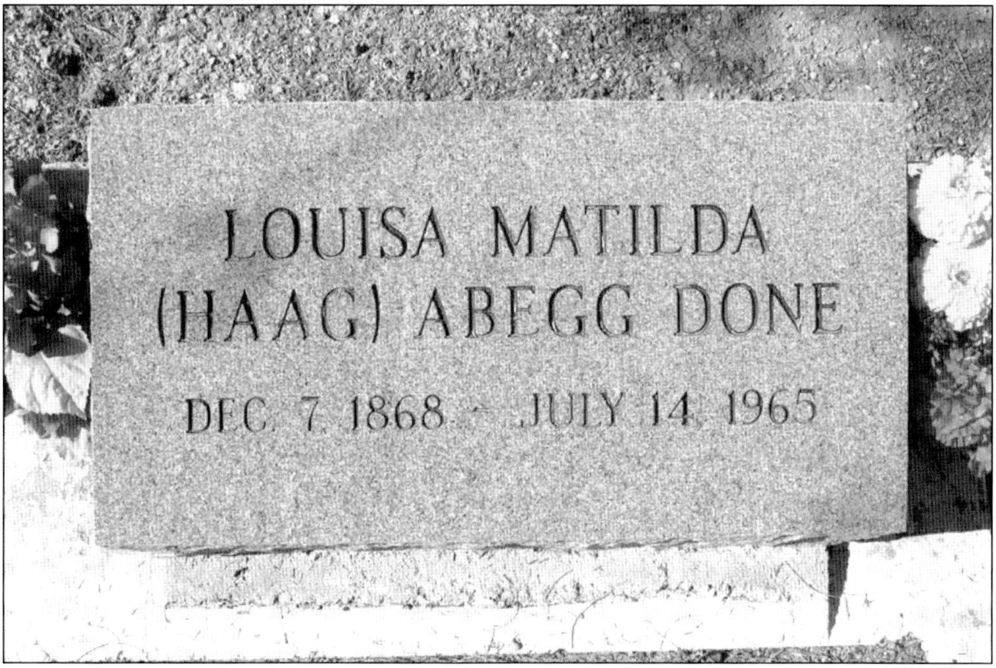

Louisa Done served as the Binghampton Relief Society secretary for 22 years. She was an avid genealogist, researching her German ancestors, and she worked in the LDS temples in Utah and Arizona. She lived to age 96 and died in Binghampton in 1965. She is buried in the Binghampton Cemetery.

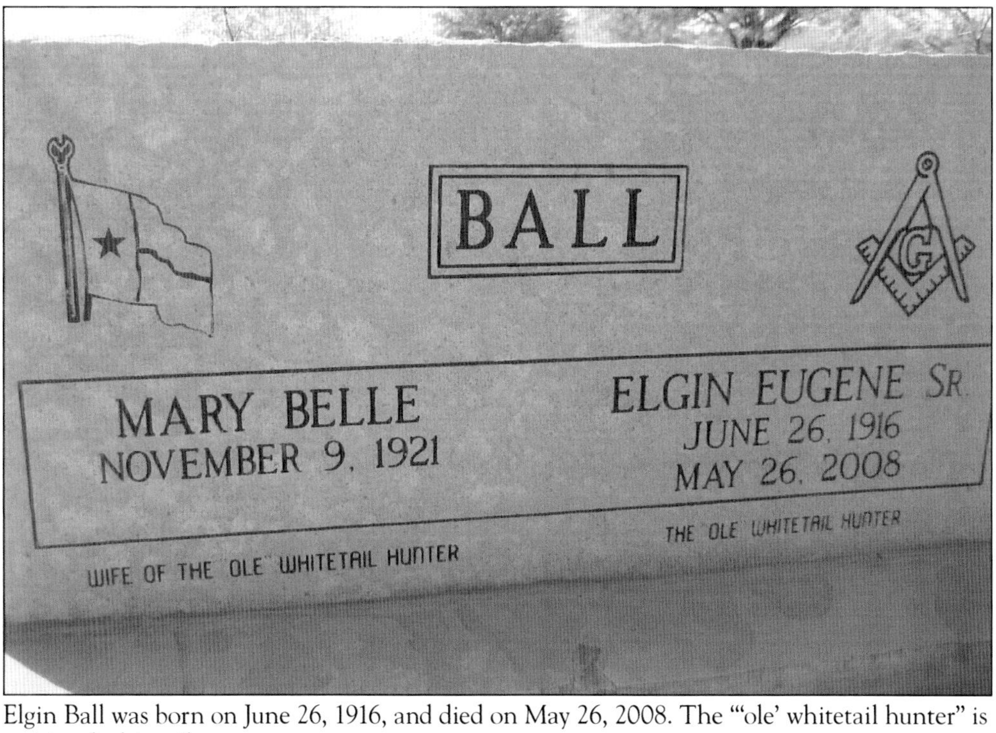

Elgin Ball was born on June 26, 1916, and died on May 26, 2008. The "'ole' whitetail hunter" is waiting for his wife.

Five

Santa Cruz County Graves and Cemeteries

Santa Cruz County sits on the border of the United States and Mexico. It is Arizona's smallest county, but it has a wealth of history and culture reflected in its graves and cemeteries. Nogales is a major port of entry between the United States and Mexico. Along this border, Fray Marcos de Niza became the first European to enter what is now Arizona. The historic Tumacácori Mission, started by Padre Eusebio Kino, has several historic graves. Spain controlled this land until 1821, when Mexico obtained jurisdiction over the land that would become Santa Cruz County. In 1848, through the Treaty of Guadalupe Hidalgo, Mexico ceded part of present-day Arizona to the United States, but the Santa Cruz County land remained in Mexican control. In 1853, the United States acquired this land through the Gadsden Purchase. In 1863, the United States created the Arizona Territory from the western half of New Mexico Territory, and Arizona achieved statehood on February 14, 1912. All of these changes were accompanied by the arrival of a rich variety of people, who in turn brought their own funeral traditions to the area.

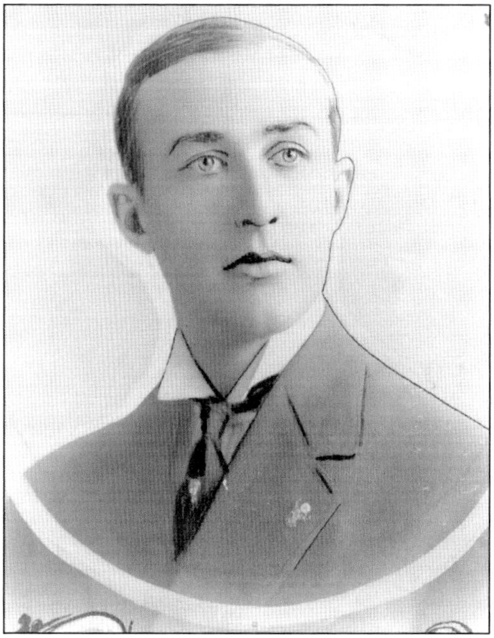

Malcolm "Mal" Wayne Eason, born on March 13, 1879, in Brookville, Pennsylvania, died in a house fire in Douglas, Arizona, on April 16, 1970. He is buried in the Black Oak Cemetery in Canelo. Eason played professional baseball from 1900 to 1906 and was a pitcher for the Chicago Orphans, Boston Beaneaters, Detroit Tigers, and the Brooklyn Superbas. In 1906, he threw a curveball and a spitball, which was legal at the time, and pitched a no-hitter against the St. Louis Cardinals. He umpired from 1910 to 1917, and during one game, he ejected all of the New York Giants' bench because they disagreed with his calls. (Courtesy of the Baseball Hall of Fame.)

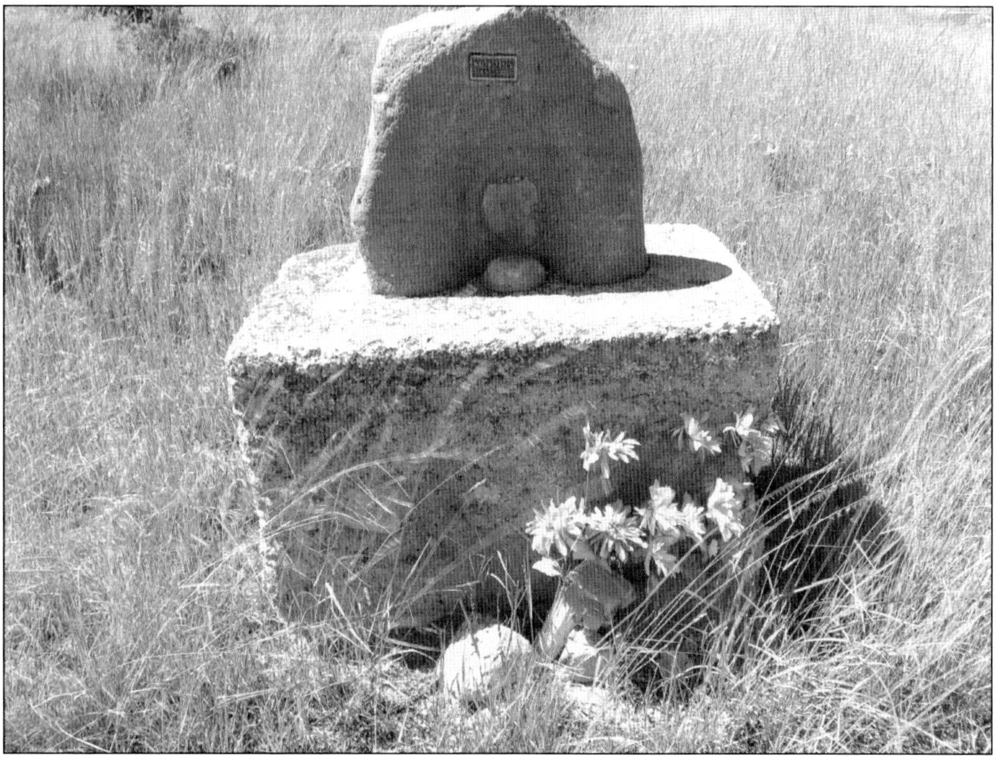

Mal Eason retired on his homesteaded land in southern Arizona, which he called the Umpire Ranch. Old-timers recalled him walking five miles every night, with his shovel and pickaxe, to the Black Oak Cemetery, where he dug his own grave. He created his own headstone from a metate, or grinding stone, which, when standing upright, reminded him of a catcher's glove. In the hollow is a stone representing a baseball.

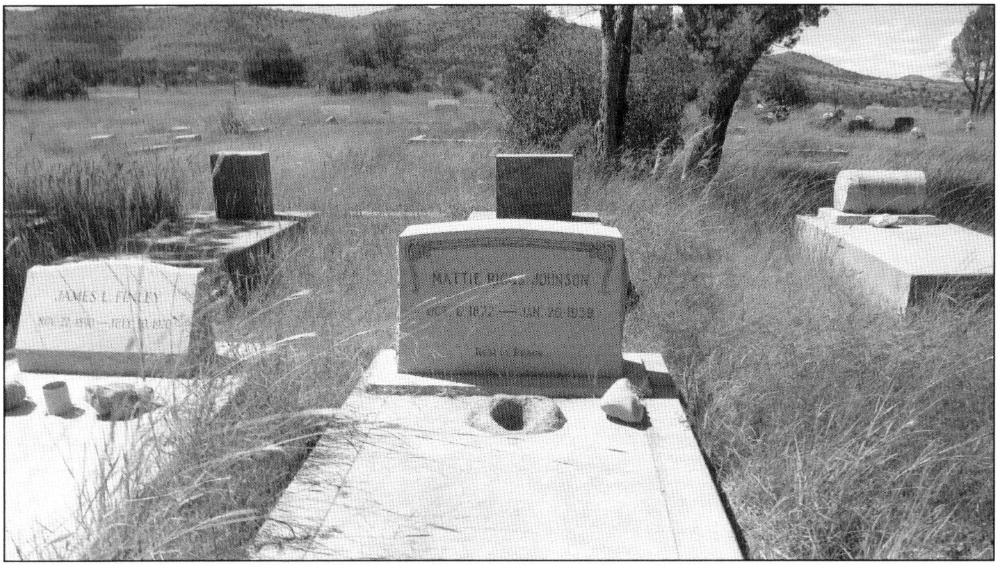

Mattie Riggs Johnson was born on October 6, 1872, and died on January 26, 1939. In 1917, she made a special arrangement with the US Forest Service to donate a 10-acre parcel of her lease for the creation of the Black Oak Cemetery. Her son James Finley endowed the cemetery with a large sum of money. Plots are free to pioneer families who lived in the area prior to December 31, 1952, or who have relatives already buried at Black Oak. Mattie was an old-time cattle woman who could ride sidesaddle as well as—or better than—any man could ride astride.

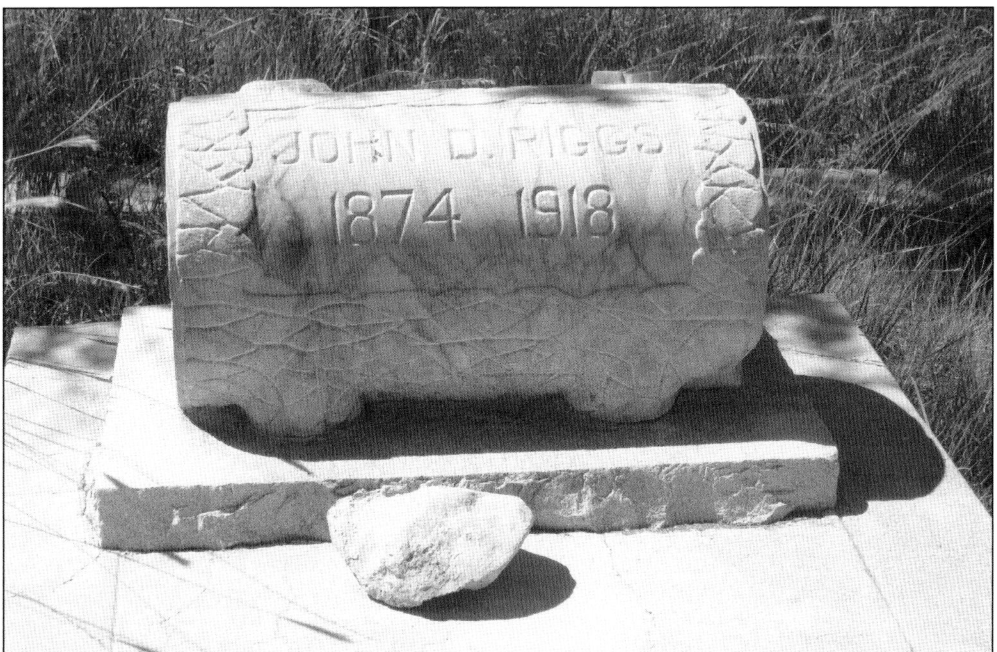

John D. Riggs was born in 1874 and died in 1918. His treestone marker in Black Oak Cemetery announces his membership in Woodmen of the World, a fraternal organization that provided its members with insurance and treestones for their graves.

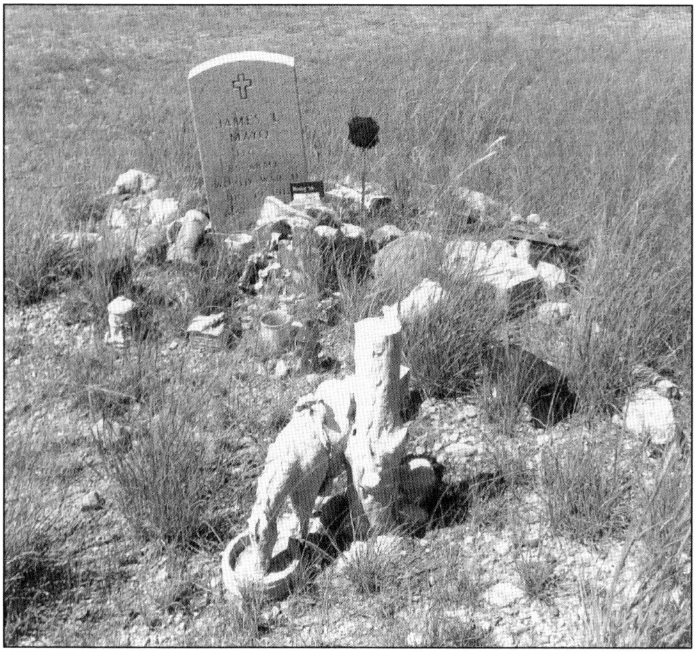

James "Slim" Mayo, born on June 19, 1912, died on May 16, 1998. His gravesite leaves little doubt that Mayo was a man who had a special love for horses. Mayo was the wrangler for the Little Outfit Ranch, a private boys' school. In 2009, alumni helped to get the Little Outfit Ranch Schoolhouse listed in the National Register of Historic Places, paying tribute to Mayo as their mentor. Mayo also kept the school's herd of 600 buffalo away from Fort Huachuca while troops practiced firing mortars and artillery.

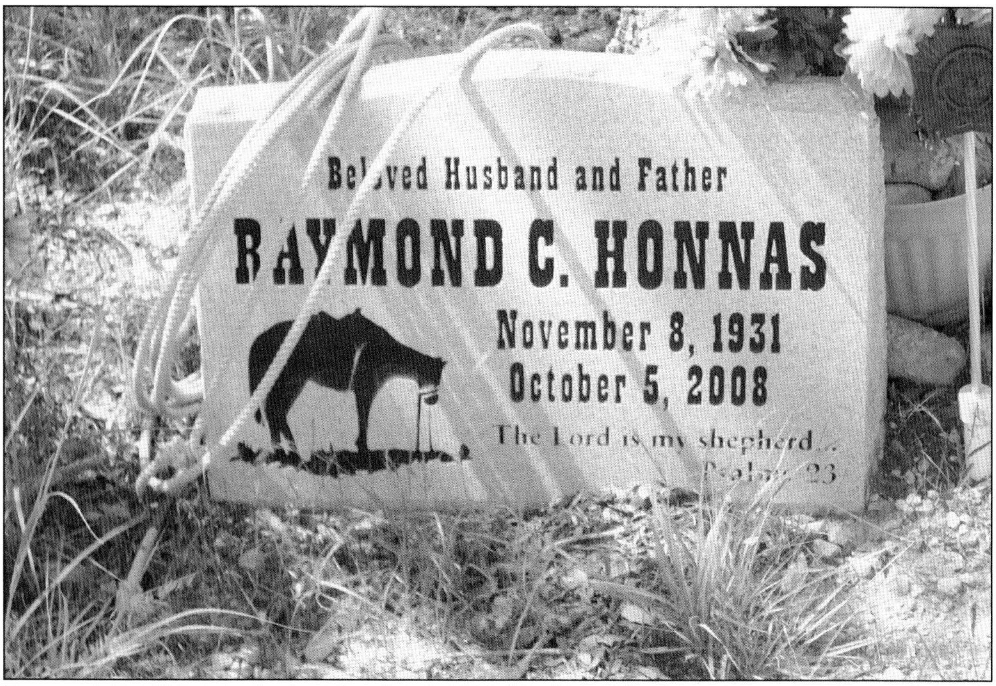

Raymond Cecil Honnas died on October 6, 2008 (his date of death is incorrect on his tombstone). He was born at St. Mary's Hospital in Tucson on November 8, 1931. He graduated from the University of Arizona with a bachelor's degree in range management and animal husbandry and ranched in the Sonoita-Patagonia and Bradshaw Mountain areas. The lariat on his grave signifies that he was in a severe roping accident. His tombstone is decorated with a riderless horse.

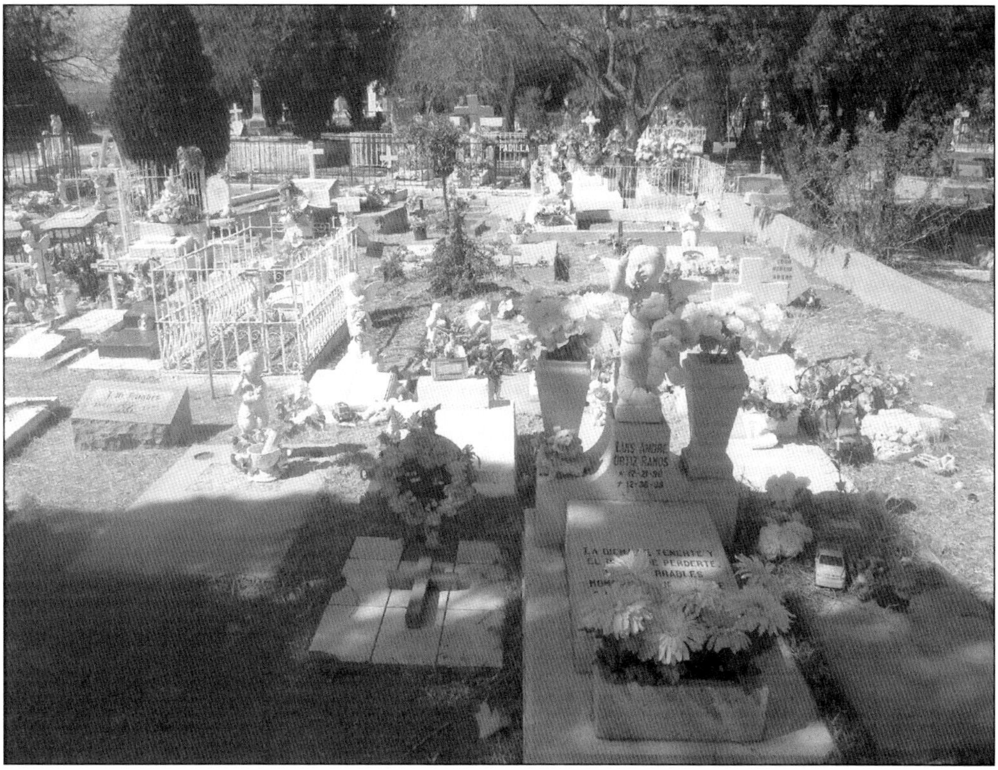

Robert James Parker was born on January 5, 1956, in Douglas, Arizona, and died on February 9, 1992. His tombstone attests to the fact that he was well-liked by those who knew him. The Parker name is associated with the beautiful 130-acre Parker Canyon Lake located in the high, cool, rolling hills of Southern Arizona.

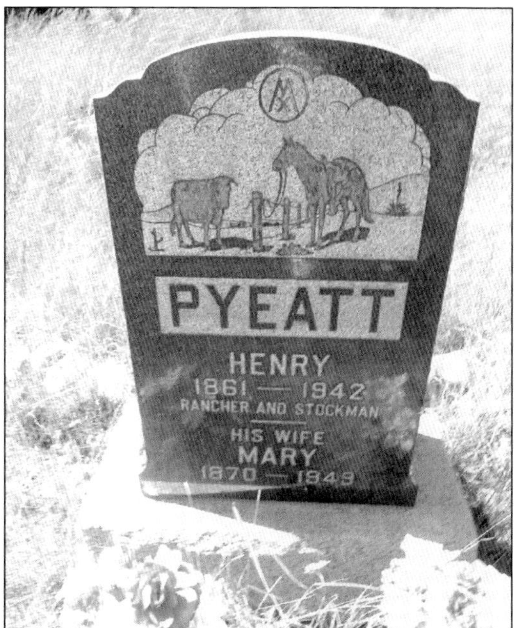

James Henry Pyeatt was born in San Saba, Texas, in 1861, and died in 1942. The gravestone of Henry and his wife, Mary, is decorated with their ranch's brand. Henry worked as a cotton-picker in Texas and as a cowpuncher in the Oklahoma Indian Territory. In 1882, he was hired as a cowboy for a company moving 1,000 head of Texas longhorns to Arizona. In the late 1880s, he bought a couple of ranches along the San Pedro River, and he is credited with bringing in Durham and Hereford cattle to improve his holdings. The Pyeatt family celebrated its 100th anniversary of ranch life in 1999.

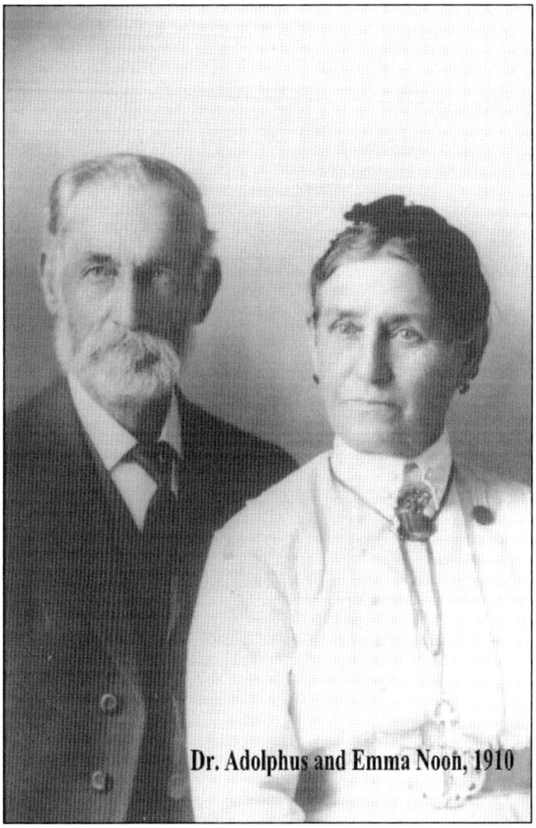

Dr. Adolphus H. Noon was born in England on June 22, 1838, and died on March 23, 1931, in Nogales, Arizona. He married Emma Catherine Slaughter in 1864. Besides practicing medicine, Adolphus served as mayor of Nogales from 1910 to 1911 and was a correspondent for the *Chicago Tribune*. (Courtesy of Mary Noon Kasulaitis.)

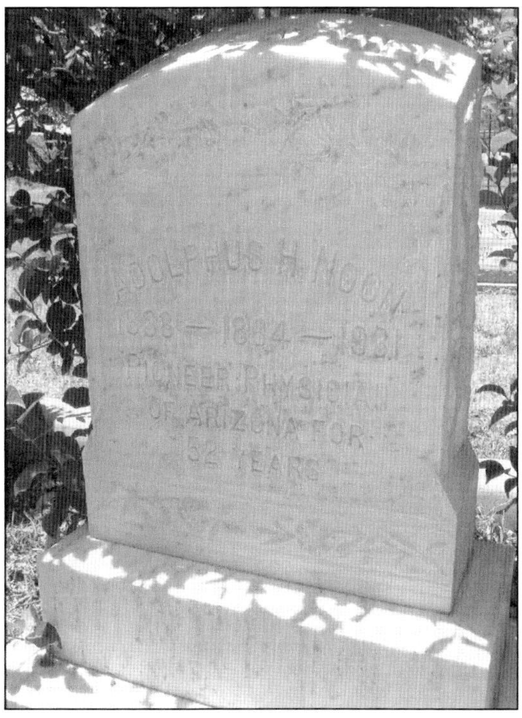

Adolphus H. Noon studied medicine in San Francisco and, for many years, was the only doctor between Tucson and Hermosillo, Mexico. Noon's tombstone is plain but carries a message of love for an early Santa Cruz County pioneer. (Courtesy of Mary Noon Kasulaitis.)

William Vann Rogers (known as Will Rogers Jr.), was born in New York on October 20, 1911, and died in Tubac, Arizona, on July 9, 1993. He was the son of humorist Will Rogers. Will Rogers Jr. graduated from Beverly Hills High School and Stanford University and served as editor/publisher of the *Beverly Hills Citizen* from 1935 to 1953. While preparing to ship out as a merchant seaman in 1935, he learned that his father had died in a plane crash off Barrow, Alaska. He was elected to the US House of Representatives in 1942 and served for almost two years before resigning in 1944 to return to the Army and serve as a tank commander.

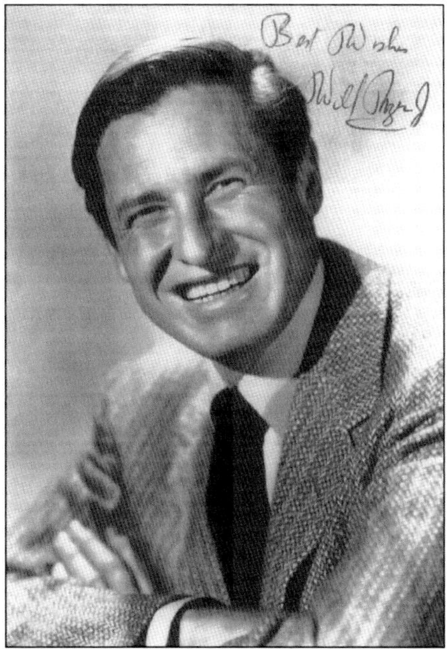

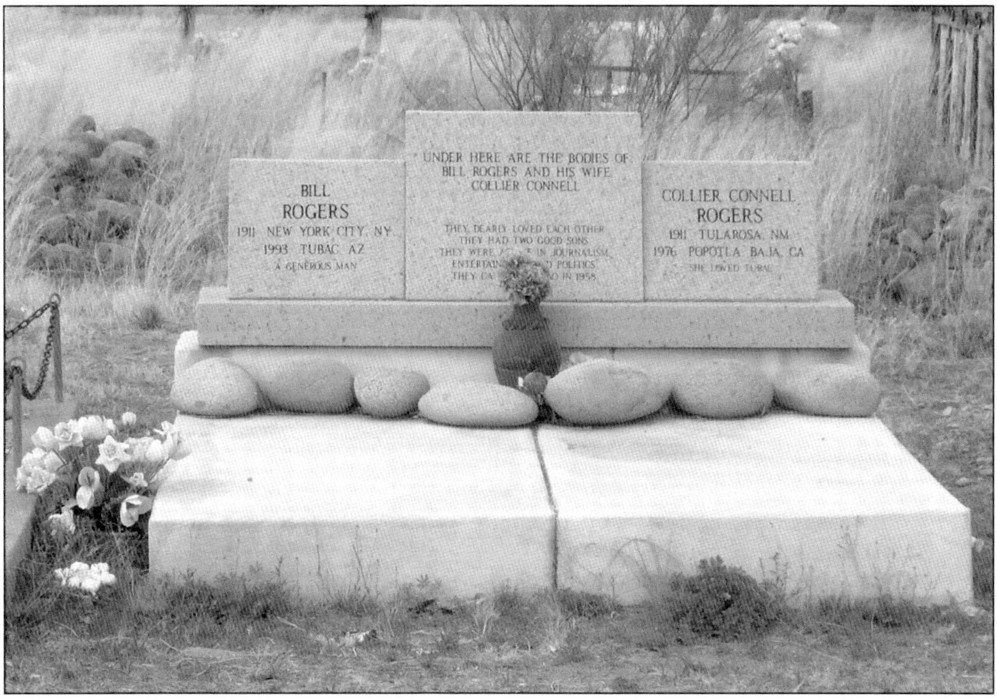

Will Rogers Jr. was part Cherokee, was active in American Indian affairs, and served as chairman of the California State Park Commission. Rogers won the 1946 Democratic nomination for the US Senate, but was defeated and went on to manage Harry Truman's reelection campaign in Southern California. His later career included jobs in radio and television, including hosting a morning talk show for CBS. On July 11, 1993, the 81-year-old Rogers was found dead of a self-inflicted gunshot wound to the head on a road near his home in Tubac. In his later years, he had suffered two strokes and heart problems and had undergone hip-implant surgery.

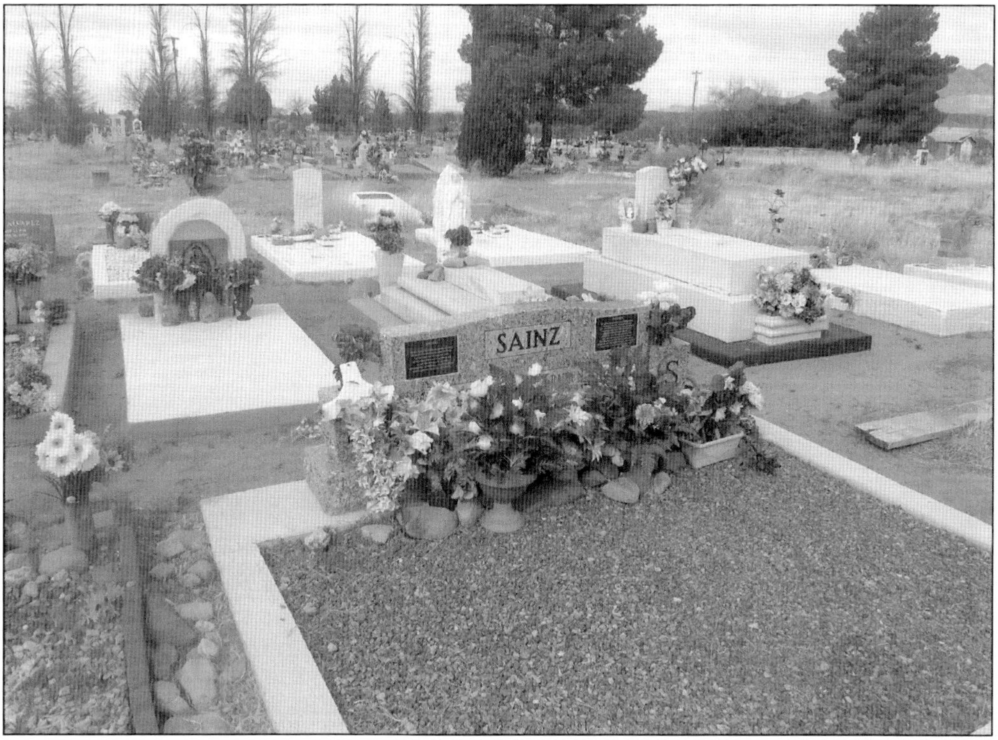

Rosa and Ruben Sainz share a typical Mexican tombstone in the Tubac Cemetery. Ruben was born in 1915 and died in 1975; Rosa was born on December 18, 1920, and died on October 19, 1995. There is a Spanish prayer on the tombstone, and family and friends continue to remember Rosa and Ruben with flowers.

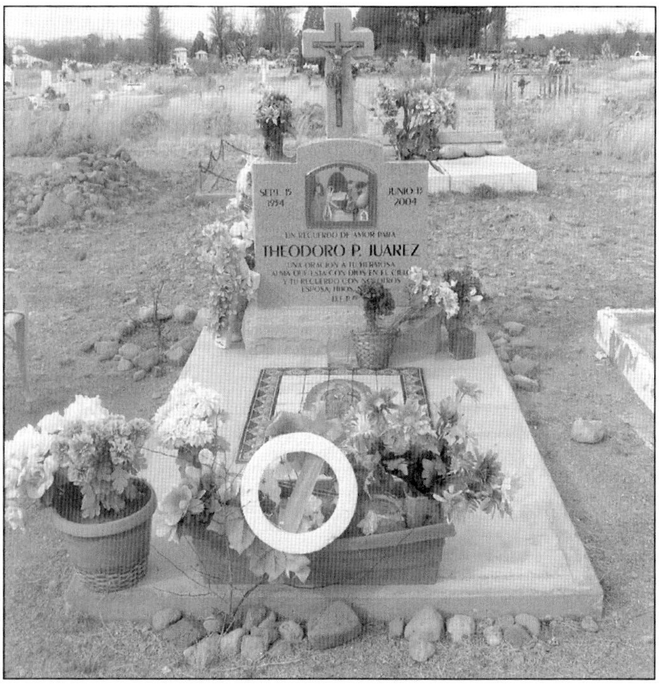

Theodoro Juarez was born on September 15, 1934, in Amado, Arizona, and died in Phoenix on June 13, 2004. His grave is adorned with the beautiful Virgin of Guadalupe (aka Our Lady of Guadalupe), a popular saint whose entire body is covered with an esplendora.

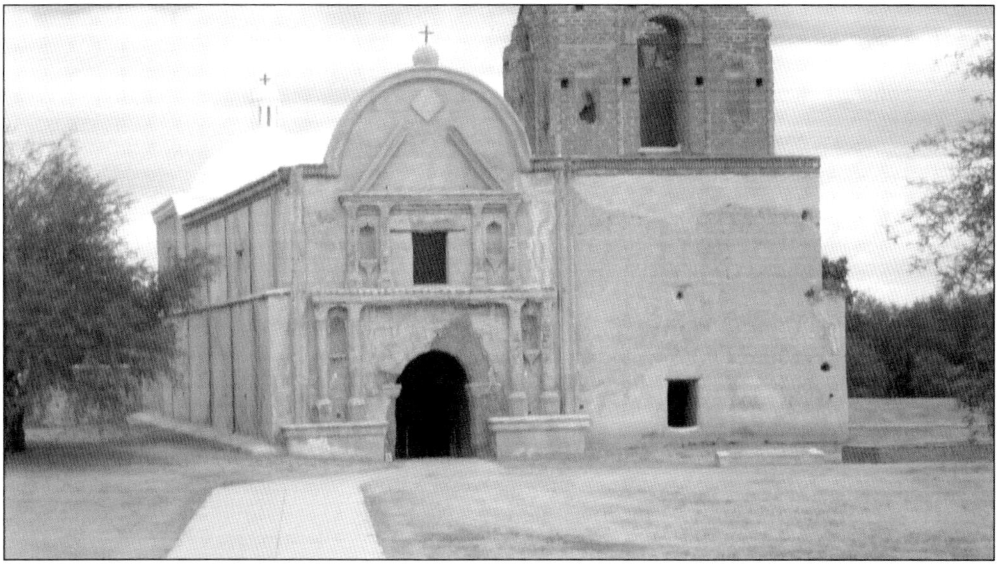

Mission San José de Tumacácori is now part of the Tumacácori National Historical Park. Fr. Eusebio Kino celebrated Mass under a ramada in this area. The Jesuits built the first church here sometime before 1757, but it was abandoned when Spain's King Charles III banished all Jesuits from the realm in 1767. The Franciscans took over in 1773, and construction of the current structure began sometime around 1800. The Franciscan mission was dedicated in 1822, but the bell tower was never completed. The mission garden has been reconstructed to be as similar as possible to the original.

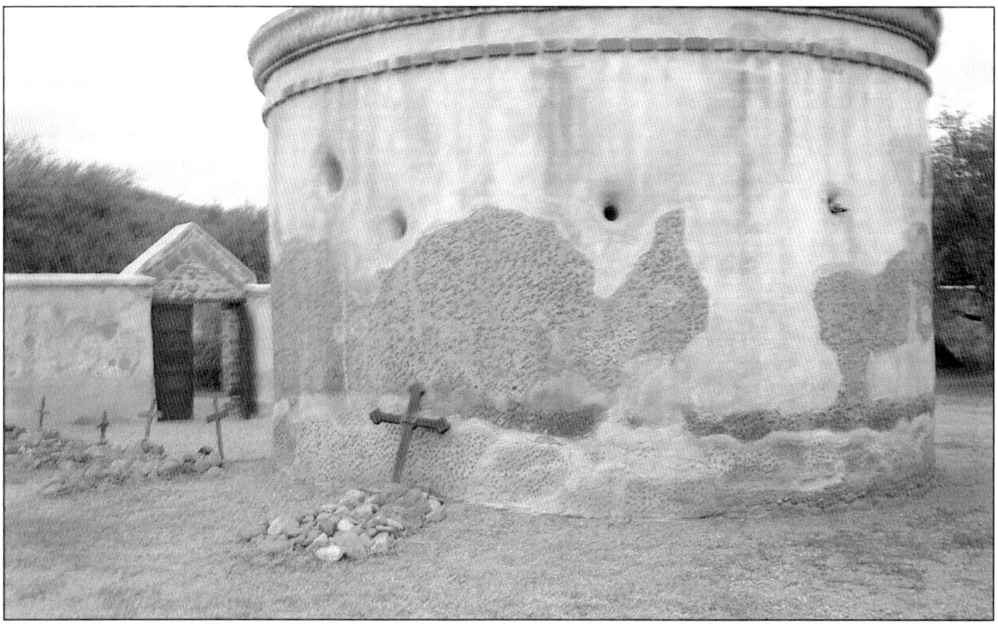

The museum inside Tumacácori National Historical Park includes information about the Indian tribes in the area and exhibits such as weapons, a map of the missions in the area, and a description of the construction of the church. The museum has one room devoted to the history of Father Kino. Just outside the Mission San José de Tumacácori church is the cemetery, along with this 16-foot-diameter mortuary chapel.

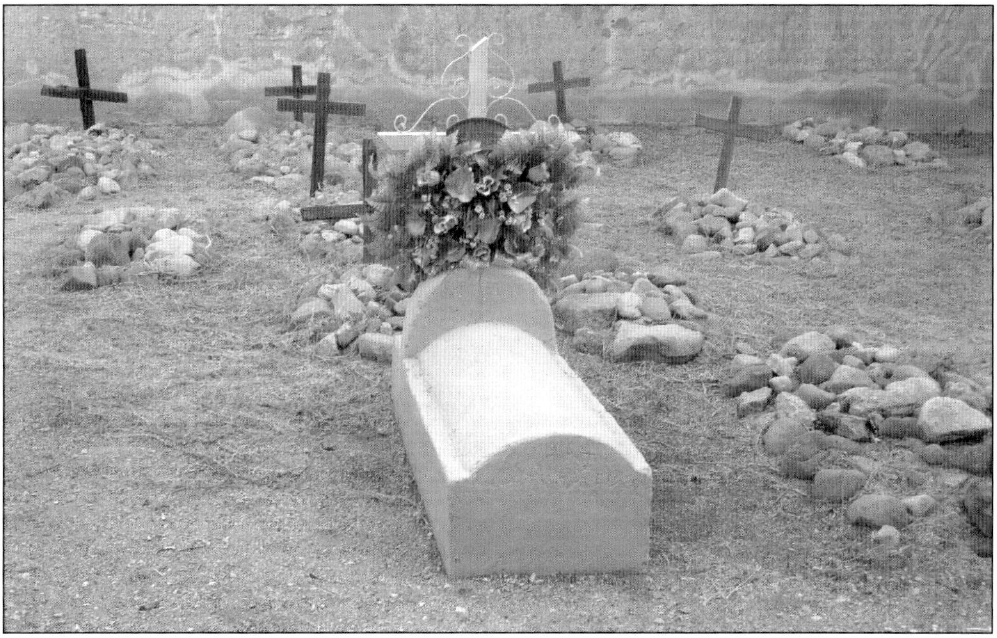

It is estimated that about 593 people were buried in the Mission San José de Tumacácori cemetery between 1755 and 1825. The last burial—and the only one identified—was that of a nine-month-old girl named Juanita Alegria, who died in 1916. Descendants of her family still place flowers on her grave.

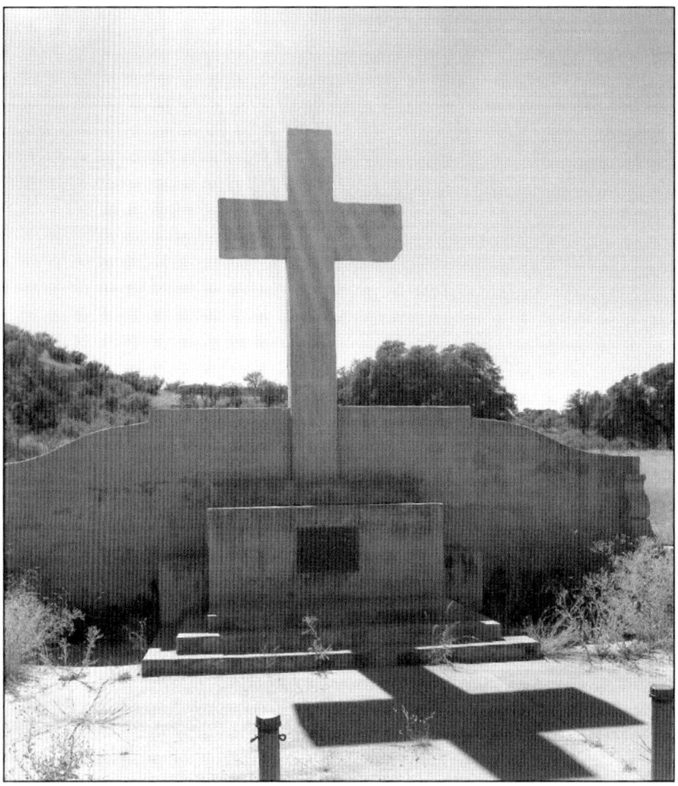

This spot near Lochiel, Arizona, is marked with a special memorial. Here, on April 12, 1539, Fray Marcos de Niza (1495–1558), missionary explorer in Spanish North America, became the first European to enter what is now Arizona.

Index of Cemetery Locations

Chapter Three: Cochise County Graves and Cemeteries

Chapter Four: Pima County Graves and Cemeteries

Chapter Five: Santa Cruz County Graves and Cemeteries

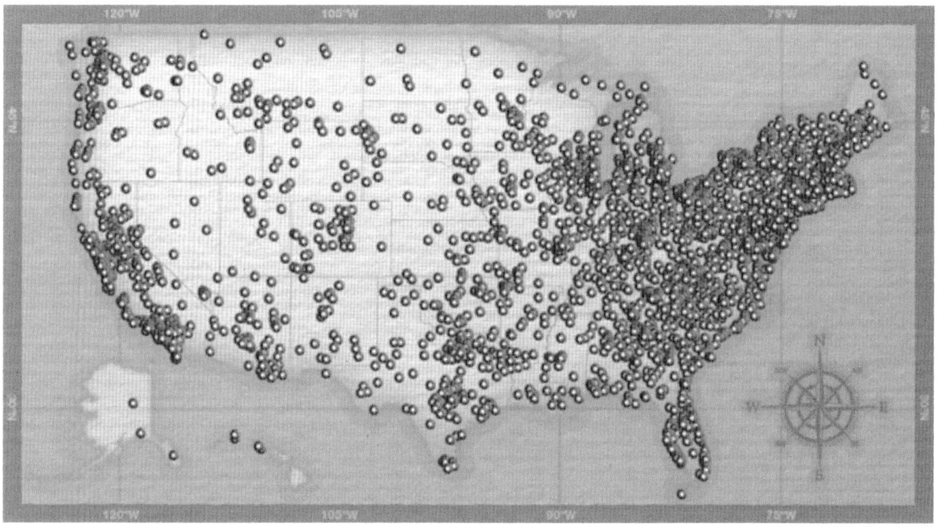